ROMANS

ROMANS

Michael Sheridan

St. Martin's Press
New York

Library of Congress Cataloging-in-Publication Data

Sheridan, Michael.
Romans : their lives and times / Michael Sheridan.
p.   cm.
"A Thomas Dunne book."
ISBN 0-312-13158-5
1. Rome (Italy)—Social life and customs—Anecdotes.   2. Rome
(Italy)—Politics and government—Anecdotes.   3. Rome (Italy)—
Biography—Anecdotes.   I. Title.
DG807.6.S44   1995
945.09—dc20   95-2070   CIP

First published in Great Britain by Weidenfeld & Nicolson

First U.S. Edition: May 1995
10 9 8 7 6 5 4 3 2 1

Contents

CHAPTER 1

Arrival

Few of the people in this book were born Roman yet their lives all became part of the city, like classical fragments embedded in the walls of buildings old and new. Even those who merely pass through Rome leave their brushstrokes on its extravagant canvas. The lifetime labours of those who stay for ever provide the broader outlines.

They are all here, ambassadors and counts, ambitious provincials clawing their way to glory, a venerable cardinal from the slums and several popes who came unwillingly from their city-states to high office. There is a poet who loathed priests, a priest devoted to poetry, in Latin, and a diarist to chronicle almost every generation of Roman decay. There is a great deal of talk about passion and a generous amount of sudden death. It is a heady cocktail, but who would not prefer it to a tepid cup of tea?

Nothing is done by halves in Rome. Nowhere is the espresso more bitter, the monuments as grandiose, the corruption as ancient and the style quite so contrived. It leaves a profound mark on the briefest of visitors. The city is a drug that seeps into the habits and conscience of all who stay, a compound of inertia and impatience in constant mutual tension, restrained by the intermittent pang of pleasure. Sitting in a traffic jam by the Forum is the definition of this state.

Few indeed are the antique Romans and the common lament in the older quarters is that *i veri Romani non ci sono piu*, there are no real Romans left. At least two-thirds of the present inhabitants trace no roots to the city, for its boundaries twice exploded, first after the collapse of the Papal States and then at the end of Mussolini's war, when people rushed from the countryside to the capital. They and their children constitute the new Romans.

It remains the custom for the grander families to possess a home in the city and an estate on the shores of the Tyrrhenian Sea or in the hills of Tuscany. They are part-time Romans.

Then there are the foreigners, most of whom like to consider themselves at least honorary Romans. Some are birds of passage, abandoned to the excesses of youth, which are readily indulged; others serve out an agreeable middle-aged tour of duty, then move on with regret, perhaps to buy the long-coveted farmhouse in Umbria or an apartment on one or other riviera.

A handful can never leave and blend into the crowds, year after year, absorbed in the pleasure of Italian life to an extent which renders the daily trials of Roman existence unimportant and postpones for ever the moment of return to lugubrious northern climes. Some may be exemplary, others pathetic.

The oldest Romans are the cats. They live in baleful disdain of all around them, curled up in the midday sun on the steps of the Capitol, foraging in the rubbish heaps of Trastevere, assembled to feast on cold pasta beneath the ramparts of the Quirinal palace where the President of the Republic resides. An old legend holds that the souls of dead generations inhabit the unkempt skeletons of the cats, so that in their eyes you see the very depths of antiquity.

That is why, for affection's sake, elderly ladies can still be found in the early morning or the late afternoon, doling out wrinkled damp strands of spaghetti into tin plates to propitiate these venerable citizens. What began as a superstition lingers as a habit. Computers hum in the salons of the Quirinal palace and motor cars built in Osaka race around its encircling warren of cobbled streets. The feeding of the cats, however, proceeds unfussed. Each day a fruit and vegetable market generates scraps fit to claw at. Their retired admirers shuffle dishes into corners where a cat can wolf its carbohydrates and fight off interlopers with a warning hiss. Roman cats are not friendly creatures.

These are not the sleek and hieratic cats that surveyed the world in solemn wisdom from the paintings of Syria and Egypt. That feline godhead vanished with the late Empire. Nor are they the silent but appreciative pets of northern Europe, pampered, combed and stroked into reconciliation with domestic harmony. Few Romans in the old city centre seem to keep cats.

No, these are ragged and disputatious beasts, quick to spit and bristle, perpetual in their search for nourishment, wont to rend the night with their howls of amorous adventure. For some reason there seem to be few cats in the precincts of the Vatican. They prefer to lurk in tangled weeds around the ruins of pagan pomp. Whole squadrons patrol beneath the arches of the theatre of Marcellus and lost souls congregate in the Jewish ghetto. Others raid the market streets towards the Campo de' Fiori.

An entire legion of cats assembles at lunchtime beneath the marble wedge of the Pyramid of Cestius, a Roman tomb next to the graves of Keats and Shelley. Munching on plates of rubbery macaroni and licking up saucers of rancid milk, they slink between the long grasses at the edge of the English cemetery to escape through the gaps in the old city wall and out into the roar of a thousand Fiats.

Impervious, it seems, to polluted air, a diet of scraps and the indifference of all but the aged, the cats retain a triumphant air. They have survived.

There is a train that reaches Rome just after dawn. It begins to slow down as the railway from Tuscany enters a lazy curve around the east of the city. The tracks unite with those from Naples, Calabria and Sicily. At this junction, the rhythm of wheels and rail gives way to an irregular clatter. The rattle of points, the sighs and groans of hydraulics and greased machinery, tell dozing passengers that it is time to wake up.

Even in an age of cheap air travel, the overnight express trains from northern Europe to the Italian peninsula are still crowded, sweaty conveyances. Tousled, whey-faced teenagers stretch themselves out of the cramped postures necessary for a night's fitful sleep, sitting upright on brown leatherette seats in second class, amid a jumble of fluorescent backpacks, olive army-surplus haversacks, plastic bags containing half-eaten stale bread rolls, empty cans of soft drinks and crumpled Marlboro or Gitane packets.

People who have made this journey remember most clearly the unromantic smell that accompanied their first morning in Italy. It is compounded of unwashed bodies, old food, French cigarette smoke, the reek of last night's cheap red wine and the peculiar plastic–electrical odour common to Continental railway carriages. There is a metallic taste in the mouth – the lavatories are, of course, all occupied and brushing teeth is out of the question – and a sour ache at the base of the stomach. One's travelling companions, with whom the most cheerful cosmopolitan acquaintance seemed a pleasure only hours before, look like down-and-outs.

Out of the windows, clouded with dust and grime, an uninspiring vision is unveiled. The train grinds past row upon row of serried apartment buildings, wildly festooned with television aerials, most balconies adorned by washing, every anonymous block a testimony to the banality of modern official architecture. There are few people to be seen before seven o'clock – the Romans are not an early rising lot, and will progress snail-like to their offices for eight or eight-thirty. Perhaps. Only the clear sky and an occasional cluster of flat-topped trees suggest that this city landscape might be anywhere more exotic than Düsseldorf or Birmingham. It is, frankly, a disappointing moment.

But then the train slides beneath a curling, rust-coloured twirl of motorway bridges, and a significant clatter of interlocking rails announces the junction where the two Italies converge and the traveller from northern Europe realises that he has most definitely arrived in the south. The South! There is a trellis of vines around the railwayman's hut between the tracks. That crumbling wall on the left is a ruined aqueduct. That curious edifice nearby is the tomb of a certain Marcus Vergilius Eurysaces, an ancient Roman magnate, who made his fortune as a baker. It is a vulgar thing, pierced with holes to resemble the wood-fired ovens in which his bread was made. A stone frieze depicts the labours involved in baking a loaf some two thousand years ago. The city gate built by the Emperor Claudius, the Porta Maggiore, looms behind it. Indisputably, this is different from the approaches to Waterloo or the Gare du Nord.

All at once Mussolini takes over from Vitruvius and the portentous flat-fronted towers and blockhouses of his Fascist architects escort you into Termini, the name given to Rome's one and only grand railway station and perhaps the most exotic terminus to be found in Europe south of Paris.

In Federico Fellini's film *Roma*, a wide-eyed young provincial (the director himself) clambers down from his third-class carriage at Termini into clouds of hissing steam and a Dantean babel of dialect and dispute.

It is the 1930s and every third person seems to be a youth in uniform. Moustachioed nuns elbow their way with peremptory grace through the crowds. Peasants dressed in black climb in and out of the carriage windows, the men handing down immense bundles and baskets to crows of reproof from their thick-set womenfolk. The young Fellini, impeccable in a cream linen suit, beams affectionately upon the proletarian chaos around him. The loudspeakers, installed by the regime, bark instructions, all of them ignored. The place is a madhouse, a microcosm of the capital which Fellini proceeds to depict in the throes of a zestful collapse.

The railways were part of the triumph of modern Italy. Not much more than a century ago, the country barely existed as anything more than a political concept. The railway bound it together and changed Rome for ever. From north, south, east and west, the tracks penetrated the boundaries of the old city, uniting at Termini where all the lines came together.

For centuries the city had slumbered within the fastness of the Papal States, unbothered by restive elements in the Kingdom of the Two Sicilies or progressive enlightenment in the salons of Turin and Milan. It was rather like Venice in its isolation, hemmed in by the coast, the marshy Maremma dividing Lazio from Tuscany, and the spine of mountains down the centre of the country. Immured in a fortress of withered papal tradition and pomp, its populace subsisted on the indulgence of the great, the gullibility of their visitors and an undemanding amount of clerical work.

All that vanished with the battles to unify Italy, the conquest of Rome by secular forces and the declaration that the city should be the new capital, a decision, some believe, that neither Rome nor Italy has yet recovered from.

The trains brought labourers, conscripts, rural families and provincial priests to the capital. They carried petty officials and functionaries of the new state to the outlying boundaries of Puglia and the Alps. Staff officers and administrators, dispatched to Abyssinia, Tripoli or Tirana, arrived at Termini with their orders in their pockets and warrants for the boat trains to Naples or Bari.

Legions of farmworkers escaped stifling toil on the vast estates of the Sicilian nobility by enduring the long, slow, train journey to the new factories of the north. Sharp young men in Calabria and Campania suddenly grasped that it was possible to achieve mobility, advancement and liberation from the narrow confines of a career in the provinces. A government job, held for life, and an apartment in Rome became the goal of every striving head bent over papers in the public examinations.

Thus Rome changed more within the seventy years between 1870 and 1940 than at any time in her history since the Renaissance, perhaps even since the end of the Roman Empire in the West. The railways transformed life for Italians more rapidly than in any other western European nation. They literally tied the country together and became the arteries through which its life-force, the people, flowed.

The scene was set for Fellini's hordes to debouch from their trains into the city suburbs created to absorb them. Through the 1920s and 1930s, and once again with the great migration of the 1950s, they poured in. North and south of Termini, the streets erected by Piedmontese builders after 1870 marched in regimented fashion beyond the walls of ancient Rome. A century later, in the late 1970s, they were lined with cheap restaurants, barbershops, cafés and pensions where students on holiday could spend the night for a pittance. You could eat a three-course meal of spaghetti, a sliver of unidentifiable 'steak', salad, ice cream and wine for a modest sum and then retire to sleep, if possible, in a room containing at least six beds and residents of both sexes. Most of the time, the arrangements were gloomily platonic.

This was the sort of area to which Fellini's young character came on his first days in the city. It was relatively modern, crowded with immigrants from the countryside, a noisy place where people ate outside at wooden tables spread in front of trattorias while trams clattered past, showering the passers-by with sparks from their primitive electrical gear. There was a simple budgetary formula for eating that persisted during good economic times in Italian cities almost until the end of the 1970s. It was this: a person might eat in a simple restaurant for less than the cost of purchasing and preparing the same ingredients at home. The buildings here were imposing apartment blocks, constructed under the pretence of resembling a nobleman's residence, with high windows and cavernous halls, broken into family units and dignified by the suitable Italian title for any such building of high or low station, the *palazzo*.

The builders must have felt the sweep of destiny overcome their finer instincts, for they swept away much that was beautiful and ancient to construct the station and its surrounding streets. We are led to believe that the land on which the concourse and platforms of Termini were laid out was once the estate of the Villa Massimo Negroni.

This was the home of Cardinal Felice Perretti, who ascended the throne of St Peter as Pope Sixtus v in 1585. The pontiff's sister – like him, a newcomer from the rude country smallholding of their youth – remained in the Villa after his election. He is said to have ignored her when she visited the Vatican in the gowns of a princess, only to embrace her with fraternal affection when she reappeared in peasant garb. She passed her years amid its formal gardens and terraces, bequeathing it to generations of careful owners. It remained as a sylvan retreat for centuries thereafter. But in the fervent rush of the Piedmontese government to modernise and to bring the railways into the very heart of Rome, the Villa was expropriated from Prince Massimo, its last owner, for a pittance. He died, it is claimed, of a broken heart as the last of its orange and cypress trees fell to the axe.

Thus did the new men in Rome cast their influence over all the north-east corner of the city, throwing up block after block of those solid apartment buildings that look as if they ought to belong on the quais at Lyon or alongside the arcades of Turin. 'There is not a single point in the entirely modern Rome which calls for anything but contempt,' complained the acidic Victorian writer Augustus Hare. 'Wide shadeless streets of featureless, ill-built, stuccoed houses, bearing foolish names connected with Piedmontese history, and a wretched square called the Piazza dell'Indipendenza ... hastily run up, with the worst materials and by the most unskilled workmen, its buildings all seem destined to perish within the century.'

Those words were first published in 1871 and remained to be proven 120 years later. In fact it was not the supremacy of aesthetics but a crash in property values in 1887 that brought a temporary halt to the building boom unleashed by unification. By then the stately gardens and terraces, characteristic of the area around the great baths of Diocletian since the early days of empire, had gone for ever. No more could one ascend the vaulted roof of that building, as Trollope did, and conclude that 'nowhere is there sweeter air, a wider prospect, more silence and desirable solitude'.

We are told constantly that this is the new Europe. And indeed there are different inhabitants in Fellini's bedlam today, for the colonised have come to haunt the heirs of their colonial masters, as you see when you pass through the ticket barriers and into the vast airy concourse.

Two utterly different societies exist here. There are the Italians and the Others. The Italians dominate – sharp-suited fellows running for the

Milan train, elegant ladies wafting towards the Florence express, worried-looking southern bureaucrats, each with a schoolmaster's small leather briefcase, legions of well-behaved children and, of course, the eternal contingent of ferocious nuns, first on to the train for Lourdes and first off it. There are the hotel touts, just as in the young Fellini's time, each wearing a peaked cap embroidered with the name of his down-at-heel establishment, plucking at one's elbow, chanting his offerings of rooms for hire, murmuring in one's ear of clean sheets and gleaming bathrooms, the airiest of salons and the most reasonable of rates; premises, naturally, frequented only by the most distinguished clients – persons such as yourself! Some of these gentlemen are honest, others less so. Giving in to the wrong one of these individuals is a guarantee that one will meet his factotum, the taxi tout, who will scoop up the traveller's bags amid a great bluster of goodwill, to carry them off to a decrepit Fiat parked near the official taxi stand and painted a shade of yellow that quite resembles the official colours. The fare, however, is likely to be even more exorbitant than the shameful amount required by the licensed drivers.

There are sellers of lottery tickets, smooth-cheeked clerics, smart young men in army or navy uniform, mountainous maternal women clutching their squalling offspring, beggars, a man predicting the end of all things and a sweet old lady with brushed white hair and a beautifully knitted sweater, sitting, as she always does, on a luggage trolley that carries all her worldly possessions. A permanent resident of Termini, she is known to the staff as its queen.

Then there are the Others. Anyone who has lived in Beirut or Cairo will suddenly feel at home. Tall, thin-featured Somalis. Ethiopians marked out by their fine cheekbones. Olive-skinned Palestinians, Syrians or Lebanese, the darker Libyans, Egyptians, Sudanese – all of them ebb and flow through the station, for it is the focal point of the eastern district of Rome where many newcomers congregate. Protected by the lax concession of visas and the vain efforts of the authorities to enforce the residence rules, they enjoy a precarious existence on the fringes of the Italian economy. Yet these Arab visitors have been familiar to Italy ever since the Mediterranean civilisations entered into commerce. Their forefathers are mentioned by the poets. One North African, Septimus Severus, governed the Empire, becoming the first and, unless history has a great surprise in store, the last Libyan to rule in Rome.

There is infinite variety in Rome now, as if the flotsam and jetsam of

Europe's commercial empires had returned to wash up on its southern shores. Two West African ladies, their voluminous figures wrapped in flowery-patterned fabric, stand shrieking abuse at each other near the ticket office. Outside, on Via Giovanni Giolitti, Senegalese and Nigerians stand guard over the market stalls on which all the pitiful consumerism of the Third World is displayed: cheap sunglasses, nylon shirts, white socks, underclothes in every variety long forgotten by the European buyer, leather-thonged skirts and a profusion of flimsy toys. The police saunter by without taking the least notice. On a Thursday evening the Filipinos come in their hundreds to meet among the buses and coaches in the sprawling piazza before the station. They are the housemaids, cleaners, baby-sitters and skivvies of the Italian boom of the 1980s. The Romans like them as domestic employees, for they are both Catholic and compliant.

The Filipinos bring bottles of beer and eat cheap slices of pizza from the *tavola calda* in Via Giolitti. This meeting is a weekly ritual that they practise around the world. In Hong Kong, they gather on Sundays in the square in front of a gleaming skyscraper that houses the headquarters of the Hong Kong and Shanghai Bank. In Rome, they seem to have settled on the bus station in front of Termini because so many must trek in from the far-flung suburbs of Monteverde and Prima Porta. Very few of them can afford a car.

Little more than a decade ago, none of these people could be seen around the station. Apart from the traditional communities from the former Italian colonies of Libya, Somalia and Ethiopia, there were few non-Europeans in the city. The character of these streets has thus changed yet again. Many of the Roman residents moved elsewhere years ago. An Ethiopian restaurant, a Korean café and several Chinese establishments have opened their doors. Innumerable bars remain, of varying seediness, while some of the same old places that have been doling out indifferent plates of pasta for decades are still in business. Nowadays the small hotels and pensions are often homes for the dispossessed and the desperate, Middle Easterners escaping one regime or another, Serbs and Croats lamenting in their common tongue, Poles and Czechs trying to scratch a living, or Africans simply fleeing.

The curious thing about Termini is that it combines the squalor of the present with remarkable souvenirs of a more optimistic era. For example, everybody knows that the trains do not always run on time. The station clocks, when they are working at all, frequently provide differing interpretations of the exact time of day. The harassed station announcers, no longer obliged to exhort the populace to feats of endeavour on behalf of the Italian empire, spend most of their working hours explaining the delay of this or that expresso, rapido or accelerato (there is no term applied to an Italian train that implies anything other than a speedy pace).

Yet symbols stand at every turn of a faster, cleaner, more efficient Italy that exists in the imaginations and, indeed, the memories of many Romans. It exists in reality, too, but far away to the north, in the plains of Lombardy and the valleys of the Alto Adige.

They include, for instance, the special letter boxes at either end of the concourse provided for post to the main Italian cities. These are emptied every hour, the sensible idea being to provide a quick mail service via the railways. Each box carries the name of its city and a postcard of the place is set into a glass holder at the front. Palermo's proudly displays its nineteenth-century opera house, framed by waving palm trees. The box for Naples carries a glorious view of Vesuvius and the bay, delineated against a spotless city sky. Bari's port is washed by a pristine sea of deepest blue. The arcades of Bologna extend in regal splendour past medieval domes and towers, unsullied by traffic. The Piazza Signoria in Florence looks as it must have done forty years ago, without a single sightseer to block the view. The cathedral of Milan strains skyward in a forest of Gothic stone so clean that its pinnacles and spires could scarcely have been touched by the breath of the motor car.

But all the postcards are badly faded, so elderly are they, and one or two have almost been eaten away by damp, so that each of these heavenly views is seen as if through gauze, like the cracked patina on a very old icon.

For many years there existed a bewildering variety of honorific passes, official reductions, cards held by prolifically fecund mothers and carefully stamped booklets retained by journalists that added up to a simple equation for the Italian rail traveller. If you were paying the ordinary fare then you were paying far too much, a dismal confession of low status or lack of connections. The inspectors of tickets carried thick black books recording, for example, the exact fare to be paid between Rome and Bologna by a disabled veteran born in 1898 who had fought at Caporetto. None of this discouraged the *furbi*, the smart ones, those who blithely occupied first-class seats reserved by elderly Contessas, or who sat comfortably in trains for which all manner of special supplements were demanded while professing no knowledge whatsoever of these requirements. Profound and theatrical debates thus enlivened every journey when the inevitable denouement took place between crabbed officialdom and the *furbi*. Nor might their outcome be predicted with ease, since a toss of blonde curls or the possession of a distinguished name could sometimes influence the result.

They say now that the railways are bankrupt and must be reformed. Reform, a word tossed around with carefree abandon in Italy, would be a labour worthy of Hercules. The scale of the enterprise alone defies any easy reformation.

The trains pull in from north and south, a constant ebb and flux of carriages, restaurant cars, sleepers and postal wagons. They connect the Italian capital to Munich, Vienna, Salzburg and Brussels. There are trains that crawl around the fertile crescent of the northern Mediterranean to Ventimiglia, where the mountains of Monte Carlo signal the beginning of the Riviera, and on to Irun, at the Spanish border. The Palatino, a long convoy of smoke-windowed French carriages, departs each evening for the Gare de Lyon in Paris. The Marco Polo leaves for Venice and Trieste every morning, cocooning its first-class passengers in agreeable luxury for the haul through the flatlands of Emiglia-Romagna, with starched linen, flowers and wine glasses already arranged upon the tables in its dining car. The Dortmund sleeper, by contrast, discharges its load amid bundles of grubby blankets and the detritus of a miserable, ill-fed night. The Italian pilgrims to Lourdes hobble on board a collection of elderly fieldgray coaches, while the Polish pilgrims to Rome spill out of a shabby khaki-hued train provided by their national railways.

Then there are the boat trains from Bari and Sicily, full of Italian migrants from the deep south, sharing the crowded corridors with the Moroccans, Tunisians and Algerians. And at 10.15 each night, except Friday, a magnificent array of ancient rolling stock heads off for Trieste, Zagreb, Budapest and Moscow, where it arrives thirty-seven hours later. The Russian sleeping cars, all brass plate and antimacassars, are a deep bottle green and a samovar hisses comfortingly in the corridor. From the snows of Muscovy to the sunlit vines of Latium ... one might have thought that they did not make railway journeys like that any more. The sight of these heavy, elderly wagons-lits is enough to drive any onlooker possessed of a scrap of imagination straight to the booking office. It might be wise, however, to stock up first on Italian salami, ham, wine, fruit and rolls from the vendors who set up their stalls at the head of the platforms.

Even the commuters at Termini are a fairly unusual lot. The railway system did not develop to serve the suburbs around Rome's old city centre, for as these grew up, propelled by greed, speed and jerry-building, there existed barely a semblance of urban planning. The unfortunate residents of the Roman suburbs are obliged to resort to the crowded, spartan and stifling public buses, or to use their own private motor cars to get around. Not surprisingly, most prefer to do the latter, with the dismal, choking results available for all to see and inhale.

A few people grew so tired of life in the metropolis that they took advantage of the local trains that head south from the capital. The principal line devolves into a single track shortly after leaving the suburbs. The train clatters through fields of corn and clumps of trees. Out of the wide-open windows, to the east, a ruined aqueduct processes across the landscape. Herds of sheep graze in the shadows of its arches. This is nothing less than the Roman Campagna as seen by Claude Lorraine. On a clear evening, the Alban hills provide a backdrop of Elysian pleasure. Then the train – an affair of a few carriages, no more – begins to wind up a gradient, through vineyards so profuse that their fruits almost brush the sides of the coaches. Small farmholdings and villas of recent construction begin to dot the hillsides, then around one final bend, the train comes to rest in the little station at Frascati.

The towns and villages on the slopes of the Alban hills, known as the Castelli Romani, provided refuge from the city's furore for many a long year. In classical times, they were favoured by Horace and others who longed for a pastoral retreat and possessed either the money or the patronage to allow it. The architects and cardinals of the Renaissance caused lavish villas to be raised on the sites of the old Roman retreats. The Villa Aldobrandini in Frascati, built by the cardinal of the same name, attracted the talents of Giacomo della Porta and Carlo Maderno. Painters of the school of Domenichino frescoed its salons and the most sensitive tastes were applied to its ample gardens. The modern Frascati grew up around these pleasure domes. At dusk, its inhabitants gaze out from the town's belvedere, or from their balconies, towards the ochre haze that marks the distant city, sipping Frascati's straw-hued wine and rejoicing in their distance.

The plague of the motor car, the teenage moped and the delivery lorry have infiltrated even this citadel of tranquillity. All is relative, however. The air in the Castelli is silken and pure after the miasma of Rome. A fortunate band, then, are the few hundred people who have decided to live up here and risk the constant railway strikes on their daily journey into the city. Only a few trains each day ply the route. Of an evening, the station offices close early. Signs of decay are apparent in the buildings and the tracks. And every so often there are murmurings that the service may close, for it makes no profit at all.

That would be a shame, for it would rob the world of one of its more unusual commuter routes. Upstairs at Termini there is a surprisingly good bookstore, at which it is possible to buy the works of Horace or Tibullus, translated into the modern, living descendant of their tongue, and then, for the price of a hamburger, to ride through the very landscape which inspired their verses.

Admittedly, few passengers prefer this refined enjoyment. The favourite reading on the Frascati train is *La Settimana Enigmista*, a weekly compendium of crosswords, quizzes and brain-testing riddles, poetry of a kind.

Then there are those who scan the small advertisements in the *Porta Portese*, a publication whose pages contain every item available at the Roman flea market of the same title, and much more. There are messages from retired civil servants in search of companionship. Ladies of a certain age, divorced or abandoned as often as not, require distinguished, seigneurial gentlemen to retrieve them from loneliness. Any number of men in their early forties place advertisements. Inevitably described (by themselves) as *ragazzi* – boys – their marital status always seems somewhat uncertain but their zealous pursuit of *amore* is beyond doubt. Of course, there remains the small but faithful band of advertisers who seek the company of the same sex, the wardrobe of the opposite sex or a combination of the two.

Indeed, upon arrival at Termini one need not look too far for any of these diversions. On sale at the same kiosks which offer the Vatican's daily newspaper are lurid magazines of a frankness and speciality which would ensure their rapid confiscation in countries where public embarrassment requires legal redress. Nor is it too difficult to find prostitutes. In the 1950s the Italian state abolished the houses of tolerance, within whose chambers young arrivals in the time of Fellini had taken their first nervous steps away from chastity. This measure, hailed as a beacon of progress and enlightenment, promptly drove a hitherto sensibly regulated trade on to the streets and into the arms of the gangsters and pimps whose province it has remained.

The profusion of reading matter at Termini is unmatched anywhere else in Rome, for here one may obtain all the local papers that make breakfast reading each morning in all important cities of Italy a grandiose sweep through world events. There is no bowing to a sense of provincial inferiority in the local press. The weightiest developments on the plains of Central Asia or the farms of the Mid-West are given careful consideration by the *caporedattore* in the offices of *La Sicilia* in Palermo. A world-weary columnist on the *Gazzettino* in Venice may digress upon the defects of the German credit system as if the Director of the Bundesbank himself were dependent upon that journal for advice. The gentlemen who edit the magnificently named *Secolo XIX* – the Nineteenth Century – of Genoa measure the prospects for Piraeus and Singapore with attentive concern. Can one neglect that worthy periodical, *L'Eco di Bergamo*, surely the only newspaper that can boast a Pope, John xxiii, among its regular contributors? Down in Naples, the latest sanguine 'settling of accounts' in the local underworld is always noted by *Il Mattino*, but so considerable are the ties that link the city to the New World that equal, if not excessive, space may be devoted to party politics in America.

Then there are the precise observations of the Swiss-Italians who produce the *Corriere Del Ticino* in their canton around the northern lakes. It is a small newspaper of breathtaking seriousness, right down to the masthead, a faithful imitation of its grander, world-famous rival, the *Corriere Della Sera* of Milan. Bundles of the *Corriere Della Sera* appear in Rome in the small hours, for of all the papers read by exiles in the capital, it has the greatest audience. Many Romans take it in preference to their own daily paper *Il Messaggero*. Perhaps, like the faded postcards on the letterboxes, it provides a mental link to that mythical land where everything proceeds on time, is administered with fairness, is untainted by clerics and is, in a word, serious.

Milano, una città seria. How often is that expression on the lips of the Romans! You can see the Milanese bustling on and off their trains at Termini. They are the people buying the Italian magazines with the new-fashioned English names, *Business, Capital* and so on ... sometimes with a copy of *Le Ore*, the predominant pornographic magazine, tucked between the balance sheets. Within *Le Ore*'s pages readers were once treated to a view of a radical deputy in the Italian parliament stark naked, on all fours, presenting her rump to the camera. Nothing like that would happen in Milan, of course. Much too serious. The Romans were reassured to learn after the great upsurge of scandal that even the corruption in Milan is on a serious scale. Then it emerged that the magistracy in that city was of similar mettle and dozens of the rich and powerful perpetrators ended up in prison. Distressingly serious, that. The Milanese dress is a little more understated, more classically Anglo-Saxon in style, a little less flamboyant, the men's suits less clerical in cut than the old expensive Roman tailor's outfits, the women's business skirts and jackets somewhat more severe than would please the appreciative glance of the Roman male. The Milanese are indeed serious. They are the people who look exasperated instead of merely resigned when the Termini announcer broadcasts the news of a delay of four hours or an outright cancellation due to an official union strike, an inter-union dispute, a landslide in the Appenines, building work on the periphery of Naples, or a string of coaches lost altogether somewhere between Messina and Reggio Calabria.

Yes, Milan is serious and Rome is merely in serious condition. But if it is with some relief that the Milanese eventually board their trains back to the north, it is with little envy that the Romans watch them go. A very efficient place no doubt, but one would not want to live there. The weather is foul and there is all that seriousness to cope with.

So, across the concourse, out through the high, airy booking hall and into the Piazza Cinquecento. Within the confines of the station, the sunlight was broken into streaks, diffused by glass or shaded by the roof over each platform. Once outside, despite a solid canopy that overhangs the station façade, it bursts in full strength through a filter composed of dust and airborne grit, the fumes of a myriad exhausts and a clamour that might rouse the dead from the long-interred gardens of the Villa Negroni below. Swarms of bee-yellow taxis struggle into the resemblance of an organised line, frustrated by the dilapidated pace of elderly travellers burdened with luggage, the insistent rush of grave individuals in Milanese suits, and the insidious presence of the *furbi*, fresh from their illicitly occupied first-class seats.

Just as a traffic light in Rome is said to be a recommendation, so a taxi queue is something suggested rather than imposed. It provides a school for that version of courtesy which masks an unpitying struggle for survival. The threat contained in eye-play, the deferential shuffle of person and bag that outflanks an interloper, the muttering of complaints over standards of civic behaviour (carefully directed towards nobody in particular), the swift interposition of one of the *furbi* between old lady and open taxi door, the subsequent, dramatic appeals for public support, the indifference of the driver, the fury of the person abandoned and the triumphant slam of the door as the conqueror speeds away, eyes fixed rigidly ahead to ignore the glare of disapproval – all are instructive exercises in the arts so necessary to daily life in Rome.

All around the Piazza Cinquecento stand symbols of the post-war Italian miracle – not monuments (there are few to the makers of modern Italy), but massive advertising hoardings erected atop the buildings around the piazza. In most countries, one might expect the boring old multinationals to dominate public awareness. Of course, there is no utter escape – Canon copiers, Coca-Cola and their ilk all proclaim their qualities from rooftop and wall. But what are these unfamiliar titles and acronyms? ENI, Snaipem, INA, Snamprogetti ... and Candy. Candy? Ah, the Italian electrical firm. ENI? Ah yes, that luxuriant plant, the state-owned oil conglomerate, supposedly to be chopped up and sold off. INA? Why, it is a vast insurance concern. As for all those other bewildering names, well, they can come later. A visitor from remote and poor parts might well look on in wonder at the confident spectacle offered by the Piazza Cinquecento and conclude that here was the heart of a mighty realm indeed, a country so important and wealthy that it lived within its own economic empire.

Alas, there is an element of mirage in this vision. The great Italian financial and business concerns grew with astonishing speed upon the unification of the country. They prospered through the liberal governments before 1914, did mightily well out of the First World War, came to an understanding with Mussolini and were bailed out of the Great Depression. Then came the seeds of political control and patronage, sown within the boards and governing councils of many companies in which the state had taken a majority shareholding. After the Second World War, the new democratic parties attached themselves to this plentiful source of influence, with predictable consequences.

Now many of these edifices are riddled with decay, their proud insignia the symbols of public bankruptcy, their experiment in state intervention a lamentable show of its deficiencies. At the same time, however, others remain solvent, well-managed entities that have won much profit for Italy and extended the skills of her engineers and bankers across the globe.

As dusk envelops the Piazza Cinquecento, the fog of carbon monoxide arises from a thousand contending buses, cars and taxis, while the travellers stream out of underground passages and into the station concourse, and the signs come to life in neon and continue to glow like beacons through the miasma. But of course, only that traveller from a remote and poor place might even notice them at all.

Across the surging traffic in the piazza and into the trees, beneath the very walls of Diocletian's baths, and here one finds an unglamorous evening *passeggiata* of *le tout* Rome, a café society without money or means to enjoy the cocktails and stuffed Gaeta olives along the Via Veneto. Vagrants, national servicemen, touts, but most of all foreigners, all the denizens of the area parade to and fro, for lack of anywhere else to go and an indisposition to sit inside their small rented rooms and sweat. The groups all cling together, the ubiquitous Filipinos cheerful enough, the Slavs glum and especially penniless, and the Arabs bright-eyed. There are cheap entertainments, ice creams, drinks at open-air snackbars. Once upon a time it may have been pleasant to stroll of an evening in the open spaces around the baths, refreshed by the fountain in the Piazza della Repubblica, admiring the girls and the florid architecture at the head of the Via Nazionale. Now it is merely sordid, with grit in the Campari, dust in the food and the constant, very new, fear of being waylaid, propositioned, abused or robbed. There are still magical and luminescent places in which to pass the twilight hours in Rome, but this is not one of them. It is time to move onwards, and inwards.

CHAPTER 2

The Problem with Latin

Beneath the gloomy skies of an October evening in the late eighteenth century, Edward Gibbon sat down to muse upon the ruins of the Capitol. He rested at the summit of the Sacred Way, once tramped by victorious consuls wreathed in splendour. The barefoot friars were chanting their litanies within the church of Santa Maria d'Aracoeli, reminding this most sceptical historian of the triumph of Christianity over the myths of Jupiter and Mithras, a sensation heightened by the roofless temples of paganism all around him.

The autumn dusk in Rome vanishes in a few fleeting minutes. As the sun descends across the Tiber behind the Janiculum, its last rays fall on ruined palaces and twisted foliage, tumbling down the western slopes of the Palatine hill. The shadows of approaching night invade the empty halls of vast basilicas. On every panelled Imperial arch the sightless marble faces recede into invisibility.

In the Farnese gardens, laid out above the rubble of forgotten audience chambers and boudoirs, groves of orange trees and cypresses murmur in a twilight breeze. Below the garden balustrade, a fountain trickles into a craftily engineered lily-pond, while huge arches set into the hillside, now supporting only earth, provide the illusion of an abandoned citadel brooding over the vale of the Forum itself. Few places on earth so readily evoke magnificence and decay.

Even in the present day, when the traffic has lapsed to a distant rumble, it is easy for the imagination to fill this sprawling archaeological garden with the echoing voices of many a mighty orator, or to people its overgrown avenues with the flitting shapes of long-departed courtesans and kings. How much more evocative it must have appeared two hundred years ago, strewn with monumental reminders of vanished power, the graveyard of a civilisation that continued to hold the intellectual world in its grip even when its own life-force was many centuries spent!

Gibbon resolved that evening to embark on a work that was to occupy him for almost twenty years. When he finally laid down his pen, on 27 June 1787, he had written a work of six volumes that transformed conventional ideas about the decline and fall of Rome. One French thinker said Gibbon had erected a bridge between the ancient world and the modern era. The historian himself saw it as a chronicle of crimes and follies, culminating in a victory for barbarism and the imposition of a new religion, a triumph of superstition over a civilised ruling order. The calm and permissive society of the ancient world, he lamented, became the dominion of scheming priests with their deluded followers. It thus had crumbled to destruction.

Gibbon had by then removed himself to the gardens of a lakeside house in Lausanne, the better to contemplate in rational tranquillity the collapse of a world to which he attributed the finest method of human government ever practised. He claimed in a famous passage that man had enjoyed no happier or more prosperous time than during the period between the death of the Emperor Domitian and the accession of the demented tyrant Commodus. That would be a short interval indeed, enduring from AD 98 to 180, a mere intake of breath in the long centuries that elapsed from the ascendancy of Tiberius to the extinction of the Empire in the West in 476 and the eventual capture of Constantinople by the armies of Islam in 1453.

For the rest, it was a dismal catalogue. When famine and pestilence did not ravage the extremities of the Empire, hordes of barbarian tribes constantly tested its frontiers. Inflation, a debased coinage, corrupt tax farmers in Asia Minor and the gluttonous consumption of the Roman masses were among the factors that contrived to undermine the structure of government. At the heart of the Imperial system there festered rottenness and evil. No man could count himself secure under the whim of a Caligula, no Emperor might sleep soundly for fear of an over-mighty Praetorian, no Senator dared to make the chamber resound to a denunciation of the status quo, while poets wrote only in allusive verses of their discontent and the approved historians contented themselves with evocations of a distant golden age of Republicanism and virtue.

Gibbon spared neither the rulers nor the ruled in his description of their pride, their degeneracy and their ruin. He noted 'without surprise or scandal' that the introduction of the Christian religion had some influence in the decline and fall of Rome, but cautiously set its dep-redations against the canvas of a fatally undermined regime, doomed to collapse of its own inertia. Again and again, throughout the volumes, a philippic directed against the church with viperous skill is succeeded by a mollifying passage recalling, in rather watery fashion, the virtues deriving from its predominance.

There is much apology for reciting the details of each wretched act of schism or persecution of pagan by Christian. Over and over, the strategic, political and institutional reasons for the end of the Roman world are elaborated to give the effect of a rigidly balanced account. Time and again, the author purports to show that he has exercised a full measure of impartiality.

This is not, however, how the *Decline and Fall* is remembered, or indeed absorbed, by the reader.

Instead the rise of the priesthood, the conversion of the Imperial family, the intolerant requirements of the episcopate and the introduction to public reverence of a theology which, as Gibbon hastened to note, buried the last remains of military spirit in the cloister, emerge from the work as the principal causes of the death of civilisation itself.

The clergy preached the doctrines of patience and pusillanimity, while the sacred indolence of the monks was embraced by a servile and effeminate age, he said. The duty of religion to provide for happiness in the next life diverted its adherents from the stern necessities of main-taining a military empire on earth. Then ignorance of the strength and numbers of the enemies of Rome, the withering away of national spirit in the Roman provinces, the rigorous effects of cold and poverty upon the barbarian races and the simultaneous enfeeblement of Roman policy all combined to bring down the mighty edifice.

This was, no doubt, the inescapable conclusion imprinted on Gibbon's mind while sitting on the trampled Capitol. The evidence of infiltration and conquest lies all around. The Church of the Aracoeli, from whose precincts the Gregorian chant wafted on that decisive evening, is itself built upon the foundations of the Temple of Juno Moneta, the earliest Roman mint. Within its walls stand columns plundered from the ruins of the Palatine, while glittering fragments of marble, once decoration for the houses of the pagan rich, are inset into its pavements.

Across Michelangelo's piazza, Gibbon would have seen the Palazzo dei Conservatori, standing on the site of the Temple of Jupiter. This was the grandest shrine of ancient Rome, consecrated some five centuries before the birth of Christ. Within its colonnades, smoke rose to heaven from the sacrificial altars while soothsayers examined the warm entrails of their victims. The Senate held its first session of each year in the Temple. Augustus restored the fabric and endowed the temple with a gift of 16,000 pounds of gold, pearls and precious stones. Domitian added to its splendour and founded a festival in its honour of music, horseriding and athletics. By the Middle Ages it was gone, its stonework ransacked to adorn chapels and basilicas.

Down the steps of the Capitoline hill stands the old Mamertine prison, a frightful place where prisoners of the state were dropped through a hole into a sealed chamber, there to die of starvation or to await the dreaded noise of their executioner, silken cord in hand, dropping through the hole after them, Here perished one of the toughest foes of Rome, Jugurtha, King of Numidia. Jugurtha fought the Roman legions in the terrain that makes up the fertile coastal parts of modern Tunisia.

Another cynical historian enters the scene at this juncture. The Jugurthine War would have remained a provincial affair of little consequence were it not for the labours of Gaius Sallustius Crispus. A corrupt administrator of Julius Caesar's time, Sallust retired to enjoy his gains and to pursue the art of history with a dilettante's pen. He reconstructed the campaign, replete with elephant charges, desert raids and primitive espionage.

Jugurtha was deceived by the King of Mauretania, an early example of the lacklustre solidarity between supposed brothers in that part of the world. Sallust recounts that he was lured to a trucial meeting with the Roman commander, Sulla. Jugurtha believed that the Roman would be deceived and taken captive. Instead he found himself betrayed and his companions slaughtered. He was clapped in chains and placed on board a ship to Italy to be led through the Forum as the prize in Sulla's triumph. Then he was stripped and cast down to the blackness of a starving death in the Mamertine.

Upon its victory, Christianity insisted on a symbolic conquest of the place – not out of any reverence for a forgotten heathen King but because the Mamertine also served for a while as the prison of St Peter. It is believed, at least by the devout, that the Emperor Nero had the Saint incarcerated there as a prelude to his martyrdom on the Vatican hill. So the most dismal cell of the Roman state was reborn as the chapel of S. Pietro in Carcere. The tourist pilgrims file by the coachload through its narrow portals, much as their predecessors did in Gibbon's time, no doubt to his irritation.

All along the Sacred Way, there stand similar examples of Christian triumphalism. The temple of Antoninus and Faustina possessed a perfect façade of monumental proportions. It hides the brickwork of a church boldly built right into the shape of the ancient holy place. Then comes the church dedicated to the Saints Cosmas and Damian. It stands within the precincts of the library that once ornamented Vespasian's Forum of Peace. Within, it is all shimmering mosaics and polished marble. Outside, two weathered bronze doors, punctured by rust-encircled holes, are framed by a perfect pair of porphyry pillars and a carved pediment.

Next to it, up a little incline, is perhaps the sweetest corner of the Forum, a fragment of building known to the archaeological textbook writers only as a medieval portico. It is much preferable to think of it as the bower of some nameless palace, once resounding to song and laughter, now interpenetrated by the vegetation, smothering in wisteria and violet, the very image of a Piranesi engraving or a landscape by Corot. Every year for at least a decade it has refreshed itself with flowering vines, acquiring an austere green-garbed beauty in the rains of winter, then bursting forth at Easter to perfume the sweaty steps up towards the Colosseum and the Arch of Titus all summer, until it withers in autumnal melancholy.

Turning at the Arch to behold the sweep of the Forum back towards the darkening heights of the Capitol, the entire effect is that of a vast garden with ruins – placed, one might almost imagine, with the suggestive skill of a master. Fallen columns and massy blocks of travertine lie among curling ferns, ilex and ivy. Whole blocks of marble, streaked and veined like sides of Parma ham, nestle in tufted grasses and daisy-beds. In the distance, the Arch of Septimius Severus rises above a curtain of foliage, splashed here and there with poppies.

The monument to Titus encapsulates the grandeur and the folly of it all, for within its arch is the famous panel that shows the Roman conquerors bearing off the great seven-branched candlestick from the destruction of the temple in Jerusalem in AD 70. In one piece of stone, the Imperial sculptor defined a clash between two traditions that was to shape the Mediterranean world. Unknowingly, he gave to the Jewish people an image of their dispersion that endured until the foundation of the state of Israel.

The Roman historian Suetonius recounts that Titus personally slew twelve defenders of Jerusalem with well-aimed arrows and that the Holy of Holies fell to the besiegers on the birthday of his daughter. Yet, in the eyes of the Jews, these auspicious events merely served to confirm the curse that fell upon Titus when he strode into their burning sanctuary. Followed by his Jewish mistress Berenice, daughter of King Herod Agrippa, he returned to conduct a Judaean triumph down the Sacred Way under the eyes of his father, the reigning Emperor.

Berenice proved an unhappy creature. She was first married to one of her uncles, then lived incestuously with her brother Agrippa. In his company she encountered St Paul, apparently without virtuous effect. She subsequently left Agrippa and embraced the Roman cause as fervently as she did its leading general. Jewish nationalists stand ready to damn her to this day. Yet Berenice was upholding the sophisticated interests of her class, an élite imbued with Hellenistic culture. It had grown rich in the administration of a Roman province and felt profoundly antipathetic to wearisome zealots.

When Titus became Emperor in AD 79 he dismissed her from his retinue. Perhaps this was not as tough a choice as one might believe, for he is said to have sent away several of his favourite dancing boys at the same time. The show of decency did not serve to expiate his curse. He survived to reign just two years, two months and twenty days. He died suddenly of a fever, after several portents of ill-fortune, at the age of forty-two.

There are many Roman arches still standing in the Arab lands, preserved and weathered dry by hot, sandy climates, with only the purest wind and the driven particles whistling past them down all the centuries. But that of Titus is sad and deformed. Weeds sprout from its crevices and the stone frieze itself, almost carbon-black, is under the care of a team of restorers.

*　　*　　*

Ascending the slope of the Palatine itself, one enters the cooler realms of the high and palmy state of Rome, where the ruling families and their minions inhabited airy palaces and strolled in sunken porticoes. Above the steamy press of the Forum, looking down towards the Tiber on one side and the proletarian district of the Suburra on another, the patrician residents enjoyed cool winds blowing inland from the sea and felt safe from the unhealthy vapours around the low-lying river banks.

Augustus was a ruler who comported himself with deceitful skills that a modern Italian politician might envy. He chose to stay on in his modest Palatine house even after becoming master of the world. The residence had been purchased from the orator Hortensius. This modest gesture was in reality an ostentatious move. It fitted in with his exercise of absolute power by deferential means. Augustus claimed to have restored the Republic. He gave lip service to the paramount authority of the Senate, but under his guidance there was little irony in the Senators' official title of 'conscript fathers'.

The scene of the first Emperor's home is now uncertain but a sign points the way to the 'Casa di Livia', supposedly the residence of his scheming second wife. Livia achieved new fame as the monster of ill-will whose dynastic plotting animated the pages of Robert Graves' fictional memoirs of her grandson, Claudius. Hers seem a humble enough set of chambers, restrained in their proportions and lined by a floor of fading, tessellated mosaic. Few visitors bother to peer inside the shaded rooms and they therefore miss a series of haunting frescos.

In one chamber, each wall has been cleverly painted to give the impression of an interior garden. Garlands of fruits and flowers hang between pillars, as if in an outside bower, while votive gifts are suspended from each leafy bough. A frieze of ochre figures on dark orange runs along the top – shadowy, almost impressionistic horsemen, animals, towers and bridges touched in with just a few brushstrokes, gowned worthies in an agora, a flimsy theatre, dancers in mid-leap, all frozen against an economic landscape of dead cities and rural calm.

Next door there is a Pompeian scene, where masked figures and graceful female devotees perform solemn acts, whose meaning is lost to us, with the stylised motions of a mime company. They move against a crimson background brocaded in gold. We can only guess whether these were, indeed, the decorative tastes of the matriarch. But it comforts the legend of her black deception to imagine her at home – one moment entertaining patrician ladies in her light garden salon, the next retiring to conspire with her son, Tiberius, under the secretive gaze of the Pompeian votaries.

With his accession to the rank of first citizen upon Augustus' death, Tiberius decided to construct the first of the large Imperial palaces which were to extend across the summit of the Palatine. Great interconnecting chambers were built, audience halls, rooms for the ever-expanding contingents of the guard, stores and promenades, gilded bedchambers and suitably appointed rooms for the consumption of fine wines and exotic delicacies. Successive Emperors, when they remained long enough on the throne to commission the architects, added to the structure laid down by Tiberius. The Flavian dynasty, the men who built the Colosseum, were compulsive builders. The principal ruins to be seen on the Palatine today are those of the palace of Domitian, brother of the unlucky Titus.

Domitian seems to have started off no better or worse than most other despots, but if the historian Suetonius may be believed, he rapidly declined into a series of bloodthirsty and lecherous vices to which only his eventual murder put an end. He was balding at an early age and prepared a manual of hair care, dedicated to a friend. 'How pleasant it is to be elegant, yet how quickly that stage passes,' he wrote. Devoted to 'bed-wrestling', as he called it, he entered his forties a paunchy, whimsical man, prey to the dire predictions of fortune-tellers and justly nervous of those who wished him dead.

As the palace rose upon the Palatine, people grew resentful. Old patrician houses were demolished to make way for it. The gross expenditure soon bankrupted the Emperor himself. He turned to extortion, the confiscation of estates and the banishment or murder of his creditors.

Meanwhile, Rabirius the architect pursued his opulent plans: high-walled courtyards, porticoes, now yawning open to the sun, fountains and costly marbled corridors. Suetonius recounts that the Emperor took his daily exercise in a gallery lined with polished moonstone, intended to reflect all that happened behind his back. Neither mirrored rooms nor paid Praetorians saved him. Terrified by his own dreams and the prophecies of soothsayers, he became morbid. There would be blood on the Moon, he said, as she entered Aquarius.

To play on this preoccupation, a steward gained admission to his bedchamber, feigning knowledge of a plot. Ever titillated by a list of conspirators, the Emperor let down his guard. The man jumped at him with a knife and stabbed him – appropriately enough, in the groin.

Watched by a fearful house-boy, the master of the Roman world rolled around the floor clawing at his assassin. Alas, four henchmen appeared and put an end to his struggles with seven thrusts of their blades.

Thus was ushered in Gibbon's period of unparalleled human felicity.

The fantasy of Domitian and Rabirius endures. In the stifling heat of a summer afternoon, it is pleasant to lie in the long grass above the ruins of their excess, and to imagine the furtive Emperor and his architect pacing the glittering walkways or contemplating the Circus Maximus, far below.

Such were the impressions left by the ruined heart of the Roman world upon Gibbon and upon the entire generation of travellers, Grand Tourists and radical fugitives, who came to rediscover it in the knowledge and appreciation of the Enlightenment. The Palatine may even be said to have shaped the tastes of the English landscape garden, for those visitors with land, wealth and intellect returned to Shropshire or Devon intent on recreating its Elysian landscape with ruins.

If any one building may be said to have captured the imagination of travellers down the centuries, however, it is the Colosseum, perhaps the least interesting monument of all. It is a gross construction. It prompts a first intake of breath by its mere dimensions but offers no subtle amusement, no pause for reflection, no refreshment to the spirit. It possesses all the humanism and charm of a football stadium.

Curiously, the Colosseum's form itself has little to do with its lack of appeal. There is nothing intrinsically amiss with the design of an arena, nothing incompatible with grace and harmony. A perfectly beautiful Roman arena forms the centrepiece of the city of Verona. Around it the medieval and Renaissance buildings of the town provide a pleasing counterpoint, and the citizens of Verona may stroll unhurriedly among the arcades, gardens and cafés encircling the ruin. In summer it becomes a marvellous setting for grand opera al fresco, and plasterboard Egyptian pillars or rococo balconies provide an odd sight as they are stacked under Roman vaults between the scene changes. But Rome long ago banished the opera to an awesome setting in the Baths of Caracalla, leaving the Colosseum to languish like an abandoned hulk in a boiling sea of traffic.

The size of the Colosseum ensured that it became the one continuous and surviving symbol of Rome through the centuries of darkness that extinguished the guttering light of the old world. Its construction occupied three emperors of the Flavian dynasty. Vespasian sought popularity by erecting a place for public entertainment on ground usurped by Nero for his private residence. Titus oversaw the middle phase of building, and the egregious Domitian brought it to marbled completion. The engineers first had to drain the artificial lake created by Nero to adorn his Golden House. One can still discern a slight hollow within which the Colosseum stands. Somehow, foundations were created in the mud strong enough to sustain the three enormous tiers, ascending in Doric, Ionic and Corinthian styles, to be topped by a tall wall inset with pillars.

Centuries of depredation did little but crumble the edges of the thing, its sheer volume of stone outliving the plunderers who carried off travertine and marble to use in countless other buildings and at least one bridge over the Tiber, the Ponte Sisto erected by Pope Sixtus IV.

At the beginning of the nineteenth century, the popes decided to restore part of the surviving external wall, motivated by the perennial desire to indulge in conspicuous public works and by the wish to preserve an amphitheatre in which so many gruesome acts of martyrdom had taken place. .

The initial works of Pius VIII were continued by the French authorities, who governed Rome at intermittent periods after the rise of Napoleon. The French were responsible for ending the long period during which the Colosseum was something of a botanical garden, dense with weeds and profuse vegetation. Piranesi's engraving from an elevated view depicted bushes sprouting from the gladiatorial exits and a semi-tropical forest engulfing the second and third tiers. One book by a local naturalist recorded 261 species of flora in the early nineteenth century. The effect of this majestic ruin, overgrown by nature and customarily viewed by moonlight, seems to have struck particular chords in the Romantic soul. Poets, philosophers and writers waxed upon its symbolic union of grandeur and dilapidation.

The stripping away of this brambly clothing around the stonework within the Colosseum left it with a curiously naked effect. Perhaps this contributed to its loss of mystique. Perhaps, too, the overwhelming scale militates against any human response to the edifice. It overawes because of its mightiness, its direct historical link with a bloody epoch in the Christian religion and its recognisable survival from ancient times. It does not draw out from man the same response as a Renaissance *palazzo* or Greek colonnade.

It has a curious modern compulsion for men of power. Mussolini levelled a way through two of the ancient fora to create the Via dei Fori Imperiali, a broad thoroughfare between the Colosseum and Palazzo Venezia, admirably suited to displays of futile military pomp. Successive popes continue to hold a Holy Week ceremony in its shadow, amid flaming torches and illuminated crosses. Refreshed by the blood of its martyrs, the Roman church has seldom ceased to remind the flock of their example.

Both Paul VI and John Paul II made a point of performing these ceremonies with excruciating care. Only the cameramen peering through long-focus lenses could see their faces deep in concentration and piety. Paul VI, in his later years, would walk up the staircase in slow, painful steps to the altar from which he might contemplate the ruined arena. The Polish Pope adopted a stance of pride. He surveyed the view in the manner of one who believed that Rome does not enjoy a monopoly on martyrdom. Rome was his province, not his wellspring. The Colosseum was but a backdrop to his own continuous performance as preacher and politician. He had put this Roman monument in its place.

Occasionally, the Colosseum can serve to remind us of the futility of all empires or the rise of new civilisations and their decay. It is, for example, a rare day when the ruins are not visited by hundreds of Japanese tourists, parting with their yen for souvenirs with as little apparent concern for price as Japanese bankers purchasing the Italian national debt. The Colosseum is one of the icons of the Japanese tourist industry's European package. One company even has its silhouette emblazoned into a logo, surrounded by formal Japanese script, and stuck as a label on all the quasi-identical pieces of luggage stacked for the group on carts at Fiumicino airport.

Quite what it is that the Japanese find to identify with in the Colosseum remains a mystery. Their fondness for other aspects of Italian art and culture requires little explanation. One can easily reconcile the aesthetics of the floating world with a preference for Botticelli. A culture reared on the temple architecture of Kyoto needs no introduction to the Renaissance cloister. The Colosseum, however, exercises a strange fascination precisely because there is no Japanese equivalent. It is unique and therefore to be coveted.

One day in 1989, an occasion of perfect symbolism took place when the leader of the dying Soviet Empire came to seal his peace with the

Pope, to solicit funds from the Italian government and to pass a few minutes in contemplation of the mighty ruin.

Naturally, chaos prevailed. The Roman traffic, denied its daily right to froth and bubble around the Colosseum, came to a halt in a stinking, hooting, snarling mass. The Italian security men, all hair gel, bulging designer suits and strutting arrogance, shouted and pushed at the baying crowds. A few nostalgic Communists, safely corralled behind a set of railings, waved red banners.

Mikhail Gorbachev, fresh from the Vatican, stepped out of his Russian limousine behind a phalanx of flaxen-haired, pale men from his secret service. It was a brisk November day and he wore a grey flannel coat. The KGB and the hair-gel brigade conducted him down an old gladiatorial entrance and into the central arena, where he gazed on the excavated ruins of the subterranean cells beneath the main floor, where those about to die were sent to languish.

Whatever Gorbachev thought at that moment, he did not choose to say. He looked around for a few minutes, then turned on his heel, walked back to his limousine and was driven away, the last glimpse, a pale, balding head and a hand waving wearily as the car vanished past the Arch of the Emperor Constantine.

It seemed that every Roman edifice was destined to decay or to be incorporated in some sanctuary of the new religion. But the dead generations of consuls and scribes had at least imparted to posterity one unblemished monument to their vanquished civilisation.

The Latin language survived in two forms. Among scholars it was studied as a perfected relic, frozen in content and form around the era when the last acknowledged classical writers performed their art. Gibbon came to it late. He deplored the teaching of language while trapped at school, which he saw as the cavern of fear and sorrow. Nor did his fourteen months at Oxford – 'the most idle and unprofitable of my whole life' – produce an awakening. Then came the years of regret. Gibbon was evidently one of those talented pupils who wither in a formal system of regulated syllabus and examination only to flower upon the discovery of private study. This did not take place until he moved to Switzerland.

Its onset was a revelation: 'At my earnest request we moved to open the *Iliad*; and I had the pleasure of beholding, though darkly and through a glass, the true image of Homer ...'

He moved with swift appreciation through the Latin works, dividing them into historians, poets, orators and philosophers. In twenty-seven months by the shores of Lake Leman, he laid the foundations of knowledge for his life's work. Such was the epitome of classical study, a task akin to making oneself thoroughly acquainted with all the objects in a museum.

The second form in which the 'noble tongue' survived was, by contrast, dynamic. The Latin language, its polished epithets and formal, lapidary periods, continued in use around the western world through the ministry of the Roman Catholic Church, whose working language of ritual and bureaucracy it remained until the 1960s. It was, in theory, a dead language. In practice it was adopted and modified for daily use within the walls of the Vatican, even for conversation, and for the preparation of formal diplomatic documents and letters. Untold millions of faithful worshippers may simply have recited what they learned by heart as children but the princes of the Church communicated in glittering and, apparently, ever-evolving versions of the tongue.

All this held true for more than a millennium. Yet in the last three decades of the twentieth century the tradition dwindled to the brink of extinction. The Latin-speaking cleric became an endangered species. Failure to replenish the ranks of Latin scholars who once crowded the benches of the Gregorian University meant that, by the last seven years of the century, very few people under the age of forty connected with the Roman Catholic Church could carry out their functions in the tongue that had been the Church's lingua franca since the dim age of the martyrs.

This dying art found an unlikely champion, in the person of an excitable, balding and burly American priest in his fifties who occupies one of the few positions remaining to Latin scholars of the highest order.

On a cool autumn evening in St Peter's Square – not unlike Gibbon's twilight, one might almost have imagined – Fr Reginald Foster descended, blinking through thick glasses, from his barely furnished office next to the apartments of John Paul II and sat on the base of the obelisk of Caligula to explain the peculiarity of his task and his gloom over the decline in his obsessive love, the language of Plautus and Martial. Fr Foster, you see, is one of the last papal Latinists. His occupation is to translate official documents, encyclicals and letters into good Latin. In the afternoons during term-time he stalks over to the Gregorian University and bullies awe-struck seminarians into the study of dry and difficult texts. If the Church awarded prizes for the abstract practice of evangelistic fervour, Fr Foster's irascible stream of rhetoric and abuse would qualify him for sainthood.

'I like classical music and I always make this comparison, it's almost like some day no one's going to be able to play Handel's harpsichord suites,' observed the priest in a piercing American tone. 'Can you imagine what that would mean on planet Earth? No one would know what this would sound like any more.

'There's a treasure there and a value that is simply being lost. I think it's simply a tragedy among so many other tragedies. An intelligent and enlightened place for Latin would be the cure for many many foolish things we're doing.'

What, one wondered, might these follies include? Fr Foster's massive head jerked up and to the right, to the papal apartments high above the piazza. 'Well of course my office is right up there with the windows open on the third floor where the Pope is – even though he's not in the house now,' he said by way of explanation, 'but I guess all this obsession with sexuality and all this other stuff they're obsessed with – this whole nonsense – and if you get off of that stuff and get down to culture and humanity and education and all these glorious things ... but they're frittering away their lives – Ratzinger and all these people on the sidelines – and this whole beautiful thing is falling apart!'

A few pilgrims had paused to listen to this oration, delivered at a volume suitable for the lecture-room and with apparent disregard for any acolytes of Cardinal Josef Ratzinger, the Pope's appointed guardian of morality, who may have been passing by from his lair in the old Holy Office behind the piazza. It seemed prudent to return to the dead genius of classical Latin and its inheritance by the Roman Catholic Church.

Fr Foster had no trouble enlisting the immediate endorsement of the reigning pontiff himself in the cause. For while greeting a crowd of pilgrims to the papal summer residence a week earlier, John Paul II had uttered a revealing remark.

'At Castelgandolfo the other week there were about thirty-five nationalities, and they were all singing songs in Croatian and Slovak and everything else and after all the songs he said, "Now let's pray together in the common language of the Church which is Latin." And he starts singing the Our Father.

'Of course very few people answered because they didn't know it, you see,' said Fr Foster. 'That's especially what I'm concerned about. And even in the office I'm telling my friends you don't realise what's happening! What has happened! Nobody under forty really knows Latin!'

His was the last group of priests to be immersed in the Latin language morning, noon and night.

'I'm kind of fifty-three. I was kinda one of the last of the generations where I had fourteen years of Latin before I was ordained,' he recalled. 'I still write notes to the rector in Latin and I still converse with the people in the house in Latin. You see, they are my classmates of thirty years ago. The students will stand by and not understand one word. They want to do Church history and they don't know three words of Latin. Now in class I have Jesuit priests who have never had one class of it!' Fr Foster's voice rose once more to a pitch of indignation. 'Now this is gonna have an effect, you see!'

It seemed that the rarified upper echelons of the Church were either unaware or heedless of the fact that Latin is dying out beneath them.

'Now these guys up there' – Fr Foster gestured again to the papal chambers where his team of translators sits – 'are writing encyclicals in Latin and certainly the Pope can handle it and he could talk in Latin and write things out in a kind of a Church talk which was so common from St Thomas Aquinas onwards. But what he doesn't realise is that from people forty down – Zero!'

Some people may regard as fanciful the notion of Latin as a spoken language, since we naturally possess no recording of what it sounded like. This, needless to say, is no impediment to its admirers.

'We more or less know what it sounded like,' said Fr Foster defensively. 'There are different theories. Was it like Chinese, singing, up and down? Was it accented? All kinds of theories. But I think we could get very close. We do have what we call the restored classical pronunciation which came in between the wars.

'The English thing was of course off the wall – you know, all that "amikaityai" – some nonsense or other! – and the Italian version was that of the later empire. The classicists decided on the restored classical "weni widi wici". Everyone will accept that today. We can get very very close.'

They did not have much time at the Vatican for the modern fashions of Oxbridge classicism. 'For many people Suetonius is practically the end of Latin literature, considered the last prose writer – 160 AD,' complained Fr Foster of that scurrilous historian. 'For example your *New Oxford Dictionary* ends at 160! But the old Lewis & Short dictionary goes up to 400 AD. I tell the students they have to get Lewis & Short. The Oxford dictionary ends at the end of perhaps the silver age of Latin. I think it's disastrous!' One suspected that he thought Protestant influence to blame.

Nor, claimed Fr Foster, was it possible to relegate Latin to a formal, lifeless instrument suitable only for the driest of official pronouncements. The vernacular tongue spoken from Trastevere to Antioch had also come down to us.

'If you look at the first comedians like Plautus and Terence, and then talk to the Italians, you can see that there was a vernacular language which was rumbling along on a parallel track with Cicero's orations and Horace and all this other stuff.

'It's that vernacular which has turned into your Romance languages and it's very beautiful to see. The Italians have the same idioms, the same word order and the same adjectives and everything.

'We don't go around and talk in Brooklyn like Shakespeare and Milton. There were two levels and how Cicero spoke to his family at home must have been very simple and fast and neat, none of these glorious periods.'

Students who volunteered for one of Fr Foster's renowned courses at the Gregorian University were obliged to consider the whole arc of Latin for two thousand years. 'Some teachers insist that the students should read Virgil. I say well then that's like doing nothing except reading Dryden or Pope! After a while you're going to say there must be something more here. People didn't talk the way these poets did.'

His idea, therefore, was to broaden the student's understanding by including authors who wrote in colloquial terms and those who practised the utmost refinement. 'Examples have come up,' explained Fr Foster. 'You can see how Plautus in 200 BC was talking on the street in what turned out to be Italian. Then, Cicero, 150 years later, is more or less what we would call our standard beautiful bookshelf Latin.'

For British classicists force-fed a diet of the *Aeneid* and the *Odes* of Horace, Fr Foster provided a brisk deflation of the idea that Latin literature flowered only under the patronage of Augustus.

'Well there was a flowering under Mussolini too!' he chortled. 'Augustus had Virgil and Horace and Livy ... we still haven't forgiven Livy for being so romantic and not mentioning his sources instead of not being coldly historical. Augustus wanted Family Values – here we go! – Roman values, blah blah, to solidify his New World Order.' He laughed, it being a few weeks before an American presidential election.

Writing and publishing were commercial enterprises, too, not merely a refined and restricted art enclosed within the courtyards and banquet-rooms of the élite. 'There was quite a business. Even in Cicero's time his friend Atticus had a business here in Rome of copyists, and Cicero talks – he was down in the country – he writes to somebody in Rome to go to Atticus, 'because he has copies of this oration and I hear it's selling well!'

'The political pamphlets – the philippics and so on – were copied out by twenty or thirty people and sold. Even Martial – and he's a doll of course, wonderful – he tells people go to this particular bookstall near the Senate House "and you will find me there". He made propaganda to sell his poems. Virgil's stuff was read in the courts ... but other people, like Mozart and his symphonies, they had to write to live. Some were sold as a way of living and other stuff I imagine was read in literary circles. A lot of people wouldn't have read these things or heard of them,' Fr Foster believed.

His own views were heretical. 'Virgil and Cicero are overdone. I don't even like Virgil myself,' snorted Fr Foster. 'Lucretius I think is neglected. So is Martial. The most neglected is our dear Plautus. He's a genius in every sense ... the ideas and the language ... the students get Plautus eleven months every year.'

One got the impression that on occasion Fr Foster's enthusiasm for the language is such that more conventional churchly considerations are rarely permitted to intrude.

'Why just the other day we were reading some Plautus, where the mother is accusing her daughter of being a prostitute,' he said with delight. 'And the daughter says: "*Is mihi quaestus est.* This is my business, how am I supposed to make money?" And of course it's very noble! She says: "I'm not criticising people who don't live like I do and not praising people who do live like I do but this is my job!"

'Even one of the students said, "My! How noble and serene the whole thing is! Glorious, simply glorious! And totally neglected."'

Fortunately none of Cardinal Ratzinger's pale-faced minions was passing by the obelisk as Fr Foster delivered these observations to a thunderous, crimson-gilded sky.

* * *

During one of the periodic fires that ravaged the fabric of Imperial Rome, the library on the Capitoline hill burnt down. The Emperor Domitian – who elsewhere has received a dreadful press – is recorded as performing a duty of lofty intellectual worth. Suetonius says that he had copies of the incinerated books sent to the capital from all over the Empire. Teams of Roman copyists were dispatched to Alexandria, where the libraries were legendary. They brought back fresh copies of lost works. 'Suetonius ...' mused Fr Foster, 'Yeeees ... Some people have been ruined by him and Tacitus – I mean Claudius, and our dear Caligula and Nero have been blackened for ever by those guys and they say they weren't really that bad. I don't think they were that bad at all.' So there we are. The Pope's Latinist does not think that the Emperor Nero was such a bad fellow after all.

All the Imperial effort in the service of literature was of little help in preserving a vast range of works from oblivion. The Latinists still mourn the pagan volumes lost in the centuries of blackness and destruction.

'Oh my Lord, you can't even think of it because you get heartsick!' howled Fr Foster, sitting on 'our dear Caligula's' plinth, racked with woe at the thought. A courting couple – he an Italian soldier, she a long-tressed teenager – looked around in alarm.

'Half of Latin literature was lost, we figure, not much of Horace, we don't have forty-eight orations of Cicero that he mentions, half of his correspondence we don't have. Cicero had a correspondence with all these people but the letters that they sent to him are all gone,' he said. 'We have only one sixth of Livy. The rest is all gone.' Some might sigh in gratitude at that, of course, but it seemed irreverent to make the point.

'We have all kinds of poets. We just know that they existed. Like some of the friends of Catullus, we know that he had all kinds of friends in a poetic circle and all their stuff is gone ... one line here, one line there.' A later author, Aulus Gellius, mentions some of these vanished poets but offers only a tantalising hint of their eradicated lives and works.

Indeed, of Julius Caesar himself we possess but little. 'Cicero in several places in his works praises Julius Caesar's eloquence. We don't have one oration of Caesar. Tragic,' Fr Foster lamented. 'Cicero heard these things and praised his eloquence more than his own. And that's all gone. It's really sad.'

It was one of the classical defences mounted against Gibbon by the partisans of the Church that Christianity itself contributed to the preservation of a part of Latin culture.

Fr Foster cited the example of Saint Augustine and the lost author Hortensius. Augustine had read a work by Hortensius entitled *The Praise of Philosophy*. It converted him, in Fr Foster's words, to 'a more or less philosophical way of looking at life and to maturity'. No text survived of Hortensius' work, although it was in circulation as late as the fourth century. The only texts that remained were those preserved through the Middle Ages in the pages of Saint Augustin's excessively voluminous works.

Defunct and dusty though the writers and poets might be, to a Latinist they are for ever flitting behind every pillar, wraith-like presences in every ruined colonnade.

'Oh my heaven's sake!' exclaimed Fr Foster in an excess of enthusiasm. 'When I go to these authors and I read these things I just KNOW these people, I can SEE them on the street. Plautus and even Caesar ... it's so real!

'I've got a beautiful edition of all of Cicero's works in one volume – a famous edition which I found one copy of. I have it mounted on a missal stand and every day, faithfully almost like my prayers, I read a page of this, you see. This is my spiritual reading. To read this stuff, especially his letters and stuff, I can just hear him talking. You can HEAR him talking! You can just HEAR him so clear and neat and wonderful!'

The works of Cicero were pleasures the excellence of which is almost universally acknowledged. Gibbon himself regarded the letters as the models of every form of correspondence, 'from the careless effusions of tenderness and friendship to the well-guarded declaration of discreet and dignified resentment'. One might be forgiven for suspecting that the productions of Pope John Paul II were not exactly of the same literary order. And, as it transpires, one would be correct.

The Pope's Latinist, a loyal and obedient servant, was obliged, of course, to make a few things plain. The tools at his disposal, for a start, must be understood in their limitations. 'Latin is extremely functional. It's utilitarian. It's not dreamy like Greek or French, just drifting off. Latin won't do that, you've got to say something and get moving otherwise it's not going to be good Latin,' he said.

'It went with the character of the people. The Romans didn't have very much imagination at all. It was the Greeks who had the imagination.

The Romans were really dumb, square-like, and once they learned something they stuck with it for centuries and the language mirrors this perfectly. Just like the Colosseum.

'I always tell the students Latin is as solid and as enduring as the Colosseum. Now there's nothing beautiful there. It's very impressive, the Colosseum, but it's total functionality.

'It's like an instrument. You use it. And even when the Romans tried to be funny, you know their jokes are not so funny at all. The Romans couldn't really laugh. You can always hear the legions walking in Latin.

'The Greeks were totally different. There was air, and breath, and spirit and breeziness in the Greeks that the Romans just didn't understand. Caesar is so lean and so linear and straight ...'.

Thus far for the language. Now for the content. Here Fr Foster drew up his sternest indictment of the new status quo (not that the status quo can be known officially by its Latin term, of course).

'I came thirty years ago and for five years every single one of my Theology classes was in Latin and we took it for granted that everyone could express himself. Not a trace of this is left. Not a trace. In 1967 they said, "We're going to do this in Italian."

'I'm glad I wasn't there to see this. They said, "No, no no, now the new thing is this" – they thought Vatican Two meant this, which of course it didn't – but the Liberation was coming and all this other stuff and they said, "We'll go into Italian." Now the students come up almost begging on their knees and say to me: "Couldn't we do a little bit of Latin at Christmas time?" '

Mellifluous, caressing, languid, forgiving, theatrical and drawn-out, Italian does not conform to the stern requirements of the Latinist. 'It doesn't have what I would say you call guts,' said Fr Foster dismissively. 'It's very milky creamy and nice.'

Thirty years ago, encyclicals and papal statements were first composed in Latin, then rendered into vernacular languages by teams of specialists. By the pontificate of John Paul II it was the other way around.

'Most of them are written in Italian by a commission,' said Fr Foster with scorn. He went on graphically to compare the output of these worthies to an embarrassing ailment. It might be kinder to them (and to him) to leave the comparison to the imagination. 'They can't shut up,' he said. 'This drivels on and on, and then they come and say "You're supposed to put this into Latin."

'And I've been quoted, against even the boss up there, like all these verbose encyclicals and other stuff, which are intolerable ... if you were to write these things, the original, in Latin, then (1) they would be one fourth, one tenth of their length, and (2) you'd say much more.'

His lot, however, was to deconstruct the reams of Italian and to render it into a Latin text which merely went into the archives for history.

Although Fr Foster did not say so, it was the tendency of the reigning pontiff to lapse into a peculiar Polish-Italian flight of metaphysical speculation, mingled with what he imagined to be up-to-date academic sociology. This would provide any translator with a nightmarish task.

If the fog of meaning is dense in the original, how can it thus be cleanly rendered into accurate English, German ... or Latin? A recent major encyclical, *Centesimos Annos*, seemed to have taxed the patience of the Vatican's officials to the limit. Fr Foster still groaned at the recollection.

'Even the Italians didn't understand the Italian. The English is hardly intelligible. All this sociological jargon, hundreds of pages of it! Someone asked me, "Did the Pope approve the Latin?" I said, "I don't know." He had to sign it because that's the official thing. I doubt whether he understood it himself.'

All the specialists got together for a drink around a table when this gargantuan work was complete. 'I said, "Man, this is for the birds! What they should do is sit down and force themselves to express themselves in Latin and they would be saying about four things and be done with it",' recalled Fr Foster. It reminded him with acute melancholy of the maxim of one cardinal long since departed to his reward: If one cannot express it in classical Latin, then it is not worthy to be expressed.

The Pope, it seemed, remained deaf to these appeals, even though he himself complained that few people were speaking Latin in the hall at a bishops' synod. Bishops used to summon Fr Foster and other Latinists to polish Latin interventions for debates, 'but that's all over now'.

One prelate, however, stood out as a beacon of enlightenment, in Fr Foster's view. He was the Cardinal Archbishop of Westminster. 'Ah, Hume, our beloved Hume. Cardinal Hume said when he retires he's coming down and he's going to do Latin in my class. These are cultured people,' he said in pleasant reflection. The mood lasted only a moment before the Dark Ages returned. 'But there are hundreds of people, even younger bishops, who just can't handle this and what are you going to do? You can't just martyr them!'

*　　*　　*

Until 1967, the office of the Latinists enjoyed its own distinctive title. It was known as *Epistoles ad Principes* – Briefs to Princes. The titles were taken away in a fit of modernism, and scholars like Fr Foster were listed by their minor official rank in the *Annuario Pontefice*, the *Who's Who* of the Vatican. The scholar who held the last title as chief composer of the Briefs to Princes is now over ninety years old. The man lives in retirement in an apartment behind the Vatican, and when he dies, the old title will expire with him. 'He's the Last of the Mohicans,' said Fr Foster, with an unerring instinct for the least apt comparison, a sign that thirty years in Rome have not touched him that profoundly.

He himself would stay for ever, 'unless I get sick or get thrown out'. There may be twenty more years of work in him, he reckoned. He has succeeded in loving Rome because, for one in his vocation, there could be nowhere else that fulfilled so perfectly the needs of the obsession and the faith at once. And each of these provided him with a little island of peace: his home in a religious house on the Janiculum hill, that bare study down the corridor from the Pope, with the crucifix above a plain table, and the lecture-room at the Gregorian University. Each day he navigated on foot across the swirling city – 'no discipline, no control and everyone has his own motor car' – hopping, from one safe haven to another.

Reginald Foster thought that nobody should have any illusions about Latin. 'It takes about fourteen to fifteen years of work, I tell my students, and they may as well reconcile themselves to that and get on with it.' Expect no real results for the first four or five years, he maintained. The rewards will yield themselves only later.

This was not an easy message to impart to the young, even to seminarians. 'Ah, everything is so fast now, the quick fix thing,' lamented the Pope's Latinist, 'especially, you know, with the American way of vision ...'.

He arose from the plinth of the late, lamented Caligula's obelisk and wandered off through the colonnades, back through the gate pierced in the walls of the Vatican City. Cicero, no doubt, awaited.

CHAPTER 3

Mrs Shelley's Roman spring

In the second decade of the nineteenth century an earnest young woman travelled through Italy, keeping a journal as she went. It is still with us, a brown leather-bound hardback book, embossed with a gilt pattern incorporating the emblem of a horn intertwined with plants.

The owner of the book was Mary Wollstonecraft Shelley, daughter of the radical philosopher William Godwin and the renowned feminist Mary Wollstonecraft, from whom her first two names derived. She had eloped with the poet Percy Bysshe Shelley and then married him. Thus, just beyond her teens, her life had already attained a tumultuous notoriety.

In years to come she would try to live it all down. But aglow with the flush of early spring 1819, no thoughts of the kind troubled the couple, pursuing their excited discovery of one city after another in the Italian peninsula. Mary and her husband were heading to Rome from Naples in anticipation of a new year, full of fresh hope and still armoured by the youthful confidence that one is invulnerable.

Much later, she wrote an inscription in the journal: 'Begun July 21, 1816. Ended with my happiness, June 7th, 1819.'

The Shelley party breasted the Alban hills south of Rome on Friday, 5 March 1819. They looked upon the far-off city with a sense of enchantment. It was their second visit to Rome. The entry in Mary's journal for that day betrayed nothing of the woes ahead. They surveyed 'the beautiful hills of Albano' and traversed the *campagna* south of the city. From far off, pilgrims could make out the glimmer of marble and the flash of white travertine through a dense curtain of pine trees. The group descended into the vale of the Tiber, entered the old city walls and rode past the Colosseum.

The journey from the Campanian countryside to Rome was arduous. Poor roads, uncertain conditions and the quantity of luggage all contrived to make it more difficult. Romantic travellers did not travel light. Not for them a bag slung over a shoulder and a pocketful of cash. They moved around the Continent encumbered by quantities of clothing, books and domestic necessities – even furniture – that would make a modern removal company shudder. All this had to be conveyed by horse-drawn carts and poorly sprung carriages from one temporary residence to another. Pestilence, discomfort and danger contributed to the experience of each journey. Shelley, who sometimes travelled with a pistol, once saw with his own eyes a murder casually committed at the roadside between Naples and Rome.

The Shelleys arrived in Rome before dark. Their first visit to Rome, in the previous year, had been brief. This time they intended to explore the city in greater depth. It was also a chance to rebuild their life as a couple.

A season of tragedy had set in for Shelley. His first wife, Harriet, had committed suicide by throwing herself into the Serpentine lake in Hyde Park. His children by the first marriage had been denied to him by order of the Lord Chancellor. Shelley pronounced a vituperative verse addressed to that worthy, 'I curse thee by a parent's outraged love.' It had no effect.

Sent down from Oxford, a hot-headed critic of the established order and a loudly self-professed atheist, the poet represented scandal where he did not evoke the shiver of revolution. Children were unlikely to be granted to the care of such a parent by the stern authorities of the time. He and Mary then had a daughter named Clara, but the child died of a sudden fever at Venice in November 1818.

Mary was cast into depression and despair by little Clara's death. But with youthful resilience, she had bounced back to enjoy the delights of life in southern Italy. On one bright December day they had visited the ruins of Pompeii, where they lunched on oranges, figs, bread and medlars beneath the portico of the temple of Jupiter. 'If such is Pompeii,' asked Shelley in wonder, 'what was Athens?'

Now they travelled with their surviving, much-adored son William, who was four. Inevitably, too, there came Claire Clairemont, Mary's step-sister and Byron's discarded mistress. She exercised a charm over Shelley until his death and, perhaps as a result, her relations with Mary veered from the affectionate to the injurious.

All these young people imagined that a Roman spring might provide their renaissance. Instead it would commit Mary to despair. It marked the turning point in her life, from a fearless taker of risks into a woman who, in her own words, walked on shifting sands. From a guarded optimist, ready to be intoxicated by life, she turned into a melancholic.

On that first day back in the city, Mary quoted in her journal from one of the numerous books upon their reading list that spring, Edmund Spenser's *Ruins of Rome*.

> Rome living was the world's sole ornament
> And dead is now the world's sole monument.

Shelley might have done better than this, even on one of his poor days. But the overwhelming effect of Rome evidently made even the banal seem poetic. The party lodged at a hotel. With scarcely a pause to unpack, they threw themselves into a round of sightseeing.

After two days they moved to rooms at the Palazzo Verospi, at 300 Via del Corso. The *palazzo* overlooked a long, straight avenue of palaces and official buildings, inset with churches and punctuated by elegant piazzas. It extended from the northern gates of the city almost to the boundaries of the Forum. The Palazzo Verospi was just about the last building in the Corso, a few minutes walk from that rambling archae-ological garden, as yet untamed and innocent of the broad avenue that would be driven across its expanse by the architects of Italian Fascism. The unhappy monument that graces Piazza Venezia today did not exist and the modern car-strangled square was but half its present size, bounded by the Palazzo Venezia itself and by a walled garden laid out under the direction of Pope Paul II. To the north, the Corso ran up to Piazza Colonna, where, by decree, all coffee-roasters in the city plied their trade around the column of Marcus Aurelius. A pungent aroma filled the air.

Today the frontage of the Palazzo Verospi houses a branch of an Italian bank and its façade is blackened by the incessant, stinking fumes spouted by buses, taxis and a fleet of dark-blue government cars. In 1819 it must have been comparatively pleasant, with carriages and horsemen clattering past, placed at the very epicentre of Shelley's Roman world.

'There are two Italies,' Shelley wrote to his friend, Leigh Hunt. 'One composed of the green earth & the transparent sea & the mighty ruins of ancient time & aerial mountains and the warm & radiant atmosphere which is interdiffused through all things – the other consists of the Italians of the present day, their works and ways. The one is most sublime & lovely contemplation that can be conceived by the imagination of man; the other is most degrading, disgusting and odious.' Rome provided both in ample measure.

It is all but impossible nowadays to conceive of the impact of the South on travellers in the age of the Enlightenment. Nor can we share the tantalising prospect of new and extraordinary sights that excited every quivering fibre of their imaginations.

We assume today that tourists to countries like Italy seek a personal confirmation of images lodged since infancy in the mind. A child has already seen colour pictures, films, or videotapes of the Colosseum and St Peter's, perhaps heard the Pope pronounce a televised benediction in a multitude of tongues from the basilica's balcony, listened to the chanting choirs at the Easter rite and laughed at Gregory Peck and Audrey Hepburn a-flurry along the Via Veneto or around the Trevi fountain. Thus, upon boarding an aircraft, taking a coach and arriving in a comfortable hotel, the visitor sets forth to visit monuments and churches with whose actual appearance he or she is already familiar.

At the beginning of the nineteenth century all these possibilities remained far-off. For those condemned to live in the wet English shires and to pass their childhood in dull northern climes the miraculous effect of the Mediterranean light could scarcely be imagined. Think of it – no photographs, no colour reproduction, no moving images, no mechanically reproduced sound, only the words of previous travellers and such tinted engravings or drawings as could be printed in books, themselves available to relatively few. Unless one had visited an art gallery and gazed upon the original oil painting or watercolour by an artist back from the Mediterranean, the senses would have been quite unprepared for what lay in store.

Rome offered a dizzying prospect of ruins and doomed splendour. In letters and poetry of the time, each word it evokes is worth volumes of sensuality. The light drenches the daily world and it suffuses existence. The stars pant in the sky at night. Flowers perfume every step and sensations dance in frantic minds intoxicated by the South. In letter after letter, people from northern Europe speak of rebirth, coming alive, instincts newly sharpened and love's pleasure brought to a crescendo. The spirit of a young person educated in the classics could not fail to be uplifted.

At the same time Roman society was almost certain to disappoint. The old families, long mummified in their manners and customs, were robbed by the papacy's temporal authority of any court or government system that might give meaning to their rank. As a result the traveller found no sparkle, an absence of exciting gossip, none of the tension and verve that marks an exchange of power or the infiltration of new men into high positions. The aristocrats played cards, held salons and performed like supporting actors on an ornate stage long abandoned by its principal player. Compared to France, England or the Tuscan states, society was complacent and dull.

It rained all over the weekend when the Shelleys moved in, very typical of the sudden, heavy showers that douse the Roman spring. That did not deter Shelley and Mary from stalking off to inspect the Colosseum, the Vatican Museums and the Villa Borghese. On 10 March they, too, ascended the Capitol, and their journal recorded the 'most divine statues' in its surroundings. 'We live surrounded by antiquity,' noted Mary.

Of the Colosseum, Shelley wrote: 'It has been changed by time into the image of an amphitheatre of rocky hills overgrown by the wild olive, the myrtle and the fig-tree and threaded by little paths which wind along its ruined stairs & immeasurable galleries.' The woods embraced its visitor and wild weeds pierced through flowers blooming beneath one's feet.

Nearby stood the Arch of Constantine, an edifice upon which the poet held pronounced views. In his opinion it should have retained its original title as the Arch of Trajan. It was disgraceful that a craven Senate should have rededicated it to Constantine, 'the Christian reptile who had crept among the blood of his murdered family to the supreme power'.

Shelley was enthusiastically infected with the spirit of pagan Rome, seeking the vindication of his own atheist principles in the proof of its extinction through Christianity. Despite their eager anti-clericalism, however, neither Mary nor Shelley had much time for the great sage. 'We go to Lausanne and visit Gibbon's house,' their diary recorded of that pilgrimage. 'I see the little summer house where he finished his history and the old acacias on the terrace from which he saw Mont Blanc after having completed the last sentence. My companion gathered some Acacia leaves in remembrance of him ... I refrained from doing so ... Gibbon had a cold and senseless heart.'

Shelley and Mary were never apt to let the heartbeat slow or allow its palpitations to fall calm. A few days after their arrival the two of them slipped out of the Palazzo Verospi late at night and walked by moonlight to view the Pantheon, a great domed Roman temple dedicated to all the gods. Its huge portals stood open, its round inner chamber then uncluttered by the pompous marble tombs of the Kings of Italy implanted there later in the century. It must have been an austere interior, with the coffered circular roof ascending to its round aperture, through which the moon's rays fell on the flagstones and the undiscovered tombstone of Raphael. 'As when you regard the unmeasured dome of heaven,' Shelley thought, 'the idea of magnitude is swallowed up & lost.' Mary remembered how the columns of the rotunda were set aglow by the diffused light of the moonbeams.

Rome was beginning to exercise its magical spell. The Shelleys saw the elderly Pope Pius VII in St Peter's. They encountered him walking on the Pincio, taking a little exercise while his horses trotted alongside in the shafts of his carriage. At the opera, Rossini was all the rage. On 18 March, the Shelleys visited the curious pyramid that marked the tomb of Caius Cestius, a Roman governor of Egypt, already then a place of succour for hungry Roman cats. It stood just on the boundary of the city walls and formed the cornerpiece of the cemetery for non-Catholics. It was a place that would recur in their writings and become a symbol of the Romantic tragedy. Shelley put down his first impressions in a letter to a friend. 'I think [it] the most beautiful and solemn cemetery I ever beheld. To see the sun shining on its bright grass, fresh when we visited it with the autumnal dews and hear the whispering of the wind among the leaves of the trees which have overgrown the tomb of Cestius ... and to mark the tombs mostly of women and young people who were buried there, one might, if one was to die, desire the sleep they seem to sleep.'

The social life pursued by most English visitors to Rome did not contain much to attract the Shelleys. They had, in any case, become accustomed to their own company. At Bagni di Lucca, in Tuscany, Mary and Claire went to the weekly balls but did not dance. 'I do not know whether they refrain from philosophy or Protestantism,' Shelley observed. At Naples, Mary recorded, 'we lived in utter solitude' and Shelley wrote to Thomas Love Peacock 'we see absolutely no-one here'. Stuffy salons full of gentlemanly English travellers held little appeal for Shelley. His elopement from England, abandonment of his first wife and loudly proclaimed atheism had made him an outcast. Nor did he have much tolerance for the recognised poets of the age, whose works won fame while his languished in obscurity. 'What a pitiful wretch this Wordsworth!' he wrote to Peacock. 'That such a man should be a poet. I can compare him with no one but Simonides, that flatterer of the Sicilian tyrants and at the same time the most natural and tender of lyric poets.'

Most Shelley lovers know that he called Italy 'the paradise of exiles'. Few recall that he also regarded it as 'the retreat of pariahs'. Yet Shelley was uncomfortable with solitude for very long. 'Social enjoyment, in some form or another, is the Alpha and Omega of existence,' he admitted. 'I most devoutly wish I were living near London,' he was to write, missing its radical society and his friends.

The party went to call on the Signora Marianna Candida Dionigi, their neighbour at number 310 on the Via del Corso. The Signora was a talented product of the enlightened minor aristocracy. A widow, she performed the duties of a mother to her seven children, was a musician, dabbled in painting and had written two books about art and the region of Lazio. Signora Dionigi's salon became a regular stop for the English, although many of them, unable to understand the patter of Italian, simply propped up the ornate chairs in silence until a suitable hour of the evening, when they arose, made a polite farewell, and departed. Mary was unimpressed. 'We saw nobody at Naples – but we see a few people here – the Italian character does not improve upon us,' she noted, archly. As for Signora Dionigi, she was 'very old, very miserly and very mean'.

Shelley wrote to Peacock in scathing terms: 'We see no English society here ... the manners of the English are wholly insupportable and they assume pretensions which they would not venture upon in their own country.' Despite the sweeping edict it seems that not all such visitors were unwelcome. Frederick North, the Earl of Guildford, apparently called twice on the Shelleys without incident. As the youngest son of Lord North, George III's Prime Minister, he might have been expected to attract the full vitriol of Shelley's dislike for the regime. Perhaps his own role as a well-known traveller and antiquarian spared him the experience.

Shelley was in no mood to hear a good word about his native country. 'I believe, dear Peacock, that you wish us to come back to England,' he wrote. 'How is it possible? Health, competence, tranquillity – all these Italy permits & England takes away.'

Yet the exaltation of Italy coexisted in the minds of both the Shelleys with a view of the Italians that would find no place in a modern journal of the politically correct.

'The Romans please me much,' Shelley recorded, 'especially the women, who, though totally devoid of every kind of information, or culture of the imagination, or affections, or understanding – and in this respect a kind of gentle savage – yet contrive to be interesting.' Meeting them socially was, he felt, 'very like an intercourse with uncorrupted children'.

Writing private letters to his male friends in London, Shelley betrayed an erotic fascination for the women of Rome. It was held in bounds of restraint by a brand of prudery that was at once both very English and quite unromantic.

Shelley gazed into the eyes of many a young lady in the course of his researches. He concluded, however, that their superficial sparkle could not substitute for the deeper charms of the northern European. They lacked 'the mazy depth of colour behind colour' which gave intellectual excitement to female beauty.

These Italian eyes were customarily set in a frame of desirable, yet imperfect, allure. Shelley elaborated: 'The moulding of the face, modelled with sculptural exactness, and the dark luxuriance of their hair floating over their complexions; and the lips – you must hear the commonplaces which escape from them before they cease to be dangerous.'

This marked an improvement on Shelley's view of one year before, when he had written to Thomas Medwin thus: 'The modern Italians seem a miserable people without sensibility, or imagination, or understanding. Their outside is polished, and an intercourse with them seems to proceed with much facility, though it ends in nothing and produces nothing.

'The women are particularly empty and though possessed of the same kind of superficial grace, are devoid of cultivation and refinement.'

The true level of such conversations between English and Italians has not come down to us. It is unlikely to have reached the rarified realms that prevailed in the Shelley household. During their first week in Rome, Mary's leisure reading consisted of the Bible and Livy, while her husband was immersed in Lucretius. In Latin, of course.

Rome was still in a distressed state after the Napoleonic wars and French occupation. Some palaces had been ransacked, churches had been stripped of their ornaments and several rich families had lost all their valuables. Life was slowly returning to the city centre but the place was still prey to rumour, infested by mutual distrust and prone to alarm.

Yet the visitors' routine pursued a quiet, civilised pace. Mary went riding regularly in the Pincian gardens and in the grounds of the Villa Borghese. At the end of March, Shelley made his way to the Vatican for a private performance of the Miserere. Ceremonial exercised a fascination upon him. The treasures of the Vatican, very often, did not. He was studiously unimpressed by the Sistine Chapel, deeming Michelangelo's *Last Judgement* a vulgar piece of artistic propaganda, 'a dull & wicked emblem of a dull & wicked thing'. It showed 'God leaning out of heaven as if eagerly enjoying the final scene of the infernal tragedy he has set the universe to act'. Jesus Christ he thought was 'like an angry pot-boy ... in an attitude of commonplace resentment'. The whole fresco he dismissed as 'a kind of *Titus Andronicus* in painting but the author surely no Shakespeare'. It had hideousness without beauty, terror without loveliness. Shelley's tastes were directed towards more sensual works of art, for example 'a Diana of Titian – the softest & most voluptuous form with languid & uplifted eyes and warm yet passive limbs ...'.

Two days after the Miserere, he was back with Mary and their son William, 'Will-mouse'. Although Shelley did not much like the basilica – 'The more I see of the interior of St Peter's the less impression as a whole does it produce on me' – he loved the sweep and drama of Bernini's piazza, colonnades and playing fountains. They filled the air with a radiant mist, he noticed, and in the sharp light of noon innumerable particles seemed to hang in the spray.

The little boy, to the delight of his parents, drank in every aspect of the spectacle, especially the animals that thronged the piazza.

'We took our Will-man to the Vatican & he was delighted with the goats and the cavalli,' Mary wrote. 'William speaks more Italian than

English – when he sees anything he likes he cries *O Dio che bella!*'

'The silken fineness of his hair, the transparence of his complexion, the animation & deep blue colour of his eyes were the astonishment of everyone,' Shelley recalled. 'The Italian women used to bring each other to look at him when he was asleep.' One day William was taken by his parents to the market in the Campo de'Fiori, a medieval piazza near the Tiber. A shouting throng moved between stalls laden with artichokes, fruit, flowers, sheeps' lungs and glistening pigs' livers. William's eyes gaped wide at the sight of a huge sea bass, and to the delight of English and Italians alike he let out a loud '*O Dio che bella!*' The fish-stalls still cluster at the southern end of the piazza: serried ranks of sole and flounder, baskets of black clams and the startling sight of the head of a swordfish, propped up to display its four-foot blade. In the centre of the square stands a grim and hooded statue of Giordano Bruno, the man of philosophy and astronomer. It marks the spot where he was burnt alive by the Inquisition in 1600 for the supposed heresies of his teachings.

The ever-present reminders of injustice did nothing to staunch Shelley's revolutionary beliefs. His loathing for authority did not remain far below the surface, fed at every step by new evidence of feudal oppression. Galley-slaves toiled in the Colosseum. Three hundred convicts were to be seen at work in St Peter's square as the fountains played gaily, 'fettered animals at work watched over by sentries with muskets,' Shelley noted. 'It is the emblem of Italy – moral degradation contrasted with the glory of nature & the arts.'

The Emperor of Austria, Francis II, had descended upon the Vatican to partake of the Holy Week ceremonies, a slow-moving cycle of ritual and dull pomp. Long before the days when leaders came preceded by a phalanx of bodyguards, the Emperor was attended by a single officer with drawn sword, who cleared his path. The Shelleys kept out of his path, 'for our English blood would ... boil over at such insolence'.

'How gracefully the old and venerable Pope fulfilled the church ceremonies,' Mary noted. The palaces of the Vatican were hung with silks, while celebratory fireworks and suppers marked the Imperial progress.

Ensconced in the exiles' paradise, the couple none the less missed their friends in London. Letters arrived on 5 April from Peacock and Leigh Hunt. It was the practice to pick up mail from the post office on the Corso, then, as now, a tiresome and uncertain procedure. Sometimes letters to and from Italy were simply lost in the mail; on other occasions a letter from England would reach some Italian city after the restless Shelley party had already departed for their next home. Collecting the post was not all boredom, however. On one occasion Shelley strolled into the post office, asked for letters addressed to him by name, and was felled to the ground by an outraged fellow-countryman who exclaimed, 'What! Are you that damned atheist Shelley?'

Both the Shelleys were great propagandists for the expatriate way of life. On 12 March Mary dispatched a letter to Marianne Hunt from the Corso: 'An Apollo – Shelley's favourite – is in the Capitol – he is in the act of being inspired ...'. She liked to remind their friends in London of the delight to be found in the Italian climate. Southern Italy, she told the Hunts, basked under 'a brighter sun than peers through the mists of your England'. There was proof, too, that the ethereal Shelley was not immune to the more prosaic advantages of residence abroad. Writing to Leigh Hunt, he summed it up: 'Italy has the advantage of being exceeding cheap, when you are once there, if you go to market yourself, otherwise the cheating makes it approach English prices.'

Easter provided its traditional attractions. On Good Friday there came the Washing of the Feet, a crowded, ill-organised affair with much pushing and shoving, angry complaints and torn mantillas. On Easter Sunday itself, the cupola of St Peter's and the piazza were lit up by rockets, catherine wheels, and roman candles, while lights were placed with cunning skill to highlight the architecture. The display was so bright that crowds gathered on the Pincio, across the Tiber, to appreciate its dazzling effect against the night sky.

'My past life ... appears a blank & now I begin to live,' Mary decided, 'in the churches you hear the music of heaven & the singing of the angels.' The season brought fresh pleasures. Mary discovered that she was pregnant once again.

By almost any standards, the Shelley ménage pursued an unconventional course. It was viewed from England with a particular horror reserved for those who combined an inexplicable preference for residence abroad with habits thought to be depraved. Yet these Roman weeks breathe a spirit of innocence. Riding, drawing lessons, visits to galleries of painting and sculpture, and evening conversations with polite Italian ladies – this was hardly the stuff of Byron in Venice, with his peacocks and catamites, his private gondolier and his mistresses, the panther-like baker's wife with her hair streaming in the rain and the masqued hostesses at Carnival.

In contrast, it sounds remarkably like a collection of serious under-graduates on a sponsored tour. The Shelleys' reading list, preserved in the same gilded notebook, provided few concessions to frivolity.

Among the Italians, they had settled on Boccaccio and his *Decameron*, together with the *Inferno* of Dante. Mary laboured through the works of Pietro Metastasio: Shelley took refuge in the *Hippolytus* of Euripides. He ploughed through the extant volumes of Livy, we have already seen him submerged in Lucretius, a particularly abstract author, and he moved on to Lucan's account of the Civil War.

Sometimes the Shelleys read together. They worked their way as one through *Paradise Lost* – Shelley read extracts to Mary after dinner, while Italian musicians played in the *palazzo*'s lofty rooms. They sat in quiet companionship to read Winckelmann's *Ruins of Rome* and his *History of Ancient Architecture*. These were then the pre-eminent books on the rediscovered splendours of Rome, the work of Johann Winckelmann, a German aesthete and lover of young men, whose scholarship and zeal secured him a place in the Vatican library.

They both laboured through the *Histoire des Republiques Italiens du Moyen Age*, by Jean-Charles Simonde de Sismondi. Mary read *Mandeville*, a novel by her father, William Godwin. Shelley's flight of imagination took him to *An Account of the Kingdom of Cabaul*, by the Hon. Mountstuart Elphinstone, a military man's vision of Afghanistan. The visions of the remote Caucasus and the far plains of Asia in Shelley's poems may well have been drawn from Elphinstone's descriptions. Both the Shelleys partook of Plutarch's *Lives*, while Mary, presumably in search of light relief after all this, read Shakespeare's *Julius Caesar* and *Hamlet*.

There were travel books, too, of a kind. Along with Spenser's *Ruins of Rome*, Mary possessed one of the latest Italian travelogues by Joseph Forsyth, a volume alluringly entitled: *Remarks on Antiquities Arts and Letters during an excursion in Italy in the years 1802 and 1803*.

Then, of course, there were Shelley's own productions to read and discuss. He had embarked on *Prometheus Unbound*, a drawn-out, lyrical expansion of the tragedy conceived by Aeschylus. Every day he set off armed with pens, ink and notebooks towards the monumental remains of the Baths of Caracalla. Erected by the fratricidal, demented Emperor whose name they preserve, the ruins lay a half hour's walk from the Corso through the Forum and past the Aventine hill. Today the massive arches and hollow chambers provide a setting for televised opera performances by Pavarotti and Domingo. In 1819, this was the poet's sylvan retreat. His introduction to the poem, though quoted with dutiful conformity in almost every study, still sharpens the appetite for Shelley's Rome:

> This poem was chiefly written upon the mountainous ruins of the Baths of Caracalla, among the flowery glades, and thickets of odoriferous blossoming trees, which are extended in ever winding labyrinths upon its immense platforms and dizzy arches suspended in the air. The bright blue sky of Rome, and the effect of the vigorous awakening spring in that divinest climate, and the new life with which it drenches the spirits even to intoxication, were the inspiration of this drama.

In truth the modern reader is apt to find *Prometheus Unbound*, like other Shelley verse dramas, rather a labour of devotion. The subject is lugubrious and monumental. The action, such as it is, moves at a glacial pace. Its chief attraction lies in its crystal language and bright images of nature, destruction and pain. Much later, from the sadness of widowhood, Mary was to recollect: 'The charm of the Roman climate helped to clothe his thoughts in greater beauty than they had ever worn before. And, as he wandered among the ruins made one with nature in their decay ... his soul imbibed forms of loveliness which became a portion of itself.'

By the end of April a new obsession had overcome the Greek drama. The Shelleys had visited the Palazzo Colonna and there gazed upon a portrait of a young woman which Shelley found inspirational. Her pretty head is turned left over her shoulder, a half-smile playing on her lips. A shift is thrown about her and her head is wrapped in cloth. The girl was Beatrice Cenci, who was executed by order of the Pope on 11 September 1599 for the murder of her incestuous and tyrannical father. Her stepmother accompanied her to the block. When the two women had been beheaded, Beatrice's brother was tortured, bludgeoned to death and quartered.

The painting, or so it was then believed, was the work of Guido Reni. 'The moulding of her face is exquisitely delicate,' Shelley rhapsodised, 'the eyebrows are distinct and arched, the lips have that permanent meaning of imagination and sensibility which suffering has not yet repressed and which it seems as if death scarcely could extinguish. Her forehead is large and clear, her eyes, which we are told were remarkable for their vivacity, are swollen with weeping and lustreless, but beautifully tender and serene ...'.

The Palazzo Cenci occupied a dark corner of the Jewish Ghetto, between the Tiber and the Capitoline hill. It is still a forbidding place, a rambling edifice of high-ceilinged chambers and thick walls. It is almost impossible to see the shape of the *palazzo* from any one angle, so closely have the other Renaissance buildings encroached around, so that it can appear architecturally overgrown and strangled. Shelley spent hours stalking around its intimidating walls.

Soon he was at work on a drama devoted to the subject. *The Cenci* pursues an implacable path through the cycle of abuse, murder and punishment. It dwells at rhetorical length upon the ill-deeds of the count and draws to its conclusion as Beatrice calls on her mother to bind up her tresses in deference to the executioner's blade. It is a slow-moving drama. Little action takes place on stage. Much of the tension is exacted through emotional speeches directed against, first, the count, and second, the pontiff. The elder Cenci's crimes are expiated by making over prime land to the greedy papacy. But his daughter's offence can only be punished by death. The Pope is stern, not to be moved or bent, as calm and keen as the engine that tortures and kills, so the poet informs us. Beatrice – young, beautiful and with blood quickening in her veins – must yield to his lethal authority.

'Can it be possible I have to die so suddenly?' she cries. 'So young to go under the obscure, cold, rotting wormy ground! To be nailed down into a narrow place; To see no more sweet sunshine; hear no more blithe voice of living things ...'.

A gloomier note began to creep into the Shelleys' daily round, even as Rome came alive with the spring. The change of weather brought malaise and irritation, as it does to Romans every year. Mary wrote to Maria Gisborne, her friend in Tuscany, on 26 April: 'We begin to feel the effects of the Roman air, producing colds depression and even fever. S. has been v. unwell lately.'

Already there existed a subtle difference in Shelley's spirit. One moment he was striding off, like a boy in the countryside, to clamber amidst the wondrous leafy caverns of the baths of Caracalla, the next he was dwelling on the Palazzo Cenci, full of its gloomy deeds of incest, tyranny and unnatural death. It is as if the dark side of the Romantic spirit had tugged at the optimism of a Roman spring, pulling it ever nearer the morbid territory where the most brilliant flowers are those on a grave and the pallor of a corpse assumes the hue of marble.

Not for nothing were his most lyrical lines the verses written under the inspiration of a cemetery. Later, he would confess: 'Ill spirits – God knows why but I have suffered more from them ten times over than I ever did before I came to Italy. Evil thoughts hang about me.' This was depression battling hope, all that Greek light and air against the cold of the wormy tomb, Frankenstein versus Ariel.

The Shelleys moved from the Palazzo Verospi to the Via Sistina, at the top of the Spanish Steps, high above the matrix of streets crowded around the most fashionable quarter for the English visitor to Rome. They lived next door to Aemilia Curran, the daughter of an Irish politician, John Philpot Curran, who had moved to Rome and painted portraits in her whitewashed studio. The spring breeze wafted through their apartment's high windows. It was thought that fresh weather was good for the health. Shelley's own belief was clear: 'The bright sun of this blue sky is of more use than a myriad of medicines.'

But the Roman spring is changeable in the extreme. In the second week of May, Shelley rose with Miss Curran to the ruins of the Emperor Hadrian's villa at Tivoli. It poured with rain on their ride back into the city.

Aemilia Curran left the only portrait of Shelley that is known to have been painted from life. Her life intertwined with the Shelleys in the manner of so many people's. Friendship deepened to intimacy within a few weeks, to be sustained for a brief, intense period, often to be remembered thereafter with a mutual mixture of misunderstanding and vague resentment. The day after their ride to Tivoli, Shelley brought young William next door to sit for her. The portrait was lost later in the century.

A few days later, as they were together in the house at the top of the Spanish Steps, the boy sickened towards evening. Mary summoned an English physician, Dr John Bell. Whatever treatment the doctor prescribed seemed to have worked. On a quiet Sunday evening, Mary sat down to write to Maria Gisborne, the Shelley's friend who lived on the coast of Tuscany. 'What weighs ... with us is that the heat of this southern climate disagrees with William – he has had a dangerous attack of worms & it is only yesterday and today that he is convalescent.'

Dr Bell had delivered a firm warning. The Shelleys should leave southern Italy at once, he said, because the hot climate was bad for a delicate child. But by late May, the summer heat had already set in, creating its usual stagnant and unhealthy atmosphere in the marshes and low-lying lands around Rome. Malaria was rife at this time of year.

But where to go? The party had seen quite enough of Naples, in Mary's view, and in any case they should head north. She would have liked to come to the Gisbornes at Livorno but worried over the sultry evenings and baking days along the coast. 'The heat would frighten me for William who is so very delicate – and we must take the greatest possible care of him this summer,' she told Mrs Gisborne. He needed to be near an English doctor. 'We have the most rooted contempt & in any case of illness the greatest dread of Italian medics,' she wrote.

For a few days they enjoyed a respite. The social round resumed, with calls on Miss Curran, walks by the Tiber and calm evenings of drawing and reading. Doubtless they discussed where to go next, but the debate failed to produce a resolution. Mary knew her husband to be 'as incapable of cruelty as the softest woman', but he could often be incapable of taking a decision, too.

On the evening of 2 June, when the boiling temperatures of a Roman summer were becoming more and more insistent, William suddenly became sick and feverish again. Dr Bell was called at once.

His prescriptions have been preserved, and frightening reading they make. Beneath the Greek for 'child' there appears a dreadful compound intended to act as a purgative, including mercury, aromatic powder of cinnamon bark, cardamom seeds and ginger. Then the boy was subjected to a stronger mixture to treat his fever: digitalis, potassium nitrate and refined sugar. Camphor and a dose of opiates were also administered.

These were desperate remedies for a small child and it is evident that William was dying when Dr Bell decided to apply them. The adults became frantic. On Thursday, 3 June, Mary recorded in her journal: 'William is v. ill but gets better towards the evening.' She and Claire wrote a joint note to Mrs Gisborne. 'William is in the greatest danger – we do not quite despair yet we have the least possible reason to hope – yesterday he was in the convulsions of death & he was saved from them – yet we dare not, must not hope – '.

Shelley said William had been 'reanimated' from the process of death by the doctor. The child persisted in a high fever, while Shelley sat over him. 'He is more exhausted by watching than I am,' Mary noted. 'He watched 60 death-like hours.'

William died on 7 June. He was taken for burial to the Protestant cemetery, in the arcadian setting his father had eulogised.

Several days later Shelley put pen to paper, writing to Peacock in London to ask him to inform their circle of this latest misfortune. 'It is a great exertion to me to write this and it seems to me as if, hunted by calamity as I have been, that I should never recover my cheerfulness again,' he scribbled.

The Shelleys slowly assembled their luggage, engaged coach and horses, then set off for Tuscany, to the north. Shelley would never see Rome again. 'It is more like a sepulchre than a city, beautiful but the abode of death,' he wrote to Aemilia Curran.

It was several weeks before Mary, crushed by the experience, could summon up the willpower to communicate with her friends. Once settled in Livorno, she sent a note back to Rome, addressed to Miss Curran. 'I never shall recover that blow,' she said. 'I feel it more now than at Rome – everything on earth has lost its interest for me.'

At the end of the month, she wrote to another friend, Marianne Hunt. 'We came to Italy thinking to do Shelley's health good but the climate is not any means warm enough to be of benefit to him & yet it is that that has destroyed my two children.

'May you my dear Marianne never know what it is to lose two only and lovely children in one year – to watch their dying moments and then at last to be left childless & for ever miserable.

'William was so good, so beautiful, so entirely attached to me – to the last moment almost he was in such abounding health and spirits ... that the blow was as sudden as it was terrible.'

Eventually, she turned once again to the diary. 'I began my journal on Shelley's birthday. We have now lived five years together and if all the events of the five years were blotted out I might be happy – but to have won and lost the associations of four years is not an accident to which the human mind can bend without much suffering.'

'Shelley is today twenty seven years of age.' She herself was but twenty-one.

Shelley inscribed the journal:

> We look on the past and stare aghast
>> On the ghosts with aspects strange & wild
> Of the hopes whom thou and I beguiled
>> To death in life's dark river.

> The waves we gazed on then rolled by
> Their stream is unreturning
> We two yet stand, in a lonely land
> Like tombs to mark the memory
>
> Of joys and griefs that fade & flee
> In the light of life's dim morning.

The rest of their story became a part of nineteenth-century legend. The Shelleys rebuilt their life in Tuscany but something in Mary had gone, never to return. 'What a blessing fearlessness is,' she recalled. 'Since William's death I have lost that feeling which was my attribute – since then I walked on shifting sands.'

She became distant and lapsed into silences. She displayed a reserve which her husband took for lack of emotion, prompting him to indulge in a series of affections which failed to improve her mood. He compared her in verse to the cold moon and mourned that the serpent, himself, remained shut out from her private paradise.

Shelley lived until 1822, producing in the intervening years much of the work that was to be his testament. He drowned at sea off La Spezia on 8 July. His body was washed ashore and cremated in a ceremony of Homeric quality on the beach near Livorno, and his ashes were placed by his friends beneath a crumbling tower at the Protestant cemetery in Rome. They first opened William's grave so that father and son might rest together, but found that it contained an adult skeleton, and the whereabouts of the little boy's remains could not be traced. His small tombstone, however, still rests on a patch of grass nearby.

'Rome is a good nurse & soon rocks to a quiet grave those who seek death,' Mary wrote to Thomas Medwin later that year. She found herself condemned to an age in widow's weeds, imprisoned by the bright memory of her past and tormented by remorse. Through the sad decades ahead she would turn over and over in her mind, and in her journal, the events of those frantic, intoxicating years. She met Byron – 'Albe', in their circle – again, but even the bravura of the noble lord could not pierce her sorrow – 'When Albe speaks and Shelley does not answer it is as thunder without rain.'

Returning to the pages of her own diary proved too painful. 'What a scene to recur to! My William, Clara ... are all talked of – they lived then – they breathed this air & their voices struck on my sense, their feet trod the earth beside me and their hands were warm with blood & life when clasped in mine. Where are they all? This is too great an agony to be written about.'

Acute melancholy, however, coexisted with the remembrance of joy, 'rapturous sensations ... when the evening star panted in the west and the heaven-pointing cypresses sent forth their fragrance ...'.

At one time, Mary determined to live at Rome for the rest of her life. Money and dull duty compelled her to return to Kentish Town. There remained little else in her life but the preservation of her husband's reputation, the belated public worship of his works and the upbringing of his son and heir, Percy Florence.

The Shelleys and their friends lived on a peculiar cusp between the ages that must have made life astonishingly full of energetic possibility and yet at every turn beset by frustration.

On the one hand, the old feudal order was expiring in blood but nothing had emerged from reform to take its place, save the grisly excess of the French Revolution. The powers of kingship, superstition and economic ignorance had appeared to reassert themselves. On the other hand, man remained imprisoned by a level of scientific knowledge that had changed little for generations, yet people were already alive to the imminent possibility of dramatic innovation.

A vast gulf separated the world that existed when Shelley drowned off the Tuscan coast in 1822 and the modern age that had entered its vigorous early youth by the time his widow died quietly in 1851. He had gone in the full flowering of the era of aristocracy and snuff-boxes; she lived out her last thirteen years in an England that was already Victorian.

Mary would live to see the railways, regular passenger services by steamships, mass-circulation newspapers, gas lighting in the home and the electric telegraph. Shelley himself died unaware that many of these inventions could be anything more than scientific speculation.

In 1860, one of the survivors of the Shelley circle, Thomas Love Peacock, recalled the storm-tossed journey of Henry Leigh Hunt and his family to Italy in 1822, when they were driven back in the Channel by foul weather and reached Tuscany months later than planned. By then industrial technology had made such progress that Peacock could blandly comment: 'In the present days of railways and steam navigation, this reads like a modern version of the return of Ulysses.'

Mary witnessed the English Reform Bill of 1832, the revolutions throughout Europe in 1848 and the slow erosion of reaction by the new bourgeois forces of the mercantile and clerical classes. If it was not the triumph of liberalism for which Shelley had yearned, it was at least a beginning.

Fulfilling Shelley's dream, and the cause in which Byron died, she saw an independent Greek state come to rebirth through British, Russian and French naval power at Navarino in 1827. She read of the ascent of Prussia over Germany, followed the collapse of Louis Philippe's constitutional monarchy in France and its substitution by the Second Republic.

From the semi-agricultural economy that still prevailed in England when the Shelleys took ship in 1818, she saw the upsurge of grim industrialisation and the dizzying expansion of the British cities. 'Hell is a city much like London,' Shelley had proclaimed, from the comparative arcadia of Florence, in 1819. Yet the metropolis he had abandoned for good one year before held not much more than a million souls. By the time of Mary's death, three million people crowded into its suburban streets, swallowing areas that had once been almost countryside, like Bayswater, Kensington and Chelsea. What a contrast to the paradise of exiles, its mountains, seas, vineyards and cities, ringed by ancient towers!

In the monochrome years after the loss of Shelley, Mary had time – too much time – to reflect upon the intoxicating effect of travel in the South on people with fertile minds who had never seen anything like the landscape and marble cities of Italy. In reading every word that is left to us by the travellers of the Romantic age, all their breathless, overdone, mildly – sometimes not so mildly – hysterical descriptions, one has to recall their wonder, their daring, and their innocence.

Generations of romantic pilgrims made their way to the cemetery by the Pyramid of Cestius, where Shelley's tombstone lies a short distance from the modest grave of Keats. Twenty years passed before Mary could bring herself to visit the grave. On her first journey back to Italy she had ventured no further south than Florence, as if the spell of Rome might awaken too many memories of her early life. Even the thought of it set off emotions so strong that she could confide them only to her journal, a place of solace in a world where 'the stars may behold my tears and the winds drink my sighs'.

CHAPTER 4

The son-in-law also rises

Few times and places can have offered more excitement to eager youth than Shanghai in the 1920s. A young Italian diplomat, freshly posted to the great port, might stroll along the banks of the Huangpu river, a waterway about as far removed from the Tiber as it is possible to imagine, with every conceivable indulgence available from the opium dens to the chorus girls in the seething streets around him, grand dinners in the vast mock-Tudor houses of the European quarter and fine imported liqueurs at his club.

These delights were well appreciated by one particular diplomat, bored with his routine life as a junior member of the consulate representing Fascist Italy. It was, however, on an exotic but innocent whim that he presented himself at the booth of a venerable Chinese fortune teller. The old seer scrutinised him. Then he uttered the grave prediction that his customer would die before the age of forty, near a wall. A prophecy of this nature, one imagines, might dampen the ardour of the most dedicated Shanghai party-goer. But it was shortly before the young man's wedding day, and few people contemplate mortality with any seriousness at such a point in their lives.

Indeed, Count Galeazzo Ciano was rarely accused of taking anything too seriously. As a teenage boy, he already displayed the vanity, insecurity and narcissism that characterised his adult life. He dabbled in theatrics and journalism, succeeding in neither. His father sent him off to the diplomatic corps in 1927. He was dispatched to a minor post in the Far East, for Italy was expanding its interests in China, as befitted a power that sought a place in the oriental sun. Then he was called back to Rome, for Mussolini had arranged a family wedding.

Galeazzo Ciano, born at Livorno in 1903, was the son of a distinguished naval officer and war hero, ennobled by the King. His father, Costanzo, was a close friend of Mussolini. Constanzo was also a shrewd and corrupt business operator who converted his patriotic credentials into a substantial portfolio of investments. His fawning relationship with the Duce became a source of political fortune.

Next, by arrangement, the young Count met and courted Mussolini's daughter, making the Italian dynastic marriage of the century to place himself at the highest level of the regime.

Galeazzo met Edda Mussolini for the first time on 27 January 1930 at a charity ball arranged for that purpose. Edda was not yet twenty, bubbly, extrovert, a woman who loathed the ordinary people yet despised the established aristocracy, whom, she rightly suspected, would never accept her. She was also the object of intense and poisonous gossip. Her father, as conventionally predictable in these matters as he was volatile in others, adored Edda with uncritical passion, a feeling she reciprocated. The young Ciano is said to have proposed to her with brief intensity and she to have replied 'why not?', and then the two went off to advise the paterfamilias of their engagement.

'Tell your readers that I am radiant with joy,' Edda advised a popular London paper down a creaky telephone line, 'but I'm annoyed that so many papers have written that I'm twenty-five, when I'm only nineteen. I'd be grateful if you could put that right.'

They were married three months later in the church of San Giuseppe on the Via Nomentana. Five hundred guests and three times that number of police guards were present at the wedding reception, an affair bedecked with roses and azaleas. Mussolini and his own wife, Donna Rachele, made their baleful presence more agreeable by modest gifts and a display of respectable behaviour, although the Duce held the institution of marriage in disdain and affected mild surprise that a daughter born to so revolutionary a family might end up as a countess.

Donna Rachele, however, was quick to conceive a righteous dislike of the adventurer, since she was a woman to whom the elegance and panache of Count Ciano acted as a jealous spur, amplifying her own manifest lack of these qualities. 'You ought to know,' she told the Count, 'that my daughter doesn't even know how to make a bed.'

The happy couple went off in a white Alfa to honeymoon in Capri. Mussolini himself accompanied them part of the way. Edda had to tell the Duce to go home. When the bride and groom arrived at the Hotel Quisisana, a paternal telegram awaited them. Mussolini could not let his daughter go so easily.

Not surprisingly, the young man prospered. Having departed from Chinese shores as a mere counsellor, he returned as Consul-General. The Cianos threw themselves into the hedonistic, cosmopolitan life of pre-war Shanghai with verve. They spoke English, charmed their dinner guests, imported fine Italian wines for their receptions and cut a heroic dash while the Japanese armies surged up to the boundaries of the foreign settlement. In 1933 they returned home by liner, suffused with melancholy, to be decanted on the quay at Brindisi. The period that Edda later recalled as the most brilliant of her life was at an end.

Upon his return, Ciano's career took wings. He was appointed chief press officer to the Prime Minister in 1933, Under-Secretary one year later and Minister of Press and Propaganda in 1935. Then, in 1936, came the bolt from the blue. The Duce, seeking a person of utter trust and obeisance to handle a critical portfolio, appointed his son-in-law Minister of Foreign Affairs at the age of thirty-three.

It is difficult today to recall the importance attached to ambassadors and foreign ministers during the 1930s, an age when commercial jet air travel and instant global telephone connections were unknown, while routine summit diplomacy by heads of government was rare. The foreign ministries of Europe still commanded the heritage of Bismarck and Sir Edward Grey, behaving as if their subtle ministrations might rework the map of the old continent. Their attitude reflected the exalted origins of most senior officials. These placed them in instinctive harmony with the perceptions of those who still provided the governing élite in most countries.

The National Socialist and Fascist governments in Europe were among the first to break with tradition and to subordinate professional makers of foreign policy to the whimsical ideals of the dictators, all of whom emerged from undistinguished backgrounds. They sought instruments, not debaters, executors, not counsellors. Mussolini intuitively selected Ciano, the possessor of an *arriviste* title, in this role. Hitler employed

Ribbentrop, a champagne salesman who appropriated a 'von' to his name.

Thus Galeazzo Ciano, more familiar with the scented boudoirs of Rome and Shanghai than with the chanceries of the Continent, became the head of Italy's diplomatic service. Down all the intervening decades, one can almost hear the echoes of the protesting ambassadors and permanent secretaries in the corridors of the Palazzo Chigi, in vain and in private, of course.

Ciano's rise was meteoric. He owed everything to the Duce. He was comfortable and therefore enjoyed stability, held office and therefore disliked risk. He felt unwilling to participate in the grand schemes for war yet was unable to sacrifice his advantages in a gesture of disapproval.

Thus intoxicated by position, influence and the unremitting adoration of countless Roman women, the Count allowed himself and his country to drift into war with only a few caustic remarks in his private diary to mitigate his despair. He first sought to advance Fascism by force in Spain, and next chose to subjugate Albania through violence. Only then, as Ribbentrop and Hitler dragged Europe towards conflict, did he discover the attractions of peace, seeing all too clearly the disaster that awaited Italy.

On 22 May 1939, Ciano, acting on the orders of his father-in-law, carelessly signed the 'Pact of Steel' with Germany, committing Italy to the side of the Third Reich in the event of war. He is said to have affixed his signature with an air of gracious unconcern. No need to bother with an Italian text of the pact, he told Ribbentrop, the version thoughtfully prepared by Friedrich Gaus, the legal expert in the German foreign ministry, would do perfectly.

Only later did he confess that the document was 'dynamite'. Three months after, Ciano discovered at a hideous meeting in Salzburg that his blunder had led Italy to the brink of disaster. A treaty imagined by the Italians to function as a guarantee of peace had in reality been transformed into an instrument of collective aggression.

Ciano was wealthy, handsome by the matinée-idol standards of the era, his straight black hair always slicked back with perfumed brilliantine (from which Hitler was said to recoil in distaste), of medium height and somewhat burly. He ran to fat as the strain began to tell. His father's riches ensured a cultivated education. He spoke fluent English – it was the language he used in private with Ribbentrop. His favourite pose was that of a languid tennis player just off the court, a young thirty-three prone to irony, sallies of humour and the distant variety of wit that so easily smoothes salon conversation. He was much more a plutocrat than a black-shirt.

Like his wife, he abhorred the masses. Unlike her he was amused by the aristocracy, especially the contessas and princesses who flitted around the green card tables in decaying palaces. He had the reputation of a heartless womaniser, too egocentric to be truly charming, too capricious to provide sustained enjoyment, lacking the necessary humour about his own pretensions that women find attractive. He would conduct his affairs with flagrant discretion. Everybody might guess, including Edda; few might find confirmation, for he preferred his women as butterflies, not consorts. His true passion was for gossip, preferably mendacious. A succession of drawing-room affections, combined with international power, plus the knowledge that one was second in line to the most powerful man in Italy and father of his grandchildren, why, it would turn the head of an anchorite.

Ciano and Sir Percy Loraine, the 12th Baronet of Kirkharle, GCMG, KCMG, FRGS, had a certain amount in common. Both men were greatly fond of the golf course at Aquasanta, in the countryside outside Rome. The greens extend past ruined Roman aqueducts, and from its luncheon terrace the Alban hills arise in parade behind a screen of conifers. Both men appreciated horses. Each felt himself part of an elect raised to rule. Neither enjoyed perfect relations with his master. But if Sir Percy had an eye for the ladies, it was one of discreet inspection alone. And while the Count considered himself in the vanguard of a new European order, Sir Percy was a product of an old civilisation that had sickened fatally in 1914 and was dying slowly at places such as Guernica and Nuremberg.

He was born in the heyday of Queen Victoria, attended Eton and New College, Oxford, fought in the South African War of 1901 and took up his first posting three years later as a junior attaché to His Majesty's Embassy at the Sublime Porte of the Ottoman Sultan in Constantinople.

By the time he met Ciano and Mussolini, Sir Percy had already served in Rome, Peking and Paris, participated in the Versailles Peace Conference, effectively run the politics of Persia as British minister in Tehran, ruled Egypt and the Sudan as High Commissioner and returned as ambassador to Atatürk's republic with its new capital, called, at that time, Angora.

His was a diplomatic career of perfect symmetry. In 1939 he was around the age at which British diplomats are today compelled to retire, when Lord Halifax disrupted his smooth progress towards an honourable exit. He was called upon to go to Rome at once. His predecessor, Lord Perth, had engaged the sympathy of the Fascist regime to such an extent that he no longer functioned as a useful emissary. Sir Percy found himself at the apex of his life as a diplomat with a brief both vital and contradictory. He was to stand up to Mussolini – but only as much as necessary to convince the Italian leader to stay out of the war.

His interlocutor, Ciano, did not pursue a dignified or traditional routine. Between the golf club, cocktails at the Hotel Ambasciatori and bad dinners at the behest of anxious European ambassadors, Ciano led an energetic and stimulating existence. He lived in the Via Sacchi, in the new district of Parioli that had arisen to accommodate the pre-war upper-middle class north of the old city walls. He saw the Duce almost every day. On occasion he even found time to visit the Foreign Ministry.

'Galeazzo Ciano was the creature of his times,' recalled Sumner Welles, the American envoy sent by Roosevelt to Italy in 1940, 'and the times in which he had his being are the least admirable mankind has known for many centuries.'

Ciano's diary traced a version of events that he was content to leave to posterity, convinced that it would vindicate his intuition and damn the Germans. Shot through with self-regard and a breathless lack of consistency, it recorded the sins of Ribbentrop and Hitler while simultaneously admitting the Count's own voracious designs on Albania and the fractured Yugoslavia. Throughout, it contrasts his cringing regard for the Duce's will against the serious, statesman-like role he adopted in the presence of Sir Percy Loraine.

Their first meeting, on 3 May 1939, was duly written up. 'I received Sir Percy Loraine, the new British ambassador. Our conversation was of a purely conventional nature, thus it was dull. However, Loraine made a good impression on me. I believe him to be a fundamentally timid man, also most concerned by the atmosphere in which he must fulfil his mission. Rome is always a difficult post for a foreign diplomat, particularly so for an Englishman who finds himself in the ambiguous role of an uncertain friend. While maintaining the façade of friendship, he must conduct a policy that is in reality hostile to us.'

Lord Perth, the Count noted, had gone out of his way to be understanding, ending up as a virtual spokesman for Italy in Whitehall.

Ciano hoped that Loraine would develop along similar lines. 'I don't rule it out,' he thought.

Sir Percy soon became acquainted with the style of Fascist diplomacy. First he presented his credentials. Then the Italian office of protocol smoothly informed him that it was desirable for all new ambassadors to lay wreaths at the Tombs of the Kings of Italy in the Pantheon, at the Tomb of the Unknown Soldier atop the monument in Piazza Venezia, and at the shrine to those who had fallen during Mussolini's Fascist revolution. Sir Percy was unenthusiastic about the third engagement. He consulted the Foreign Office.

'We do not much like this business of laying wreaths,' grumbled Maurice Ingram, the Whitehall official who dealt with the telegram. 'It seems to us distinctly odd to ask foreign representatives to pay homage to Fascist martyrs ... would the Soviet ambassador be asked to do this?'

Appeasement, however, knew no bounds. The Foreign Office discovered that the French and Belgian ambassadors had already acceded to the request of the protocol office. 'I think Sir Percy Loraine must follow suit,' wrote Sir Andrew Noble, another senior official. 'The Italians are unbelievably touchy about such matters.'

Sir Percy, it turned out, had already anticipated the judgement of his masters and solemnly fulfilled the ritual. It was duly recorded in the pages of *The Times* and the Italians chalked up another moral victory.

Charity dictates that one should remember the climate of these years. The embassy and the Foreign Office were beset by British admirers of Mussolini and all his works. There was Colonel Cyril Rocke of the Anglo-Italian Cultural Association, a body whose homage to the Italian leader stemmed from its own roots in the British Union of Fascists. Like so many amateur intermediaries in diplomacy, Colonel Rocke gained a vastly exaggerated notion of his own worth. Flushed with success after the Anglo-Italian Parliamentary Committee enlisted him to pass a message to Mussolini, he wrote to propose himself as a suitable candidate for the post of press officer in the embassy in Rome.

A horrified mandarin minuted: 'There could of course be no question of considering Col. Rocke for such a job – or indeed any job.' A polite and inconclusive letter was sent to the Colonel.

The new ambassador was thought to be a tough professional. That is why Lord Halifax, the Foreign Secretary, had selected him for the job.

Another British envoy in the Levant was to praise the reappearance of a bit of backbone in British dealings with Rome.

Quite why anybody thought that Sir Percy Loraine was the man to match the hour is still a cause for wonder. He was an old-fashioned diplomat whose *modus operandi* consisted of striking up the most intimate acquaintance possible with the leading man in the country and conducting all business through that channel. They still tell the story in the Foreign Office of Charles Mott-Radclyffe, a young attaché, who, weary of Sir Percy's grandiose effusions from Ankara – 'the requirements of His Majesty's service have once again rendered it necessary for me to sit up the whole night with the President of the Turkish Republic ...' – composed an imaginary telegram from the great man, which found its way to Whitehall.

It was an account of Sir Percy's attendance at Atatürk's deathbed and read exactly as such a telegram might – until the *denouement*, when the dying Atatürk asks the ambassador to succeed him as President of Turkey. Loraine declines the offer with regret but informs Lord Halifax with some relish of Atatürk's wish. It was, he says, ' ... unique in the annals of British diplomacy. I desire to place on record my appreciation of this great compliment that has been paid to me ... Please inform The King.' So in character was this communication that Mott-Radclyffe's pastiche is said to have convinced several grandees of its authenticity, and as late as 1968 the episode was treated as fact in the press.

In Italy, Sir Percy found his style curtailed. Mussolini simply did not receive foreign envoys on a regular basis, deeming such meetings unworthy of his rank. He preferred to deal with them through his Italian inferiors. He consented to meet with fellow dictators and the heads of democratic governments. Kings were also admitted to his presence. All this contributed grandly to the dignity with which he thought his office to be endowed. The only way to the Duce, Sir Percy soon found, was through his son-in-law.

There was a certain irony in his professional plight. Fresh from the poker tables of Atatürk and his successors, His Majesty's ambassador was, on occasion, apt to forget that he represented a constitutional monarch at the head of a parliamentary democracy. Indeed, he found much in the methods of government employed by Atatürk and Mussolini to which he could take no exception. Quite the contrary. Early in 1940, for example, he enjoyed a convivial encounter with Marshal Italo Balbo, the flamboyant aviator and dissenting Fascist. Sir Percy, like Balbo, was pursuing his own illusions until the limits of reason. He had already informed London that 'these conversations with Ciano and Balbo made me feel that that the risk of Italy's joining up with Germany has pretty well reached the vanishing point.'

Thus he confided to Balbo that he thought far too much stress was laid on the contrast between Fascism and democracy. 'It was, I thought, a superficial antithesis.' Sir Percy held that Fascism, in contrast to Bolshevism, shared the perception of democracy that the people were paramount and the state merely their servant.

'If I was right,' His Britannic Majesty's Ambassador continued, 'then Fascism and democracy were pursuing the same end by different methods.' This statement was by no means out of line with conventional thinking in the Foreign Office, where a document prepared that spring reiterated the belief of the Southern Department that 'in point of fact ... there are many aspects of the Fascist system in Italy which it would be useful to preserve'.

'I saw no necessary reason for the sympathetic collapse of Italian Fascism when German Nazism had been defeated,' Sir Percy told Balbo. The two men discussed the 'third act' of the European drama – the settlement that would obtain at the end of the war. All this, Sir Percy noted innocently, 'seemed quite novel to Balbo'. Indeed it must have done.

It was, once again, left to Sir Andrew Noble to deflate Sir Percy's political philosophising. He noted of Ciano and Balbo 'none of them are men of a very scrupulous character'.

'Count Ciano sometimes speaks the truth but he is not altogether a reliable source,' wrote Sir Andrew, adding that Mussolini had always shown himself much more anti-British than anti-French.

Sir Percy warmed to his theme of common interests. He suggested that Britain might replace Germany as the third partner in the Anti-Comintern Pact directed against Russia, thus, in effect, joining an axis with Fascist Italy and Imperial Japan. The ambassador was mystified by Mussolini's failure to reciprocate his agreeable sentiments. 'I have searched my wits to account for this obstinate streak of anti-British resentment,' he cabled to the War Cabinet. It was to baffle him until the very end.

The truth was not long to unfold. Sir Percy was presented for his first audience with Mussolini, one of only two direct encounters the British ambassador was to enjoy with the head of the regime. Ciano attended, interpreting the Duce's dialect-tinted pronouncements into French, a language all three men comprehended. Mussolini had evidently determined in advance to create an iron-fisted impression. 'His face was set in a mask, it seemed as that of an oriental idol sculpted in stone,' recorded the worried son-in-law. Mussolini began with a lengthy denunciation of Britain's policy of encirclement, correctly identifying a network of guarantees and alliances spun by Lord Halifax's men through eastern Europe to the Bosporus and the Peloponnese as a web of silken steel containing his aspirations.

In view of these manifestly unfriendly actions, did Britain's pact of good relations with Italy still stand, the Duce demanded? Why, yes, of course, said a flustered ambassador. Ciano was watching. Sir Percy reddened and seemed to splutter before articulating the foreign policy of Neville Chamberlain with all the eloquent conviction which it might merit. He pointed out – 'with a certain professional ability', the Count noted archly – that it was Italy who had altered the status quo with her occupation of Albania. Yet the British Prime Minister had subsequently confirmed the worthiness of the Anglo-Italian treaty of 1938.

Mussolini did not share his son-in-law's admiration of this argument. Britain, he complained, was removing any possibility of compromise and needlessly creating barriers to any settlement between the contending parties. If it had kept its nose out of Polish affairs, then Warsaw and Berlin might by now have settled their differences.

The affronted ambassador reacted with some vigour to this tirade. At one point Ciano feared he was about to rise and withdraw. Mussolini cut the conversation short. As the two Italians conducted Sir Percy across the room – Mussolini conventionally received dignitaries in a vast salon known as the Sala del Mappamondo – the British envoy attempted some pleasantries by way of farewell. The Duce, eyes downcast and thoughts far-off, ignored him. When Loraine had gone, Mussolini told Ciano that he had meditated long and hard before the day's performance. He had decided to clarify positions, once and for all.

The Head of Protocol returned shortly afterwards from escorting Sir Percy back to the British embassy. What on earth was the matter with the man, he wanted to know? The ambassador had talked to himself throughout the journey, twitching and nervous.

On 8 June, Sir Percy came back to confirm from the mouth of Neville Chamberlain himself that the Anglo-Italian treaty was considered by

London to remain firmly in place. Mussolini, discontented with sweet words, wanted deeds. British encirclement, her deals with Romania, Greece, Turkey and the Kremlin, all exacerbated his ire. Meanwhile the Italian intelligence services delivered to Ciano that day the results of one of their coups, this time in Hong Kong. The Count spent the evening perusing a secret Royal Navy study of British readiness against the Axis, prepared by Admiral Sir Percy Lockhart Noble, Commander-in-Chief of Naval Forces in the China theatre. He was much gratified to read the Admiral's pessimistic assessment of Britain's chances in the Mediterranean. The document asserted that this theatre of war would be dominated by the forces of Fascist Italy in the air and by sea.

The next week the Count made his way to the Palazzo Farnese for dinner as the guest of the French ambassador. The evening made a disastrous impression: a dull, useless meal of traditional diplomatic character, with the usual second-rate 'dear colleagues', presumptuous and uncertain chargés d'affaires, young second secretaries and aged aristocratic ladies. Evidently there was a shortage of Ciano's preferred evening company.

If the Count had but known it, he was himself the object of patrician disdain in the grander chanceries of Europe. Sir Andrew Noble, commenting on the award of the Annunziata to the two Axis foreign ministers, took leave to 'doubt whether the King of Italy really appreciates having to debase the highest order at his disposal by bestowing it on such men as Herr von Ribbentrop and Count Ciano'.

Mussolini and Ciano were, in one sense, ahead of their time. Concerned to break up and occupy what parts of the Balkan peninsula they deemed appropriate (with the exception of Greece, described by Ciano as 'a country too poor for us to covet') they knew that they had unleashed profound forces of national rivalry. The 3 June 1939 found them conferring over the Serbian problem with Kosovo and the claims of other Balkan pockets of trouble.

Ciano was to learn that one could not, however, employ the same tactics with the British that he had so profitably used to gain influence in Albania. The Italians had simply intimidated the prominent people they needed, then bought them off with empty titles and money. 'Wherever personal advantage may be found, the most noble sentiments will often willingly fall mute ...'.

On 26 June Ciano's father died, prompting a lengthy and self-pitying excursus in the diary, which all but abandons politics until 3 July. In London, the old Count's demise was greeted with scant sympathy. Sir Percy had telegraphed the intriguing assessment of the Polish ambassador in Rome, who from a confidential source believed that the old man's death was more significant than was thought. He was the leader and brains of 'a financial and economic organisation', reported Sir Percy, which lent colour to stories in Rome that the Ciano family had profited handsomely from their Axis connections.

Sir Andrew Noble was ready with a caustic minute to Sir Percy's telegram which encapsulated the way at least one faction in the Foreign Office regarded Ciano *père et fils*. Noble had seen it all before during his own tour of duty in Italy and harboured few illusions.

'Count Costanzo Ciano was, even before the rise of his son, the leader of what was known as the "Gruppo Ciano" which was widely assumed to have accumulated a large fortune by the misuse of official information if nothing worse,' he wrote, with all the outraged integrity of a Whitehall civil servant. The greatest corruption took place when the old man had been Mussolini's Minister of Communications from 1924 to 1934, a decade of personal enrichment.

'Count Galeazzo Ciano, whose scruples are no more delicate than his father's, may have been inclined to adopt a pro-German policy partly by the prospect of personal profit: I would not put it beyond him,' Sir Andrew continued. 'I do not think that Count Ciano's financial operations would bear too close investigation.'

In 1939 it was one thing to utter such sentiments behind the walls of the Official Secrets Act, quite another to let slip any public hint of them.

Lord Halifax duly sent a telegram of condolences. 'I have learnt with deep regret of the death of your father, whose brilliant services to his country in peace and war will long be remembered ...'.

Ciano's teletape reply that day is preserved on a blue cable form attached to Lord Halifax's outgoing message. The noble lord's sentiments were 'much appreciated'. Such is diplomacy at its most urbane.

The Danzig question was now looming over European affairs.

A few days later the British ambassador popped up again. 'As a good neophyte ambassador, he has a mania for talking to the Duce,' the Count observed. 'This morning, claiming he had a personal message from Chamberlain, he succeeded in having himself taken to Palazzo Venezia.' He ushered Sir Percy once more into The Presence. The results were no better than those of the last encounter between the two men. Chamberlain's message – seen by Lord Halifax as an admonition of necessary sternness – made no impression on the two Italians. It denounced the German claims against Danzig and warned of the dangers to peace arising from the policy.

The Duce, said Ciano, rebutted the arguments line by line. 'Some of his arguments were really brilliant,' he thought. Mussolini argued that Poland was a poor country to talk of morality since it had dealt the last blow to a wounded Czechoslovakia after Munich. 'Tell Chamberlain that if Britain fights for Poland, then Italy will take up arms for Germany!' the Duce commanded. No clearer message might have been imagined. Sir Percy, claimed Ciano, said almost nothing in the face of this onslaught. 'His second visit to Palazzo Venezia produced no more brilliant results than his first!'

By 12 August, however, Ciano realised in horror that it was he who had been duped. Italy was inexorably being drawn towards war on the German side, years before Mussolini's imaginary legions might be properly armed and equipped, and at a time when the country's fragile economy was almost bankrupt. The Count was confronted in Salzburg with Hitler and Ribbentrop at their most belligerent. In vain did Ciano politely point out that Italy was simply not in a position to wage war.

Ribbentrop, who was brusque, did not appear to listen. After several funereal meals in the company of the German Foreign Minister, the hapless Italians were allowed into the presence of the Führer. Hitler received his guests in the large living room of his house. The uncomfortable group stood with him around several tables strewn with campaign maps. With a sinking heart, Ciano noted the German leader's grasp of military strategy and tactics. He was cordial and spoke calmly, becoming excited only when he broke off to urge the Italians to deliver a *coup de grâce* to Yugoslavia as soon as practical.

'I realised quickly that there was nothing more to be done. He has decided to strike and strike he will. Our arguments carried not the least influence to stop him.' The war, Hitler stated, must be carried out while both he and the Duce were still relatively young men.

When Ciano and his entourage glumly boarded their train back to Italy, the Count had time to realise that his vaulting ambition and careless disregard for the effects of his actions had drawn him into a fatal set of consequences. The atmosphere of his meetings with Sir Percy Loraine would never again be quite so light-hearted.

Five days later Ciano held a desperate meeting with Mussolini in which he 'fought like a lion' to prevent an immediate agreement by Italy to march at Hitler's side. Sir Percy saw the Foreign Minister during the hot Roman afternoon. It was just after Ferragosto, the mid-August holiday. The streets were deserted and the fountains played to empty piazzas. Mass foreign tourism had not yet arrived in Italy. When the Romans went away on their Fascist-sponsored holidays to the beach at Ostia on the narrow-gauge tramway from the Porta San Paolo, the city fell into a torrid stillness.

Ciano did not hide his preoccupation. Good sense was needed to avoid the crisis. Good sense there was, responded Sir Percy briskly, but not of the variety that would lead to a Europe periodically hostage to the diktats of the German Führer. If the crisis came England would fight, and if it came to that he would like to participate in person. Only one thing saddened the British envoy and that was the prospect that their two countries might be at war for the first time in their long history. 'I made no answer,' remembered Ciano that night, 'but I think he understood that I, too, wanted no such thing.'

By 23 August, the engine of crisis, stoked by Colonel Beck and the Polish junta, fuelled by Hitler's critical timetable for hostilities, desperately restrained by Daladier and Chamberlain, was humming at full pitch. Mussolini at last appeared to suffer cold feet, now that the moment of commitment to German designs seemed near. 'The day was charged with electric tension,' noted the Count. At his insistence the Duce authorised the communication to Percy Loraine of an Italian peace plan under which Danzig would be restored to the Reich as a preliminary move before an international peace conference.

Ciano paints the British ambassador as presenting a far from imperturbable face to this hopeless overture. 'I do not know whether it was the heat or the emotion of the moment, but Percy Loraine almost fainted in my arms,' he wrote. The envoy was revived in a lavatory of the Palazzo Chigi. Sir Percy's message to London concerning this meeting did not mention any such drama. The next day an increasingly gloomy Ciano noted that Italian peasants grudgingly went to the colours cursing 'those German buggers'.

On the 27th, Loraine was in again with a masterpiece of Foreign Office subtlety which showed that, between fainting fits and self-interrogation, the ambassador had finally understood how to play to the Duce's personality. Lord Halifax requested and required none of his customary prerogatives. He sought the understanding of Italy for a series of initiatives towards peace, coming in person to the telephone to sooth Count Ciano and thus the Duce's vanity. Irked only by a few patronising articles in the British press, by 29 August the dictator had moved away from an impetuous desire for sudden war.

It remained for Ciano to play the peacemaker – in vain, of course, since he had known since Salzburg that Hitler and Ribbentrop were intent on war. All day long on the dramatic 30 August, Loraine was on the telephone to the Foreign Minister. Finally he came to the Ciano household in Parioli during the evening. Mussolini was convinced that the German blow would soon fall and Italy's neutrality hung around his neck like an ego-bruising albatross.

The next day both Mussolini and Ciano panicked. They feared that Britain and France might launch a pre-emptive strike upon the outbreak of hostilities and thus precipitate Italy into a war she did not want. Yet at the same time Mussolini could not bring himself to declare non-belligerence before the war began. The lights, meanwhile, were doused throughout Italian cities for fear of air raids.

Father and son-in-law conferred at the Palazzo Venezia. Ciano drove back up the Via del Corso to the Palazzo Chigi and summoned Sir Percy. By his own account, after bringing the ambassador up to date, he pretended to give in to an outburst of heartfelt frankness. 'Why do you want the impossible? Have you not understood that we shall never start a war against you and France?' Sir Percy's eyes misted over – according to Ciano, that is – and he grasped the Foreign Minister's manicured hands. 'I've known this for a fortnight and have telegraphed my government to this effect. The events of the last few days shook my trust. But I am happy I came to Palazzo Chigi tonight.'

The *Wehrmacht* marched on Poland at twenty-five minutes past five the next morning, while both men slept.

The phoney war ushered in a polite interlude of mutual deceit. A saccharine note from Lord Halifax arrived on 6 September soothing the dignity of an ever more ruffled Mussolini. A further emollient letter was delivered on 13 September, replete with the fulsome sentiment that His Majesty's Government was content 'to leave everything to the Duce's judgement'. Ciano, however, responded by a warning to Sir Percy that Britain should avoid peremptory demands that might infringe upon Fascist dignity. The Duce approved of this *démarche*.

The social round resumed in the autumn as if untroubled by the death of Poland. Sir Percy and the Count ran into each other at the Acquasanta golf club on 18 September. The ambassador was not in a good mood, having received news of the sinking of HMS *Courageous*. Ciano, meanwhile, was immersing himself in the intricacies of Fascist politics and preparing himself for a speech to the Italian parliament on 16 December. The discourse, of which he was mightily proud, was to provide his death warrant.

During the autumn of 1939 Ciano became ever more convinced that the early German victories would evaporate and that Britain and France would win the war in the end. Occasionally Ciano would try to convince himself that he was a ruthless man of steel, noting on 22 September that, while he had complained of a particularly mindless outburst of Fascist violence, 'I am very far from deploring beatings, when they are administered for sound reasons.' But the more he reflected and, presumably, the more intelligence reports he read, the deeper grew his conviction that Hitler was doomed. Mussolini, however, believed the opposite, placing great faith in a speech by the Führer which appeared to offer an olive branch to the western democracies. Ciano did not share this naïve belief, noting on 6 October: 'I have too much regard for Britain and France to believe that they will fall into this trap. The war is far from finished today: it will soon begin in earnest'.

Three days later he mourned 'my passing youth'. He was thirty-six years old.

Throughout the winter Mussolini's pique was heightened by the British naval blockade, which prevented German coal from crossing the North Sea to Italian ports. Ribbentrop, glad to make a gesture, swiftly organised shipments by rail across neutral Switzerland. The British ambassador, still playing Lord Halifax's soothing game, even travelled to Malta to discuss with the Royal Navy means of alleviating the blockade as a reward for Italy's non-belligerence. 'He is ever more understanding,' wrote the Italian Foreign Minister.

By now the Duce was suffering deeply, so concerned at the evident lack of preparation alarmingly evident among the Italian armed forces that he was feeling the symptoms of a new stomach ulcer.

Despite every measure of mutual assurance, however, both Loraine and Ciano had come to realise that their efforts could be set at naught by the whim of the leader. They had a long talk on 18 January 1940, recorded in Ciano's diary. The ambassador talked formally for a while and then sought to unburden himself. Ciano encouraged him to speak, and Sir Percy said that he had become painfully aware that the Duce's attitude to Britain was one of fundamental hostility. It was as if the veteran diplomat had reached this realisation as he spoke the very words. 'The Duce must understand that the England of today is not the country it was a year ago: it is strong and ready for anything.'

The son-in-law did not respond. But he noted his agreement with every word the envoy said.

The confusion in motives between the two men was to spring from this meeting. Loraine evidently believed that he had constructed a relationship with Ciano which transcended the links between the Foreign Minister and his patron, father-in-law and dictator. This was, of course, wishful thinking.

One evening in February 1940, while England lay under the blackout and the survivors of 1939 eked out their existence in the smoking embers of the Polish state, the two men met in the salon of the Colonna family, a gracious series of apartments in the Piazza Santi Apostoli. The ambassador told Count Ciano that coal supplies from Germany to Italian ports would shortly be intercepted by the Royal Navy. Then they diverted themselves with small talk among the fragrant inhabitants of the *salotto*, content in their mutual understanding.

Back at the Foreign Office in London, cooler counsels were available. 'Not the least of our problems in estimating the development of Italian policy,' wrote Sir Andrew Noble, 'is that Sir P Loraine has no access to Signor Mussolini, who is now almost entirely withdrawn from outside contact. We therefore have to rely on Count Ciano as intermediary; he is not entirely to be trusted and shares the common Italian failing of always wishing to say nice things to his audience.'

At the Political Intelligence department of the Foreign Office, a shrewd official named George Martelli summed up the problem facing a gentleman like Sir Percy, reared in the era of Queen Victoria and matured in the diplomatic service during the golden years of Edwardian England. 'As you know,' he told the officials handling Sir Percy's hapless telegrams, 'the Fascists completely reject the traditional conception of Anglo-Italian friendship which they say was founded on British patronage of a picturesque but weak country. It is necessary to avoid any appeal to the sentimental associations of the past.'

As if to underline this very point, Mussolini refused an overture to sell weapons on commercial terms to the British. He was dwelling already in a fantasia of economic unreality, deaf to the pleas of his advisers. For years, the Duce proclaimed to the Grand Council on 12 February, the economists had predicted disaster and yet the regime had carried on. He had noted the comforting, if debatable, thought that no government had ever been toppled for economic reasons alone.

Ciano, that night, set down these pompous declarations but added, feelingly, that the Duce had failed to note 'that we have eaten our way through twelve billion lire in foreign securities and five billions in gold. Now our reserves are down to a miserable 1,400 million, after which we shall have only our eyes to weep with.'

It was the day after that he told Sir Percy that Italy would not sell arms to Britain.

At the end of March, Sir Percy still felt able to write to Lord Halifax in optimistic tones. 'I do not think there is any immediate danger of a sudden move on the part of Signor Mussolini to enter the war on the side of Germany, unless of course the Germans gain some striking success.'

Meanwhile the efforts expended by the Foreign Office to placate Mussolini knew no bounds. In April 1940, the Italian embassy learned to their horror that the deposed Emperor Haile Selassie had been invited to attend a dinner at the British Legion in Bristol. Evicted from Abyssinia by the Italian invasion, Haile Selassie pursued an exile existence, a permanent reminder of the impotence of the League of Nations and a witness to the use of poison gas and random massacre by Mussolini's proconsuls in Africa. Presumably the ex-servicemen imagined that the Emperor, as a living symbol of the victims of aggression, was a suitable guest. Not so, it seems.

First of all the Italian ambassador called on Rab Butler, then serving at the Foreign Office, to demand in perfunctory tones that the 'Prefect' of Bristol – a title which does not exist under the British system – should order the dinner cancelled. It was insulting, held Signor Bastianini. 'I informed the ambassador we could not do things like that here,' Mr Butler recalled.

A few hours later, however, this magnificent indifference had lapsed into an undignified scramble to avoid offence to the Italian dictator. Marquis Fracassi, the Counsellor, appeared in a froth of indignation at the Foreign Office, where he was received by a Mr Bowker. The Marquis uttered a 'solemn warning' that if the dinner took place there could be serious consequences. Relations between Britain and Italy would suffer, while tempers – and one temper in particular – were running high in Rome.

Mr Bowker acted promptly, as his report shows. First he called Charles Peake at the FO press office, who ensured that the London newspapers were to publish nothing about the dinner. Then Mr Bowker got on to the Chief Constable of Bristol and through him summoned an amazed functionary of the British Legion, a Mr Ware, to the telephone. The dinner was by then in progress, with Haile Selassie and the old soldiers tucking into their first course.

'I told Mr Ware that we were astonished to hear that the legion had arranged such a dinner without consulting the Foreign Office,' Mr Bowker recorded. He ordered Mr Ware without further ado to prevent the Emperor from rising to deliver his speech. 'Some pretext must be found for relieving the Emperor from speaking – he could, for instance, have a sore throat,' he suggested. Mr Ware evidently protested that this could do little good as the American consul was present and was also expected to speak. Mr Bowker, by now in full flow, was not put off. The consul was to be told very firmly that his remarks were to be of a general nature and he was to 'make no reference whatsoever to the Emperor, or to Abyssinia, or to Italy'.

Alas, three local newspaper representatives had already attended the dinner, photographed the Emperor and prepared reports of the occasion. This too did not deter Mr Bowker. The Chief Constable was ordered to contact the local papers to suppress the story and to forbid the publication of any photographs. 'Excellent' minuted Mr Butler on the margin of Bowker's report, using his characteristic blue crayon.

A mollifying telegram was dispatched to Rome and Marquis Fracassi was contacted to hear of the Foreign Office's strenuous efforts to avoid displeasure to his master. The spectacle of a British official reciting with hopeful supplication to a Fascist diplomat a list of suppressions, interference and censorship undertaken on his behalf must have been a singularly edifying one. Unfortunately it did not suffice. Mr Bowker recorded the Marquis' response.

'He expressed appreciation but said that since it had not been possible to cancel the dinner, he feared that the action we had taken would not be enough to prevent the consequences which he feared.' Mr Bowker lamely pointed out that 'everything possible had been done' to meet the ambassador's representations. The incident, however, undoubtedly gained Mussolini's attention and fed his resentment of British policy. History does not relate how the unfortunate Haile Selassie reacted to his enforced silence, or how Mr Ware of the British Legion coped with the embarrassment of it all.

The increasing Anglo-Italian tension did not appear to infringe on the personal friendship between Ciano and Loraine, who met each other socially all the time, on 18 February at the Colonnas' and the next day formally at Palazzo Chigi. Ciano did not hide his admiration of the British raid on the *Altmark*, a German prison ship off Norway, when commandos liberated a load of POWs. It was, said the Count, in the traditions of Drake and Raleigh. One might almost still hear Sir Percy purring on his way back to the embassy that day.

There was, however, an element of perfidy in these unctuous conversations. For while Sir Percy was penning his telegrams back to London, Ciano was reading them clandestinely. The Italian secret service had penetrated the British embassy and its communications were no longer secure. On 31 March, Ciano confided to his diary, quite casually, that he had read 'one of the usual telegrams lifted from the British embassy' in which an American envoy's impressions of Mussolini had been given to Chamberlain.

The British already knew that some of their communications were open to compromise. In those leisurely times, unbelievable as it seems today, diplomats sent their less urgent communications to London in the post. Nothing secret was supposed to be put in the mail. But a reading of British embassy press summaries, or a glimpse of its routine reporting of public events, could assist the Italian Foreign Ministry in forming a picture of the preoccupations and interests of the embassy.

The Italians, therefore, arranged for all diplomatic postal dispatches to be opened and read by their intelligence services. One day in the spring of 1939, however, a clerk became careless.

Thus the British embassy in Belgrade was surprised to receive by post a 'strictly confidential' report from the United States consul in Trieste, while the American embassy in Rome was taken aback to find in its morning post a copy of a press summary from the British embassy in Rome to their opposite numbers in Yugoslavia. Telegrams flew back and forth between London, Rome, Belgrade and Washington.

Sir Noel Charles, in Rome, informed the Foreign Office dryly: 'I ...

intend to take an opportunity to tell the Italians that they really must be more careful about seeing that documents are put back in their right envelopes.'

'We got some amusement from your letter,' replied the functionary of the day in Whitehall. The embassy was authorised to buy a Crampon machine to staple its envelopes firmly closed in future.

It is now clear that the British knew that Ciano was reading at least some of the telegrams from their Rome embassy. In August 1939 Sir Percy even suggested that telegrams sent in the Foreign Office 'R' code should be regarded not as confidential, but as documents composed with a view to their being read by the Foreign Minister. His idea was that the Count might therefore learn of the ever-deeper esteem with which he and the Fascist regime were held, and thus refrain from joining the war on Germany's side.

Even the protagonists of this doomed policy had reservations. Sir Alexander Cadogan observed: 'I must say that we think it unlikely that it will deceive the astute Italians!' An even more sceptical official noted: 'I am afraid that this idea of sending telegrams of this kind in code for the benefit of the Italians is one that will not deceive them for a moment and thus is liable to do more harm than good, and I think we should discourage Sir P. Loraine from sending any more.'

At the same time the British, too, had their spies at work. Ciano's doctor also treated D'Arcy Osborne, the British envoy to the Vatican. The man relayed to Osborne many of the inner thoughts of the Ciano circle. Osborne passed them on by telegram to the Foreign Office, where, although the identity of his source was not disclosed, the officials worked out quickly who it must be.

Nor did Sir Percy allow his cordial relations with Ciano to restrain his private assessment of the Duce, the son-in-law and his wife. Here he is in a letter of 14 March for the eyes only of Lord Halifax and the Prime Minister: 'Mussolini is beginning to go down the hill,' he wrote. 'The Duce runs, rides, swims, plays tennis and drives just as much as ever,' said the ambassador, 'but to little avail. This self-justification is a well-known sign of senescence. Also he overdoes himself with his mistress.'

'The one human creature he was really fond of, his daughter Edda, has disgraced her and him. She has become a nymphomaniac and in an alcoholic haze leads a life of rather sordid sexual promiscuity.'

One can imagine Lord Halifax's lips pursing in austere disdain at this communication. What on earth must Neville Chamberlain have made of it?

On 27 April, Sir Percy's ministrations to the egos of Mussolini and his son-in-law assumed paramount importance. Rab Butler told his officials: 'We have been asked by the Chiefs of Staff and War Cabinet to use all the arts of our diplomacy to keep Italy out of the war ...'.

That month the young Italian journalist Luigi Barzini of the *Corriere Della Sera* was arrested by the Fascist police. The news of Barzini's arrest spread among Italian correspondents in London, where it created a mood of despondency.

His crime, it seemed, had been to inform the British that their Rome embassy had been penetrated. With incredible insouciance, some functionary had set this, too, down in writing and it arrived on Ciano's desk via the very network that Barzini had intended to dismantle. (For good measure, he had also told the British that Mussolini was a madman and that Italian journalists wrote only what they were ordered to.)

Barzini had spent part of February in London, where he had been entertained at table by Lord Perth on the 12th. Evidently it was a convivial Bloomsbury occasion at which much alcohol flowed. According to Perth, the Italian journalist claimed that Italy was moving towards the allies and away from the Germans. He sought to undermine the Foreign Minister.

'Little Ciano is about as important to Il Duce as Mr Duncan Sandys is to Mr Churchill – Lord Perth reported his guest as saying – 'he is a good boy, a nice son-in-law and a reliable executant. No more. The talk about anti-Fascist and anti-Duce elements grouped about Ciano ... was wishful thinking.'

These prescient words did not make much of an impression at the Foreign Office. 'All very Italian,' noted Sir Andrew Noble with his usual scathing understatement. 'I hold no brief for Count Ciano, who is a nasty bit of work, but it is sufficiently clear that he and the other moderates are not at all in sympathy with Signor Mussolini's policy.' At the Political Intelligence department, Rex Leeper added: 'He [Barzini] seems to have been talking big in his cups ... but if he talks in this way the [Intelligence] department might keep an eye on him.'

The mandarins concluded that Signor Barzini was 'not an attractive character', although he meant well. It was agreed that Charles Peake at the news department should offer him a few special stories 'to keep him buttered up'.

If this was the kind of memorandum that leaked out to Mussolini and Ciano it is little wonder that Barzini was merely exiled to an island and a minor miracle that no worse a fate befell him. He survived to become one of the most prominent journalists in post-war Italy and the author of a best-selling work about his own people, *The Italians*, entitling his chapter on Mussolini 'The Limitations of Showmanship'.

Sir Noel Charles, in contrast to his superior, never seems to have entertained the least doubt that Mussolini would go to war and that Ciano, for all his masquerade, would go along with him. Sir Noel was not quite as blue-blooded as Sir Percy, but he was a third baronet, educated at Rugby and Christ Church, who had served in France in the Great War, winning the Military Cross and a mention in dispatches. He adopted a brisk approach to Fascist Italy.

In the spring of 1940, the ambassador returned temporarily to England, where he took up residence at the International Sportsmen's Club in Upper Grosvenor Street. Sir Noel became chargé d'affaires, in which capacity he displayed a coolly realistic view of the Italian regime almost entirely absent from Sir Percy's prognostications. On 18 April he addressed a letter to Lord Halifax. Like all such communications from the embassy it is to be found still in pristine condition in the Foreign Office files, its heavy blue embossed paper unfaded, the typewriter imprint as fresh as if it was written yesterday and the signature appended in a confident Royal Blue ink.

'Within the last ten days the Italian press has deteriorated rapidly and completely,' he wrote. It had become 'completely Goebbelised'. The Ministry of Popular Culture had ordered a change in attitude and the newspapers now adopted a pro-German and anti-British line without question. At the same time local Fascist authorities had been ordered to step up their propaganda against Britain, claiming that the British intended to keep Italy a 'prisoner of the Mediterranean', bottled up by the Royal Navy at Gibraltar and Suez, denied her place in the African sun and choked by the naval blockade.

Sir Noel learned that reports from Italian correspondents in London had been 'tampered with and altered' to fit the new line. As a result many Italians no longer believed in their own press and the embassy's own digest of news reports had become greatly sought-after, 'all the more remarkable in view of the fact that, for reasons of policy, it is written in English alone'.

*   *   *

On 1 May, the Admiralty ordered all British ships to avoid the Mediterranean, a cautionary move in case vessels were caught at the outbreak of hostilities with Italy. Sir Noel went in to see the Count, aiming to sooth ruffled feelings. Ciano, too, was in emollient mood. Sir Noel telegraphed the Foreign Office to report that the Count played down the frothings of the Italian newspapers and had said that Sir Noel was not to worry about the abuse.

'Italy was carrying out her obligations towards Germany by means of propaganda and not with guns,' Sir Noel reported the Count as saying. 'He repeated that the Italian government had no warlike intentions and there was not likely to be a change of policy for some time to come.

'I asked what that meant exactly: did it mean that we would get a fortnight's warning or did it mean a month?'

Ciano obfuscated. Sir Alexander Cadogan, upon reading the account of this exchange, noted: 'the Italians reveal their venality with an engaging frankness'.

On the same day, in London, Loraine wrote a private note to Lord Halifax. 'It seems impossible to know how much time, if any, remains for us to dissuade Italy by diplomatic action ... I will not yet despair of the possibility of doing so'. He returned to Rome renewed in his determination.

Those within the Foreign Office who had no time left for the policy of Sir Percy and his ilk were emerging from cover. Sir Robert Vansittart minuted to the Foreign Secretary: 'Mussolini's decision to go to war is a clear case of syphilitic paranoia.'

Then came the German offensive in the West, and with it vanished the last chance of persuading Mussolini to renounce his share of the spoils. Loraine and his masters knew what was happening.

Just before the attack on Belgium and Holland, Ciano and Loraine met to review the position. Neither found it palatable. Ciano wrote in his diary that Sir Percy had assured him that his government wanted to make every possible effort 'honourably and in good faith' to keep the peace with Italy. Ironically, Ciano's report of the encounter seems quite balanced, while Sir Percy's own account makes it sound as if he delivered an abject apologia.

'We had recognised the Italian Empire in Ethiopia, we had concluded the Anglo-Italian agreement, we had recognised the absorption of Albania ... we had hoped these friendly gestures would bury past hatchets ... seemingly it had all been unavailing,' he recorded. Ciano had remarked –

'I must say very gently' – that it did not look as if all was going well for the allies. Mussolini for his part remained faithful to his obligations towards Germany and rejected any political conversations with Britain or France. This did not mean, said Ciano airily, that Italy would cease to be non-belligerent in the near future. Much, said Sir Percy, clinging to his illusions, might depend upon himself and upon the Foreign Minister. No, said Ciano gently, it was too late for that. 'Signor Mussolini had taken charge.' What, inquired Sir Percy, might England do now? 'Leave us alone' said the Count. In his diary Ciano did not lie to himself. 'These declarations – ordered by Mussolini – perturbed Sir Percy, who, regrettably, left my office far from reassured.'

Luigi Barzini, it seemed, was right. The intemperate young foreign correspondent had understood what grave and secret diplomats had not. In the end Count Ciano was the Duce's son-in-law, no more, no less.

Ciano, characteristically, recalled the German offensive in the West chiefly because it was preceded by a poor dinner at the German embassy and an annoying dawn call from Hitler's importunate ambassador Von Mackensen. On 10 May 1940, the British, French and American ambassadors called on the Count to seek enlightenment about Italy's next move, on 10 May 1940. André François-Poncet, foreseeing the collapse of the Third Republic, was tired, red-eyed and rather dishevelled. Sir Percy, apparently now determined to rise to such occasions, remained haughtily indifferent. At one point in the conversation he simply stated to Ciano that Germany would be destroyed, at which, noted an alarmed Count, 'he adopted a firmness unsuspected in one usually so phlegmatic and courteous a gentleman'. For a second, recalled Ciano, all the toughness of his race was in his look and his words. There were no fainting fits.

Sir Percy's telegram that afternoon did not stress these aspects of his call upon the Count. Instead he continued to dwell on the amity and goodwill between them. 'I saw he was longing to be convinced that we could hold fast, against his judgement ... I saw that he would like to believe it but he could not.' Ciano saw him to the door, where 'he took my hand affectionately in both his hands and said "One day, though I hope not, I may have to tell you disagreeable things. But one thing you may be absolutely certain of: I shall never cheat about anything I say."'

Back at the Foreign Office, Philip Nichols dryly minuted: 'Count Ciano frequently lied to us before ...'.

The next day Rome was plastered with anti-British posters. One of

Loraine's junior diplomats, accompanied by the naval attaché, attempted to pull one down, whereupon they were assaulted by a crowd of Fascist sympathisers. This ill-judged move rapidly developed into an incident. The diplomats took refuge in a hotel, accompanied by two American journalists, while the mob bayed for justice outside. A flurry of phone calls to the embassy and the foreign ministry produced Sir Noel Charles, who was pushed and insulted by the throng, then an official from Count Ciano's staff who calmed tempers all round.

By daylight, telegrams winged their way between London and Rome while Sir Percy once again called on Ciano. 'Since he adopted a rather arrogant tone' – the Count wrote that night – 'truly in contrast to our excellent personal relations, I answered sharply, refusing to give any explanation ... emphasising the fact that while the British Army is fighting hard, British officials would be better to go to bed rather than to go bar-crawling until four in the morning.'

Sir Percy did not pass on this arch observation to London. He told the Foreign Office that Ciano had unblushingly stated that Italy had a free press, that the junior diplomat had no right to tear down the posters and that the subsequent assaults were 'only natural in the circumstances'.

To underline how little of Sir Percy's message had got through to the dictator and his son-in-law, neither man professed to attach any importance to the accession of Winston Churchill in place of Chamberlain. Mussolini treated it with irony.

Three days later D'Arcy Osborne, the British minister at the Vatican, filed a 'most confidential' telegram to the War Cabinet. The Superior General of the Jesuit Order, a Polish Father, Wladimir Ledochowski, had learnt from military sources that Italy was on the point of entering the war and might do so within a week. Osborne did not quite know what to make of this prediction, covering himself with the observation that 'I have recently heard it suggested that his 74 years are telling on him'. Fr Ledochowski died in the Vatican at the end of 1942.

It was in that week that the embassy in Rome told its consular officers throughout the peninsula to advise British women and children who had means of living in England to leave Italy 'while travel conditions on the Continent are comparatively good'.

One yellowing file in the Foreign Office archives was named 'straws in the wind'. The British consul in Menton had gone across to Bordighera, where dozens of retired English gentlefolk on the Italian Riviera were shutting up their villas to depart. In Baghdad, the embassy learned that the local branch of the Banco di Roma had begun to refuse to enter any major commitments, and the city bazaars were full of murmurs that Italian subjects were about to leave Iraq. From Egypt, Sir Miles Lampson reported that the Italian consul-general in Alexandria had transferred most of his funds by telegraph home to Milan. In Santiago de Chile, two members of the Italian embassy were overheard boasting at their national club of the mass air attacks that would be launched against Malta immediately upon the declaration of war. The British military attaché in Rome had already told the Director of Military Intelligence that the Italian military commissariat had started to buy supplies for cash at short notice. The British School in Rome, which maintained a proud tradition of archaeological research and a library of that genre of English literature inspired by a love of Italy, had already closed.

In the first two weeks of May, Sir Percy seems to have haunted the chambers of the Palazzo Chigi like a ghost from Munich. Of one interview with Ciano, described by the Foreign Minister as 'of no great importance' he told Lord Halifax: 'Count Ciano's attitude has never been more friendly to me.' At the same time Ciano declined to arrange an interview with the Duce, claiming that his father-in-law was simply too infuriated by the reporting of the foreign press to contemplate an audience with any ambassadors. Lord Halifax wrote to his envoy saying that it seemed clear that Mussolini was about to take the plunge. 'You will be exploring in your own mind any possibility of delaying action that might be open to us ...'.

On 16 May, Sir Percy brought a new message from Churchill to Mussolini. This time the ambassador wisely did not seek to deliver it in person. Ciano found it dignified and noble. Perhaps fortified by these sentiments Mussolini, too, did not object. But two days later he ordered a response to be delivered which Ciano found needlessly harsh. It is preserved in the British files. Mussolini revealed a vendetta against Britain dating back to the League of Nations sanctions over his invasion of Abyssinia in 1935. These, he reminded Churchill, were moves against an 'Italy engaged in securing herself a small space in the African sun without causing the slightest injury to your interests and territories'. On receiving the Duce's reply, Sir Alexander Cadogan observed: 'I don't quite see how we could have expected anything better.'

The *Wehrmacht* was sweeping victorious across northern France and the British Expeditionary Force was falling back on the coastal ports.

Mussolini believed his hour had come, and Ciano, it seems clear, had now chosen wearily to indulge him. Sir Percy had arranged for the War Office to send him optimistic daily reports of the fighting in France and these he diligently put into Ciano's hands to convince him of the need to stay out of the war. Their tidings, even under the most persuasive rewriting, could scarcely have made a favourable impact.

'Ciano's demeanour,' thought Sir Percy, '[gives] me the impression that he regards himself as having a sort of personal alliance with me to prevent the calamity of an Anglo-Italian war.' That very day, Ciano was confiding to his diary his wish to make 'a clear agreement' with the Germans over their war aims and his plan to meet Ribbentrop to extract a written statement of what booty would accrue to Italy at the end of hostilities.

On 27 May, André François-Poncet again came to see the Count with the shreds of national dignity clinging to his person. A deal was possible over Algeria and Tunisia, he informed the Italian minister, one which might recognise Italy's aspirations. Since the rallying cry of Fascism also included Corsica, Nice and Savoy, this was too little, too late. Nor did François-Poncet help by emphasising that Corsica – almost visible from the Ciano coastal estates on a clear day – could not be included since it constituted an imperishable part of France. He had also failed to live down the reputation, noted in a Foreign Office memo, that 'few French ambassadors to Rome have been able to curb their delight at being witty at Italy's expense'.

Ciano no doubt had cause to reflect on his belief, recorded back on 24 November 1939, that 'with the French, as with heaven, one can always reach an accommodation'. He declined the offer with scorn.

The next day it was the turn of Percy Loraine to realise that his long game was at an end. 'A painful conversation' thought the Count. The ambassador had come for further interminable debates about the coal blockade. Loraine blanched when Ciano told him their countries were on the brink of war. 'If you choose the sword, the future will be decided by the sword,' he said eventually.

For all his misapprehensions, Sir Percy was a prescient man. He told Ciano that if the allies won the battle of France, the war would end within a year. If the Germans triumphed over France, then the conflict would last at least three years but would doubtless conclude with an allied victory. Britain would answer war with war, he said, repeating that he found it sad that blood would flow between the two countries. Ciano, too, found it melancholy. Loraine's face was sad, the Count thought, and his eyes appeared to dim.

He was too old a professional not to know when the scene had been set for him to complete the formalities of his exit from it, and from history. With the zeal of the convert, he returned to the embassy to draft his telegram. Ciano had promised to give him due warning of the declaration of war. 'It was the eve of great decisions,' the Foreign Minister had said, 'the Fascists did not break faith.'

'I asked him and Signor Mussolini to make no doubt that war would be met with war. He said that they understood this ... he himself knew the strong fibre of the British race.' Ciano said that 'his personal friendship and regard for me made it very disagreeable for him to have to speak to me as he did today'. Sir Percy urged London to forget any idea of placating Mussolini with concessions. 'Their success presupposes a degree of reasonableness and moderation on the part of Mussolini which in my opinion he does not possess ... Mussolini must always be met with a stiff lip and a firm hand ... charity and liberal-mindedness merely increase the arrogance of Mussolini's militant realism.'

Churchill and the War Cabinet decided that if the French, in their desperation, wanted to offer Mussolini a deal they must do so on their own account alone.

A Foreign Office official, ruling out a suggestion from the Turkish government that an appeal be made to Italy for reason through the offices of the French government, noted: 'The day for making appeals to Signor Mussolini through third parties is over.'

On receipt of decoding of these telegrams, Lord Halifax and his minions were left in no further doubt. The Foreign Office proceeded smoothly to give one of its displays of bureaucratic perfection that seem like a Rolls-Royce engine in operation. Telegrams went out warning every relevant embassy of the Count's words. Many diplomats could not believe that the Italian Foreign Minister had actually given advance warning of the outbreak of war. The ambassador in Athens queried London's telegram in amazement, while the embassy in Bucharest – possibly bearing in mind the Atatürk joke – sent back a request for confirmation that the message was not a spoof concocted in the Foreign Office. 'Even though the relations between Count Ciano and the ambassador are of an unusual character,' acknowledged the head of the Southern Department, 'even this scarcely explains the Italian communication.'

Still the surrealist air of peace at any price prevailed. In the very last week of May, the Foreign Office was still considering the possibility that an Anglo-Italian film might be made at the Cinecitta studios in Rome. It was to be called *The Mask and the Face*. Its production would underline the goodwill between the two nations, some officials believed. They wanted the actor David Niven to take the leading part. Anxious memoranda went back and forth: could Mr Niven be released for the role from the wartime commission he had so patriotically taken up? The idea died a merciful death. Fighter planes of the Aeronautica Militare roared low over the Roman rooftops, while Fascist officials ordered practice blackouts at two-thirty in the morning.

There remained only the declaration of war. Mussolini wished to dispense with such a bourgeois formality, but Ciano insisted. On 3 June, relations with the British became frosty, although both men strove to keep up the veneer of personal amity. Loraine, evidently counting on the intimacy he had developed with the Count, said that Germany would be defeated and that he personally would wish to fight in the war. Ciano responded that he did not wish to discuss the matter. 'Now that my country is at war, or will be very soon, I had no wish to join in his predictions, nor could I permit myself such a discussion,' he confided to the diary that night.

Sir Percy still failed to pass on these impressions to the Foreign Secretary, true to his habit of reporting only those personal asides from Ciano which enhanced the impression of his close friendship with the Count, while omitting the ominous, the aggressive and the impolitic.

On the 7th, matters resumed their normal cordiality. Sir Percy, ever the keen horseman, was rather concerned for one of his colts that would have to remain in Italy. A secondary matter, it seemed, was the issue of safe passage for himself and his staff. With the air of a seasoned diplomat, which, by now, one supposes he was, Ciano said that he had made all the necessary dispositions, as if drawing comfort from the observation of the traditional courtesies. Sir Percy left one remark etched in the Count's memory from that remarkable encounter. The British, he said, were not in the habit of being beaten.

Ciano read the declaration of war first to François-Poncet on the morning of 10 June. 'It is a dagger blow at a man on the ground,' responded the French envoy. 'I thank you, however, for using a velvet glove.' François-Poncet said he had seen the conflict coming for two whole years, since Ciano's signature on the Pact of Steel. The French ambassador could not resign himself to considering Count Ciano, or any other Italian, an enemy. Perhaps if he had read Ciano's arch observations about the quality of his dinner-parties things might have been different. But for now it was only warm Latin sentiments. 'The Germans are hard taskmasters,' he warned Ciano. 'You too will find this out.' Ciano did not reply. He was wearing his gaudy aviator's uniform, the better to preen himself at Mussolini's side later that day. 'Don't get yourself killed,' said the French ambassador, and left.

Sir Percy Loraine exited from Count Ciano's life in the understated manner in which he had entered it. Perhaps he knew by now that the urbane welcome in Palazzo Chigi exemplified *bella figura*, little else. He confined himself to writing down the exact words used by the Count in the declaration of war. Was it a statement of intent or a formal declaration? he asked. Informed that it was the latter, he took his leave. Ciano accompanied him to the door of the minister's suite in the Palazzo Chigi. The two men shook hands for a long time, apparently in silence, and then Sir Percy was gone.

His telegram read: 'The Italian Minister of Foreign Affairs informed me at 4.45 p.m. that the King of Italy will consider himself in a state of war with His Majesty the King as from zero hour one minute 11th June.'

Mussolini and Ciano took to the balcony overlooking Piazza Venezia to be seen by the awe-struck crowds. The Duce's speech ran to thirteen pages, taken down by the Reuters' correspondent and sent to London in rushes of a few paragraphs at a time. In the files, all the pages are still attached to Sir Percy's earlier telegram of the day as they were ripped one by one off the Reuters' teleprinter at the Foreign Office, giving a flavour of the excitement of a hot summer night.

The Dominions were warned by the Ministry of Defence just after midnight in a one-line telegram: 'War has broken out with Italy'.

Lord Halifax, laconic to the end, sent a flash telegram to British embassies and missions around the Empire and the world. It read simply:

WAR TWO.
HALIFAX.

That night Count Ciano wrote in his diary: 'The adventure begins. God help Italy!'

*   *   *

Having failed by every means to persuade Mussolini to stay out of the war, Ciano then wholeheartedly wrapped himself in the *Tricolore*, performed a few posturing missions as a combat pilot and continued to serve as Foreign Minister of the junior Axis partner until his intrigues proved his undoing. Mussolini removed him from the Foreign Ministry and appointed him ambassador to the Vatican, a post he held until the disintegration of the regime and his own imprisonment, trial and death sentence on the charges of 'betrayal of an ideal'.

Count Ciano went to his death before a muddled firing squad in the ditch that surrounds the castle at Verona on the freezing morning of 11 January 1944. The hills and battlements around the ancient city were gilded with snow and the breath of the condemned men hung in clouds in the air. Elegant to the last, though nervous in his strides, Ciano's bulky frame was encased in a beige overcoat from Caraceni, the élite Roman tailors.

The victims were tied in crude fashion to chairs, with their backs to the platoon – a platoon of wretches, the Count had called them in the last pages of his by then notorious diary. A photograph exists of the moment before a ragged fusillade blew the life out of most of those bound to the chairs. Evidently there had been a ghastly few moments of delay and confusion, for alone of all those about to die, the Count had summoned up the guts to twist around to face his murderers. His sharp features, familiar from countless newsreels of the Devil's decade, the 1930s, peer out from beneath a broad-brimmed hat.

The first volley failed to kill him outright. A film that has recently come to light from the archives shows the platoon fumbling, aiming and firing again at the men sprawled on the ground. Then Father Chiot, the confessor who had administered the last rites to the condemned, placed a bunch of violets on Count Ciano's body.

Sir Percy Loraine left Italy with all the honours accorded to diplomatic staff in time of war, but he returned to his country to find that no honour awaited. Churchill did not want to see him. As a man who epitomised the Halifax style of diplomacy, he shared in its disgrace. His views on the conduct of the war were no longer sought. The twelfth baronet took up a certain number of posts open to the great and the good, but resentment at his treatment pursued him to the grave. He died in 1961.

Harold Nicolson knew Sir Percy in Istanbul and left a satirical portrait of him as Baron Bognor, 'the perfected model of a British diplomatist,' black and manly suits, striped shirts and stiff collars, grey silk ties and well-brushed grey hair.

'It is people like you,' Nicolson tells his creation, 'who make diplomacy ridiculous. You simply aren't real at all. You have got no reality. You're merely bland: that's what you are, and you're smug, you're bloody smug: absolutely bloody.'

Loraine/Bognor responds in character to Nicolson's indictment. 'I see,' he remarked blandly, 'that George Clerk is going to Prague.'

Sir Noel Charles, the chargé d'affaires, found his scepticism rewarded. He served as ambassador to Brazil then returned as the High Commissioner to Italy from 1944 to 1947, presiding over its painful reconstruction and the birth of the Italian Republic. Obviously, Sir Noel had taken to the Mediterranean world, for he retired to Chateauneuf de Grasse, in Provence, and died there in 1975.

And Edda, poor vain, tipsy, fast-living Edda? In the early 1990s she was still alive, greatly venerable in age, residing in the Ciano apartment in Via Angelo Sacchi, in Parioli, reclaimed from a generous Italian state eight years after the war. Upon Ciano's arrest she had fled to Switzerland, and after his death she made public the notorious diary. The Swiss then handed her back to Italy, where she served a brief term of internal exile on the remote island of Lipari.

In the post-war years she returned to Capri, the scene of her honeymoon. Indulging her penchant for the bizarre, she took up a long relationship with Pietro Capuano, a jeweller known as the dandy of that tolerant island. Her home was a villa near the ruined pleasure dome of the Emperor Tiberius, a man who would surely have relished the doings of the Ciano set. She divided her time between Capri, the Ciano country home in Tuscany and the Rome apartment, forever courted by nostalgic old Fascists and dilettante aristocrats.

In 1981 Capuano died. So, too, had one Ciano son. The other lived in Central America. Only Edda's daughter, Dindina, remained nearby, and she had suffered an unhappy marriage. Through the torrid Roman summers and the brisk winter chill of the Tramontana, the old lady barely moved out of her top-floor home. It was full of photographs depicting Mussolini, and a lifesize bust of Galeazzo, placed on a side-table, contemplated the salon. There were films and tapes of the years of fame and recorded cheers of the throng doubtless played in the apartment's spacious rooms. But could it be that above it all, in Edda's ears, there crackled the constant, tinny echo of Shanghai jazz?

CHAPTER 5

The Vatican of Pius XII and John XXIII

A bronze statue of Pope Pius XII stands in an alcove along the right-hand aisle of St Peter's basilica, next to the *Pieta* of Michelangelo. Pius seems to be submerged in a vast robe drawn around him. Its broad borders are inlaid with fleurs-de-lis, holy books and cameos of the apostles. It is sealed with a huge oval clasp on which a metallic sun gives off a dark glitter.

One bony hand protrudes from beneath the folds of this splendid gown, making a reticent gesture of benediction. Crowning the Pope is a huge mitre of intricate richness. Angels support his tiara. Between the robe and the mitre – which quite overwhelm the entire statue – is the pontiff's head. The wire-rimmed glasses, which Pius wore in life, make it resemble a staring skull, a forbidding effect deepened by the hollow cheeks and cadaverous, pinched mouth. This is neither the benevolent Holy Father nor the distinguished statesman of the Church, but altogether something austere and exotic, as remote from modern western life as a statuette of some long-interred ancient deity.

The sculptor may have been fiercely honest. Perhaps, on the other hand, he did not realise the effect he had created. In the cool recesses of St Peter's an unsuspecting glance at this statue can raise the hairs on your neck. Fortunately, a benign marble Innocent XII stands in an attitude of paternal warmth just behind Pius, and one may move on with some relief to contemplate less introspective monuments to the popes of the Renaissance.

Yet if any sculpture in the entire precincts of the Vatican can be said to summon up the man, this is it. Pius XII, Cardinal Eugenio Pacelli, elected in 1939 at a conclave of paramount interest to the governments of Europe, was one of the strangest individuals ever to rule the Holy See.

The British and the French sought a pontiff who might continue the condemnatory line pursued by Pope Pius XI towards the dictators. The late Pope had anathematised the Nazis with the most outspoken encyclical of this century, *Mit Brennender Sorge*, a document which analysed 'with burning sorrow' the persecution of the Church under the Third Reich. It was said that on his deathbed he had been preparing a speech of even stronger tone, which might sustain the cause of the *entente* and make it very difficult for Catholics to support the Axis cause.

The British minister to the Holy See, D'Arcy Osborne, and his French counterpart murmured pleasantries at receptions and ceremonies. Not surprisingly, the British believed that discretion would prove the best policy, while the French lobbied without cease. In the best tradition, a degree of pragmatic realism lay behind this virginal rectitude on the part of His Majesty's representative. There were, London noted, sixty-two cardinals. Only one was British. Thirty-five were Italians. The French, unimpressed, calculated that with six of their own cardinals and three potential allies they might muster the number necessary to hold the balance of power. Both the French diplomats and their men of the Church displayed a cheerfully unscrupulous attitude towards the workings of the Holy Spirit. One French cardinal, arriving for lunch at the legation, enquired over aperitifs – with only a mild touch of irony – how did the government expect him to vote?

For these very reasons, the Italian and German ambassadors served notice on the Vatican that whoever was elected as pontiff would do well to observe an absolute neutrality in the conflict looming ahead.

In the event the lobbyists exerted precious little influence over what was an inevitable result. Cardinal Pacelli was elected on his sixty-third birthday in a conclave so lacking in competition that one of his supporters felt that only 'a handful of dust' was against him.

Cardinal Pacelli's elevation appeared to please both camps. He had served as Secretary of State to Pius XI, therefore the western democracies thought him likely to endorse the previous Pope's attitude against the dictatorships. But even before the conclave went into secret session, the Cardinal was quick to assure Mussolini's ambassador to the Vatican that the famous deathbed speech would vanish into the secret archives. There, indeed, it remained until Pope John XXIII chose to disinter selected parts of it in a letter to Italian bishops published in 1959.

Here lay the seeds of a balance so inscrutable that it was to torment the papacy throughout the war and severely to diminish the reputation of Pius XII thereafter. The allied ambassadors took refuge inside the Vatican itself when hostilities began between Italy and the western powers. When allied troops arrived at the gates of Rome in 1943, it became the turn of the German ambassador and his staff to be granted sanctuary within its precincts.

Pius was frequently caught between conflicting pressures. The allies wanted him to condemn Axis atrocities and the invasions of peaceful states. The Germans and the Italians repeatedly tried to extract from him a condemnation of the allied bombing raids on their cities. Neither proved successful. In September 1942, the allied envoys trapped inside the Vatican presented a collective *démarche* to Cardinal Maglione, the Secretary of State, requesting that the Pope speak out against the grim events unfolding in Poland. The British note mentioned the 'merciless persecution' of the Jews. At this time, only the vaguest stories of what was to befall the Jews of Europe had filtered out. But at least one British MP had raised the question of gas chambers. The American State Department did not yet believe that Jews were being gassed, but it knew they faced deportation and hard labour.

Pius did not respond with any public statement. He told the diplomats that censorship would block the effectiveness of his words in Germany and Italy, that he had spoken out already in broad terms, that his condemnation might hurt those he was trying to help, and that the Vatican's private works on behalf of the persecuted might suffer.

The Curia stuck to its belief that public protests on behalf of the Poles and the Jews would serve no purpose except to make life more difficult. It was adhered to even on the morning of 16 October 1943, when the Gestapo descended on the Jewish ghetto, not fifteen minutes' walk down the banks of the Tiber from the Vatican. They rounded up more than a thousand inhabitants, members of one of the oldest of all Roman communities. Their safety had been underwritten by the popes for generations, in return for their submission to the rule of the Papal

States. Mussolini had been half-hearted in his measures against Jews. This deportation served to satisfy the annoyance of those German officials who despised the lukewarm anti-Semitism of the Italians. Only about fifteen of the deported Roman Jews ever came back.

The Pope remained convinced to the end of his life that he had justly condemned the crimes of the Nazis and Fascists with all the force at his disposal. His opinion was not shared by the governments in Washington and London. To the allies, the Vatican's unbending neutrality, its unwillingness to condemn the specific and its preference for lamenting the general, its obscure language and its allusive phrases all signified a historic failure to adopt a moral stand.

To the Pope and his advisers, however, there were more complex issues at stake. It was sometimes forgotten that Pius XI, even in his most censorious moments, had never neglected to condemn atheistic Communism with the same fervour as he applied to the German regime. Many in the hierarchy considered the threat to Christianity from the Soviet Union a more worrying prospect than authoritarian rulers who might still respect the position of the Church. The Vatican, it will be remembered, had its differences with the Fascists in Italy but it reached an accommodation with Mussolini through the binding provisions of the Lateran Treaty.

The Vatican considered pastoral concerns as well. It had to consider the loyalties of millions of Catholics in Germany and Italy. Until the day of liberation, Pius XII was pleased to receive in audience whole contingents of the Afrika Corps. When they retreated to the north, he effortlessly changed pace to grant blessings to the American soldiers who crowded into the Vatican in their place.

There was also the matter of the Vatican's own survival as an independent neutral state. Dependent on the Italian government for food, water and electricity, it had no serious means of defending itself against a military occupation. Pius had dispatched written orders to the head of the Swiss Guard that no resistance was to be offered against any invader. Occasionally, Hitler frothed at a distance about the nest of spies within the Vatican. Successive German ambassadors would then respond with cleverly worded telegrams intended to persuade Berlin that violent action might prove unwise.

Most of all, Pius XII regarded himself as a potential mediator between the warring powers. He thus adopted no role that might jeopardise his good faith, even when it was long clear that the allied doctrine of unconditional surrender had rendered his services useless.

Behind the austere, passionless speeches of Pius XII lay no lack of humanity. Instead his manner reflected a cerebral unconcern for the demands of rapidly unfolding political events. The Vatican, as D'Arcy Osborne wearily pointed out to his masters in Whitehall, simply did not view contemporary politics with the urgent attention required by a secular government. He thought it operated in a fourth dimension, outside of time.

Osborne himself, though not a Catholic, had been immured for several years within the Leonine walls and must, therefore, have made these observations with the attitude of one who was perforce not merely an observer but an inmate. He thought the attitude of the Vatican derived from the medieval conception of sanctuary and the notion that the Church was above all nations and alliances.

The Pope, observed this most British of civil servants, did not contemplate or resolve a problem simply by considering its immediate, temporary aspects. By habit and tradition, Vatican opinions were formed in the light of infinite and boundless considerations. 'They reckon in centuries and plan for eternity,' he believed. Within its chambers, the House of Savoy was reckoned a mere interlude and the twenty years of Italian Fascism a passing affair.

A flavour of life inside the Vatican under Pius lingers in the blue pages of D'Arcy Osborne's guide to personalities. There was Count Dalla Torre, editor of *L'Osservatore Romano*, 'said to have been pro-German in the Great War ... the possessor of so cryptic and involved a literary style that his articles have to be paraphrased rather than translated'. There was at least one Irish monsignor of firebrand Republican persuasion. Another adornment to the papal court was the Master of the Pope's Music, Mgr Lorenzo Perosi. 'As he suffers from bouts of insanity, he is kept in the background,' the envoy noted.

Few, alas, were those who shared D'Arcy Osborne's gentle understanding of the celibate clerics whose company he shared in wartime. If the British minister politely regretted the 'prolix and obscure' generalities of Pius XII, others were less urbane in their judgement. Indeed, one might argue that the pontificate of Pius never truly recovered from its inability to forestall disaster in 1939. Its perceived unwillingness to condemn the most systematic atrocities in modern history thus added to the conviction of many that the clique of elderly men inside the Vatican had failed to raise the Church against an affront to all its values.

After the shock of the war, Pius seemed to retire into a meditative calm. He made few appointments and allowed the Church machinery to run itself. He held only two consistories of bishops, one in 1946, the second in 1953. These were not occasions very notable for debate. The college of cardinals, supposed to number seventy prelates, declined to a complement of fifty-three, many of them of great and venerable age. The Pope responded to the Atomic Era and to the imposition of the Communist Iron Curtain across Europe with suitably worded reprobation. In 1949 he decreed excommunication for any Catholic who actively supported Communism and in 1956 he produced three encyclicals to denounce the Soviet invasion of Hungary. But his anathemas lacked fire, and it was as if he had expended all his reserves of zeal in the locust years of the dictators.

In outward forms, the papacy retained its splendour. Little had altered since the high baroque style adopted during the Counter-Reformation. Even the most English of Victorian travellers could not fail to appreciate the rare quality of the ceremonial, however disapproving they might be of its idolatry. The papacy provided a spectacle found nowhere else in Europe. Take the account of Easter in one nineteenth-century guidebook:

At last the clock strikes. In the far balcony are seen the two great showy peacock fans, and between them a figure clad in white, that rises from a golden chair, and spreads his great sleeves like wings as he raises his arms in benediction. That is the Pope [it was, in fact, Pius IX at the time]. All is dead silence, and a musical voice, sweet and penetrating, is heard chanting from the balcony; the people bend and kneel; with a cold gray flash, all the bayonets gleam as the soldiers drop to their knees; and rise to salute as the voice dies away, and the two white wings are again waved; – then thunder the cannon – the bells clash and peal – a few white papers, like huge snow-flakes, drop wavering from the balcony; – these are Indulgences, and there is an eager struggle for them below; – then the Pope again rises, again gives his benediction, waving to and fro his right hand, three fingers open, and making the sign of the cross – and the peacock fans retire, and he between them is borne away – and Lent is over.

Such oriental refinement persisted through the Edwardian era, the First and Second World Wars, the collapse of Fascism and the installation of the Italian Republic. It was preserved in spite of all that changed around it: the Concordat with Mussolini, the Great Depression, mass rail travel, universal suffrage, the Bolsheviks and the newsreels.

Indeed, Pius increased the ostentatious display mounted for his own coronation in 1939, believing that the first pope crowned under the new Concordat with Italy should be installed in a style that brooked no inference of temporal decline.

In 1950, my father was among tens of thousands of devout young Catholics who hitch-hiked, bicycled, rode trains or simply walked to Rome in response to Pius' proclamation of a Holy Year. The tradition of the Holy Year dated back to 1300. Boniface VIII, responding to the loss of Palestine, called upon Christians to make a pilgrimage instead to the basilicas of Rome, promising indulgences and absolution to the devout. The announcement provoked perhaps the greatest influx of people into any city in medieval times. It has been calculated that two million pilgrims came to the sanctuaries and churches, and that 200,000 visitors were present at any one time in Rome. Witnesses saw men and women trampled underfoot in the press to view such marvels as the handkerchief with which St Veronica wiped the sweat from the face of Christ. Heaps of gold and silver were poured into the treasuries of St Peter's and St Paul's, where two priests were said to stand, night and day, with rakes to collect the offerings tossed on to the altar.

For Rome, the first Holy Year was an event of overwhelming financial gain as funds replenished the coffers of inn-keepers, bankers and traders of all kinds. It signified, too, a resurgence of popular contact with the Church and thus brought a windfall of revenue for relics, indulgences, fees and tributes. So lucrative and agreeable was the first Holy Year that it was decided to proclaim one at intervals first of fifty, then of thirty-three and finally of twenty-five years.

It was, no doubt, with similar revivalist hopes that Pius XII issued his proclamation for 1950. It marked the first time since 1939 that so many pilgrims were able to come to the Holy City. A carefully ordained programme of masses, processions and benedictions repeated the cycle of devotion followed by the popes for centuries. The penniless camped in white canvas tents erected in the grounds of Foro Italico, the Olympic stadium built to glorify the achievements of the Duce's athletes. The Pope was borne aloft through St Peter's Square in a sedan chair, protected by a thicket of halberds and fanned by the drooping tendrils of the customary ostrich feathers.

The liturgy, interminable though it frequently seemed, was performed in Latin, whose phrases were ground into the memories of every member of the congregation and were, of course, intelligible to all. Whether they hailed from Patagonia or Belfast, every person present could follow the Mass in their missal, and if they did not understand every lapidary turn of phrase, they knew its meaning by familiar association alone.

In 1954, Pius became seriously ill. He was sustained through his poor health in later life by frequent injections of living cells taken from ground lambs' tissue, provided by a secretive Swiss consultant. Access to his presence was regulated by a fearsome German nun, Sister Pascalina Lehnert, whose influence was as inexplicable as her manner was graceless. The Pope's nephews and other relatives clustered around the centre of authority, worming their way over the years into positions of comfort. Pius confided diplomatic activity to the head of the Secretariat of State, Monsignor Domenico Tardini, a desiccated upholder of all that was immutable. But it was typical of Pius that despite Mgr Tardini's uninspiring years of toil, he never made him a cardinal or, indeed, elevated him to the title of Secretary of State.

Pius received subordinates on their knees, and aged prelates were known to sink querulously into a posture of genuflexion if they picked up the telephone and heard the sibilant voice intone, 'Qui parla Pacelli.' The pontiff required his underlings merely to execute his will, not to collaborate in shaping it. The Church was universal, centralised, governed by sharp, if drab, bureaucratic minds and insistent upon fidelity and obedience from the sanctuary of St Peter's to the remotest villages where Mass was celebrated.

The Supreme Pontiff made no pretence of collegiality. Indeed, he permitted the college of cardinals to wither away as age and infirmity removed one distinguished member after another. He exalted, instead, the magisterium of the Church, its absolute authority. This he deemed to be incarnate in his own person. Members of the Roman Curia and the Vatican's diplomatic staff were moved at a whim from one place to another. Others gathered dust for decades in positions for which they were profoundly unsuitable. Obedience and acceptance became familiar sacrifices for clerics in the service of Pius XII. Angelo Roncalli, who was to succeed Pius as John XXIII, languished for years in Bulgaria and Turkey. In 1954, Giovanni Battista Montini, a subtle official in the Secretariat of State, was exiled to the archbishopric of Milan, without the cardinal's hat which normally accompanied such an appointment. He would return to Rome as Pope Paul VI, importing a Milanese entourage in the sweetest form of bureaucratic retribution on his tormentors in the Vatican.

There were some who prospered under Pius XII. None epitomised the successes of his reign better than Alfredo Ottaviani. He was born in 1890, the son of a baker from Trastevere, the working-class district down-river from the Vatican. He entered the Pontifical Roman Seminary as a youth and was ordained a priest in 1916, having performed brilliantly in philosophy, theology, and civil and canon law. He proceeded to teach law and philosophy at the Propaganda Fide and was picked out by Pius XI, who elevated him to the post of Under-Secretary of State, just as the Vatican's accords with Mussolini were coming into force.

He had risen to the rank of monsignor and was to become the most reactionary of all the cardinals, reviled by progressives and regarded by some as a modern incarnation of the Inquisition. This, in fact, he was, being the head of the Holy Office, and he cheerfully acknowledged the labels attached to him. Unable to disguise his distaste for Britain and its policy in the Mediterranean, he was forever bestowing blessings upon Mussolini's troops and applauded their civilising mission in the heathen realms of Africa.

Ottaviani possessed a head that looked as if it was carved of granite, like one of the busts of his ancient Roman ancestors in the Capitoline museum. His hair was cropped close to his skull and his eyes were deep-set, above a nose that jutted out in characteristic Roman fashion. His jowls were massive. His robes were invariably splendid.

Cardinal Ottaviani regarded himself as the master of a rearguard action against modernism. The motto on his coat of arms said *Semper Idem*: always the same. He was reared in the Church that stood on the principle that 'Error has no rights'. He counted as friends men of his own age and timeless outlook – prelates such as Cardinal Ruffini of Palermo, who was reputed to close the windows of his palace as he was about to address the Sicilian bishops, to prevent unwelcome interruptions from the Holy Ghost.

Cardinal Ottaviani, good Trasteverino that he was, never left the city of Rome for more than a short period and worked all his life in the Roman Curia. Here, he believed, was the repository of all authority and goodness in the Church. He had moved to the Holy Office in 1935. According to an approved biographical note, 'he showed singularly clear vigilance, deriving from his love for the Church and his vigilant defence of the purity of the faith.' He was lauded for his doctrinal work in contribution to the dogma of the Assumption of the Blessed Virgin Mary into heaven.

When it came to the time of challenge and change in the 1960s, the Cardinal, though almost blind by then, was at first magnificently unruffled. An excitable, reforming Jesuit – so one version of the story goes – lectured the Cardinal upon the need for collegiality and fraternal decision making in the Church as a substitute for the grim dicta of the Holy Office. It was time, said the Jesuit, for the Church to return to the shared authority of the apostles.

Cardinal Ottaviani considered the prospect. Then he remarked that he had studied the Scriptures at some length and could find only one instance of unanimous collective action by the apostles ... 'and they all fled', abandoning Jesus in the garden of Gethsemane.

Nobody could accuse him, then, of excessive reverence towards the saints. Indeed, he was said to joke that the works of St Paul would not have passed the scrutiny of the Holy Office.

Critics maintained that the Roman Curia was hidebound and ignorant of pastoral needs. To the Cardinal, nothing could be further from the truth. 'It seems a contemporary of the apostles in its glory,' he said, 'so full of life that it seems to have been born yesterday, high and yet humble like a mother, and misunderstood only by those who do not know her.'

When it came to the enemies of the Church, Cardinal Ottaviani did not let his sword sleep in his hand. In the 1940s, when progressive French clerics became worker-priests, sharing the experiences of the industrial proletariat, he addressed a horrified series of demands to the French episcopate. Could these priests truly say their Divine Office? Why should they say Mass in the evening and not, as tradition held, in the morning? What, moreover, of chastity? (The Cardinal, it seemed, held an exaggerated notion of the temptations available on the factory floor.) The Holy Office disapproved.

Cardinal Ottaviani embraced with enthusiasm the pact between the papacy and the Christian Democrats to banish the Left and install a right-thinking government in Italy after the Second World War. 'You can say what you like about the Divinity of Christ but if, in the remotest village of Sicily, you vote Communist, your excommunication will arrive the next day,' he promised.

At the same time, he regarded with horror any deviation by the

Christian Democrats from what he regarded, perhaps with some naïvety, as a path of duty and Catholic conscience. Giulio Andreotti, who epitomised the loyal party functionary, recalled an 'incandescent telephone call' from the Cardinal, who had learned that Andreotti and the Christian Democrat leader, Alcide de Gaspari, were to become founder members of the Italian chapter of the Rotary Club in 1945. 'He believed that the Rotary Club was nothing more than an anti-clerical Masonic lodge,' observed Andreotti, adding, with customary slyness: 'I was much amused many years later to find myself at a Rotary meeting at which none other than Cardinal Ottaviani was among those receiving awards.'

Historians of Christian Democracy, recalling the murders and scandals of the P2 Masonic lodge during the 1980s, might well credit the old Cardinal with a good deal more insight than this witticism acknowledges – particularly since so many of the honourable Andreotti's friends and acquaintances appeared to figure in the Masonic ranks.

Informed in 1960 that the President of Italy was about to visit Nikita Khrushchev in the Kremlin, he ascended the pulpit of Santa Maria Maggiore to describe the Soviet chief as 'the leader of all those who every day turn back to killing and crucifying Christ'. His speeches were to be collected and published under the title of *Il Baluardo* – the bastion.

A few years later, the Cardinal was reposing on his prelate's chair during a speech by Cardinal Montini, later Pope Paul VI, to the Second Vatican Council. Montini said that mercy, charity and the conduct of an outwardly Christian life were the right methods to confront error. Strictures and hell-fire would no longer do. An Italian magazine reported Cardinal Ottaviani's murmured response to this encapsulation of modern teaching: 'I pray to the good God that I may die before the end of this Council – so that I can die a Catholic.'

He did his bit to stem the tide. In August 1962, having examined the works of the Jesuit philosopher Pierre Teilhard de Chardin, the Holy Office issued a warning that the perusal of these recondite volumes could damage Catholic minds. But the Cardinal was flailing against a prevailing current. He prepared four significant documents for the Council, heavy with scriptural justification. They dealt with 'The Sources of Revelation', 'The Moral Order', 'The Deposit of Faith' and 'The Family'. None of these would be accepted by the bishops.

Cardinal Ottaviani made a querulous exit from the Council, fulminating in Latin against those who had removed the might from his office. He gave the supporters of liberalism ample material with which to caricature his life and work, a vocation which they all pursued with a singular absence of charity. Yet something great and ancient clung to his personage, a weight of history and conviction so massive that perhaps one has yet fully to appreciate its absence from the modern Church.

God did not grant Ottaviani's wish to die a pre-Conciliar Catholic, for he survived for many years after it concluded. When he did finally go to his reward at the age of eighty-eight, Giulio Andreotti eulogised him accurately. 'He was an exemplary figure of the Roman priest and he died a poor man, in contrast to others ranked among the progessives and modernists.'

Pius XII lived on until 1958, while palace life behind the Leonine walls developed an atmosphere of febrile intrigue and slight madness reminiscent of the decaying courts of old Peking. In his later years, Pius ruled as a high priest of his own cult, performing private ceremonies before congregations composed only of his own cardinals, an unearthly smile wreathing his pallid features. The Pope was very fond of his pet canaries, which lived in their own cage in his apartments. He confided to his subordinates that he had seen Jesus Christ in a vision, an event which would one day be produced to aid his cause for sainthood.

When he died, it was as if a pall had lifted from the Church. He had already chosen his dying words and confided them, in advance, to Cardinal Giuseppe Siri of Genoa. They were '*Depositum Custodi*' – I have kept the faith.

One progressive Italian priest summed up the feelings that might be voiced now that Pius was safely in paradise. People were weary of too much learning, too much power; he said, they were tired of greatness, prestige and words.

The conclave of October 1958 awoke to such cries and elected Angelo Roncalli as Pope John XXIII. Pope John's election was hailed, in retrospect, as the turning point. He did not at first appear to promise much to those who had endured the twilight years of Pius XII. He was already old, born in 1881. He had manifested no signs of disobedience or discontent under the *ancien régime*. His attitude to the rule of Mussolini and to Italy's role in the conflicts of the 1930s and 1940s was shot through with uncertainty. Nobody rated John very highly as a theologian, and some considered him a worthy cleric who had not outstripped his simple origins. Nor had he laboured in the Roman Curia. His conduct of diplomacy in Sofia and Istanbul had failed to arouse any acclaim for his genius. His tenure as Papal Nuncio in Paris had been spent in a vice between the implacable will of Pius XII and the insufferable dignity of Charles de Gaulle. He was happiest when installed as Primate of Venice, a position that would recur in Church history as the seedbed of a shorter, more poignant, papacy.

But, like many extraordinary men, John possessed one simple, compelling idea and was gifted with a stroke of genius to put it into practice. That idea was best expressed in the Italian word *aggiornamento*. It can be translated as 'bringing up to date', or 'modernising', but in its more poetic sense it means 'bringing into the light of day'. John recognised that the late Pius XII was the last of the papal Pharaohs and that henceforth one could not reign in darkness from the seclusion of the pontifical salon.

For an elderly Italian bishop, little known outside his own diocese and the rarified circles of diplomatic life, John achieved a great impact upon world opinion. It helped, of course, that he came in the time of new leaders in America and the Soviet Union, both then seen as young reformers of their own systems. His appeal for peace during the Cuban missile crisis appeared on the front page of *Pravda*. These were times of optimism. The Italian economy was rebounding once more after the first wave of growth in the 1950s. People who had grown up eating only bread, pasta and vegetables when the Pope was a boy found themselves slowly entering a new age of prosperity.

Throughout the major western nations, unequalled progress was being made towards material comfort. Inflation was a thing almost uncounted. Middle-class families were able to purchase affordable, spacious housing. Fuel prices remained low. Travel by commercial jet airliner was just beginning to shrink the globe – a factor not to be ignored in the convocation of future conclaves and meetings. The glum procession towards Vietnam, hyperinflation, mass unemployment and industrial decay had commenced, but it went almost unnoticed. The season of assassinations and the violent racial fissures in American society were unseen nightmares ahead.

In this atmosphere, John decided to hold a Council of the whole Church. It was a bolder move than it sounds today. The previous Vatican Council in 1870 had been an unedifying affair. It was summoned to acclaim the authority of Pius IX, it lacked any proceedings that might truly reflect the word 'conciliar' and it was remembered chiefly for its endorsement of the proposition that Pius' announcement of the Immaculate Conception had been infallible.

The Second Vatican Council convened on 11 October 1962, ushering in a promise of humanitarian change in Roman Catholicism. Its deliberations were to take the Church out of the age of the *Index of Forbidden Books* and the iron rule of the Holy Office, into a world where dialogue was held in greater esteem than anathema, and self-examination of the Church itself was preferred to vain efforts to convert the unwashed. John XXIII did not live to see it through, however. Already very old, he had developed cancer. His massive peasant constitution enabled him to fight it off through a calvary of suffering, long enough to set the tone and allow the conciliar debate to develop. He penned a significant encyclical, *Pacem in Terris*, a document that defined the attitude of the Church towards a world dominated by nuclear competition between Moscow and Washington. He died on the evening of 3 June 1963, with the last words of the Mass for the sick, said by the Cardinal Vicar of Rome outside in St Peter's Square, drifting up to the papal apartments.

Pope Paul VI inherited the Council. It was a difficult task to rise to the heights of John XXIII, who – it was said with tiresome frequency – had thrown open the windows of the Vatican. A great deal of nonsense has been written about Pope John, much of it by those who seek his posthumous endorsement for their own liberal interpretations of what the Second Vatican Council did, did not do, or should have done. The chief victim of much of this hagiography was the man who succeeded him.

John emerged only in his very last years as a cleric dedicated to change. Until that time he had conformed to Curial mores in a manner befitting a servant of Pius XII. He was on the record as deploring both authoritarian rule in the Church and paternalism. Yet in his description of those ills he asserted the need for firmness and dignity. When it came to the fundamental conflicts between the creatures of Cardinal Ottaviani and the bright-eyed advocates of progress, John inclined to the conservative cause without overtly expressing hostility to the reformers.

He has been described, very shrewdly, as an enabler. He permitted the limited propositions advanced by reformers to mature and to enter into the body of discourse at the Council. He seems to have opened his own mind, towards the end, to embrace the need for a broader transformation of Catholicism than he had imagined even when he called the Council. Perhaps the experience of listening to devout men from all over the globe, speaking of the hopes and fears among their congregations, did much to clear his head of a generation of Curial orthodoxy.

It was left to Paul, an infinitely more subtle mind and every bit as humane an individual, to unite the irreconcilable aspirations of both factions, an unhappy endeavour that left nobody fully satisfied. Public opinion, unjustly, still holds to the notion of the Good Pope John and the remote, unfeeling Paul, no doubt because one excited great expectations and the other had to reconcile them with political reality inside the Church.

Perhaps, too, John embodied the aura of a more hopeful age. In poorer Catholic households from the Philippines to southern Italy, you can still see his picture on the wall next to that of John Fitzgerald Kennedy, as if these two lost leaders of the early 1960s could somehow return the world to a state of happiness.

And if you should enter St Peter's on any morning of the year, go up to the great *baldacchino* erected by Bernini above the altar, turn right and descend the steps that lead to the crypt, lined with the marble tombs of the pontiffs. Only before that of Pope John will you find fresh flowers each day and see people kneeling in prayer.

CHAPTER 6

From Paul VI to John Paul II

Standing in St Peter's Square, it is hard to escape the conclusion that the very architecture still conjures up a vanished kingdom. One thinks of Gibbon – no friend of the papist – who summoned up its atmospheric power like this:

> Those who survey with a curious eye the revolutions of mankind may observe that the gardens and circus of Nero on the Vatican, which were polluted with the blood of the first Christians, have been rendered still more famous by the triumph and by the abuse of the persecuted religion. On the same spot a temple, which far surpasses the ancient glories of the Capitol, has been since erected by the Christian Pontiffs, who, deriving their claim of universal dominion from an humble fisherman of Galilee, have succeeded to the throne of the Caesars, given laws to the barbarian conquerors of Rome, and extended their spiritual jurisdiction from the coast of the Baltic to the shores of the Pacific Ocean.

H.V. Morton sought a more concise acclamation. St Peter's, he thought, was 'a church that makes provincials of us all'. Friend or foe, everyone, it seems, has recorded their impressions of the place. Cardinal Wiseman obviously regarded it as an antechamber to heaven. 'In summer the great square basks in unalluring magnificence in the midday sun,' he wrote. 'It's tall obelisk sends but a slim shadow to travel round the oval plane, like the gnomon of a huge dial; its fountains murmur with a delicious dreaminess, sending up massive jets like blocks of crystal into the hot sunshine and receiving back a broken spray, on which sits serene an unbroken iris ...'.

George Eliot was overcome. 'The Piazza ... gave me always the sense of having entered some millennial new Jerusalem, where all small and shabby things were unknown,' she declared in 1860. 'Does your heart not pound at the very approach to this sanctuary?' enquires a heroine of Madame de Stael's, while the author herself compares it to music petrified in stone. 'Who does not feel his heart expand?' asked Mendelssohn, 'it appears to me like some great work of nature ... for I never can realise that it is the work of man'.

Byron penned his own sweeping demand:

> Since Zion's desolation, when that He
> Forsook his former city, what could be
> Of earthly structures in His honour piled,
> Of a sublimer aspect?

The place has its detractors. Protestants, and those northern Europeans less prone to grandiose emotions than the authors above, discovered a host of faults. Thackeray had been unimpressed, announcing that he found the front of the basilica merely 'supportable', provided that the dome overawed the viewer and drew his attention away from its 'ugly and obtrusive' façade. The design was held to lack unity. This is true. The origin of its masonry, torn from tomb and temple alike, was denounced. 'No more wanton or barbarous act of destruction was ever deliberately committed,' complained one (Protestant) author, while an Italian authority of the nineteenth century pronounced that 'the rebuilding of St Peter's alone, from the pontificate of Martin v to that of Pius vii, caused more destruction, did more injury to ancient classic remains, than ten centuries of so-called barbarism'.

The air of mystique had gone by the time Paul vi supervised his own Holy Year in 1975. The rotund exclamation of Italian vowels at the end of each line of prayer replaced the resounding clarity of the Latin. Translations, usually in the language of committee rather than genius, helped the foreigner understand the vernacular Italian Mass. Paul VI walked of his own volition, clad in a pure white robe, into the audience hall designed by Nervi. Its external proportions were thankfully hidden by the southern curve of Bernini's arcade. Inside it evoked the atmosphere of a Swiss airport or a parliament in Scandinavia. The pontiff appeared on a stage. All admissions were governed by tickets and places were allotted for groups. Security men in dark suits and badges muttered into radios. There were no ostrich feathers to be seen.

The Holy Year had been Paul's last prominent liturgical role and he had carried off its lengthy obligations with painful duty. It marked the first time that the style and ceremonial favoured by the progressive bishops at the Second Vatican Council had truly been inaugurated in the traditional shrines of Catholicism. In the portico of St Peter's, the panelled brass door opened by the pope at the onset of each Holy Year was closed once more. A plaque commemorating the Holy Year of Paul VI was added to the array of similar tablets set into the walls. Yet, to many Romans, a certain solemnity had been lost. They had been used to the barbarian splendour of the old ways. The simplicity of the new liturgy merely contended against the magnificence of its setting to produce an effect of confusion.

Such were the expectations aroused by the Vatican Council that it was, in the end, almost bound to disappoint. The Council lasted from October 1962 to December 1965. It was, by papal reckoning, the twenty-fourth Ecumenical Council in the history of Christendom. It was certainly the most prolific, generating sixteen conciliar documents, 27,000 pages of verbatim record and over a hundred miles of recording tape. Apart from its own paperwork, it gave rise to millions of words in newspapers, magazines, devout periodicals and diocesan circulars. Books were penned to analyse its substance, yet many years after its proceedings ended, at least one acute observer, the late Peter Nichols, found it lacking in historical import. 'Like many other people, I mistook it for the greatest religious event of the century,' he wrote.

The Council reforms abolished the universally recited Latin Mass and brought much doctrine and teaching into the industrial age. They transformed the episcopacy from an instrument of rule into a method of pastoral care. But to Pope Paul's eternal discomfort, many priests and nuns streamed out of the doors so hopefully cast ajar. Debate engendered challenge, morality became a subject for enquiry rather than credo, and the proud dignity of his office and its hierarchy became diminished when it was not subject to ridicule. As late as the 1950s the word of the parish priest went unchallenged by observant Catholics, not only in places such as Poland and Ireland, but in the dioceses of America, Britain, the Netherlands and Germany. That which was not specifically permitted by catechism was safely deemed to be forbidden. All at once, the reverse came true.

When Paul restated the Church's traditional opposition to artificial birth control in 1968, he ignored the advice of a panel of his own lay and clerical experts. Critics took it as a sign that the *aggiornamento* was at an end. Cardinal Ottaviani professed satisfaction. But the encyclical did not silence debate on the issue, as the denizens of the Holy Office might have imagined. Rather, it opened a new and uncomfortable issue of obedience for Catholics. In the rich Catholic countries of the West, its effect was to drive many away.

For years the Pope had suffered from an old man's infirmities, accentuated, no doubt, by a melancholy cast of mind and a profound sense of disappointment, sadness that a reign begun in the light of renewal should have decayed in a clamour of dissent, incomprehension of the desires unleashed in a new age, and guilt at his own inability to effect by goodness alone the healing balm necessary in a society wracked by political discord and violence. Paul was much underestimated and effortlessly wise. But in his personal torment, his self-doubt and his unwillingness to enforce by command the discipline that he believed should stem from conscience alone, he had become most unfashionable. His throne would later be occupied by a shrewd politician who demanded obedience and operated the mechanism of charisma with confident ease.

The Pope's energy had noticeably ebbed away earlier in the year after the kidnapping and murder of Aldo Moro, the Christian Democrat leader. Paul had offered himself to the Red Brigades in substitution for a man he genuinely thought to be an influence for good. His quixotic gesture, devoid of practical reality, had been ignored. The small coterie of priests around him noticed that he would watch the news on Italian television with woe, lamenting the critical episodes of violence which Italy was enduring, and turning to prayer as his only response.

It was a very medieval death. Paul had repaired to Castelgandolfo, a papal pleasure dome that sits on the brim of a volcanic lake high in the Alban hills. The air is clear there, free of the foggy miasma composed of dirt and carbon monoxide that plagued his wheezing lungs amid his low-lying, unhealthy domains on the banks of the Tiber. On the sharpest of days, his elderly eyes might discern the Michelangelo cupola of St Peter's, like an egg, shimmering above the haze of fumes and dust.

No privacy cloaked his decline. In the first week of August, when the stifling conditions of late July are usually beginning to ease, Paul felt severe discomfort caused by a chronic arthritic illness. From then on, his every intimate agony became the subject of a public bulletin issued by his doctors, Mario Fontana and Renato Buzzonetti. On Saturday afternoon, 5 August, he became feverish. The doctors called in a urologist from one of the leading hospitals in Rome. He diagnosed acute cystitis and a treatment was begun. On Sunday morning the pontiff failed to appear, as was normally his wont, before the summer pilgrims who would assemble in the small courtyard of the palace at Castelgandolfo. Prostrate in an upper room, he was suffering a high fever. Outside, the devout fell on their knees in prayer.

By this time the modern apparatus of public demise had been placed in readiness. But even as the Pope's life drifted away, Italians, indeed the world, scarcely seemed to pay attention. Paul performed the daily functions of a dutiful and conscience-stricken Vicar of Christ, yet his later pontificate, like that of Pius XII, drifted into a melancholy stillness. He had almost slipped from notice since the upheavals of the Second Vatican Council and the bitter debate over his encyclical on artificial birth control in 1968. A lonely, introspective man by nature and vocation, he excited no popular acclaim. In any case, it was the beginning of the continental month of vacation, and in 1978 traditional working practices still governed the habits of a vast majority of Italian families. The nation had gone to the beach.

If you stand on the edge of the lake at Castelgandolfo when the sun descends into the Tyrrhenian Sea, an agreeable, timeless vista comes into being. The whole of the Roman plain unveils itself, unwinding towards the sinuous course of the lower Tiber and the filigree sheen of the coastal strand. The aqueducts and columns of antiquity recede at darkness back into the folds of a classical landscape. Clusters of lamps, each at first like a colony of fireflies, unite one with another to form roads, junctions, suburban plots and shopping arcades. The distorting glaze of extreme heat has given way to the calm clarity of a summer's evening.

Thus it was in the last days of the Pope's life, as doctors, priests, secretaries and officials bustled in and out of the dying man's room. The prayerful vigil of those gathered around the precincts of his villa became intense. At about a quarter past six, the doctors noticed that the pontiff's blood pressure was rising at an alarming rate. Then, in the words of the bulletin issued later that night, 'there followed rapidly the typical symptoms of insufficiency of the left ventricle with the clinical picture of acute pulmonary oedema'.

The world's most famous heart surgeon, Dr Christiaan Barnard, was later to utter sharp criticism of the rather homespun medicine provided to the head of the Roman Catholic Church. The Pope was not even taken to hospital, and even though many Italian hospitals can still cheerfully be represented as Dickensian workhouses, up-to-date cardiac treatment was available in 1978. His life might certainly have been prolonged. The Vatican doctors, however, admitted no doubts. Instead, the scene at his sickbed recalled the improving portraits available of domestic death in the nineteenth century, when Patriarch, Kaiser or Queen would expire at home in a palace surrounded by loyal courtiers, weeping relatives and the grave ambassadors of foreign powers. Despite all 'the precise attentions which were at once applied', Pope Paul VI died at twenty minutes to ten on Sunday, 6 August.

The pontiff's body was brought down the circuitous roads from Castelgandolfo and back through the Aurelian walls into Rome. It lay in state within St Peter's on an inclined catafalque. A remarkable photograph appeared that week in the Italian weekly magazine *Epoca*. The photographer had used a long lens and by standing far back from the foot of the bier he had contrived to include in his picture the shrunken frame of the dead Pope, clad in vestments and mitre, and behind him, illuminated by shafts of late afternoon sun, a stained-glass window which forms the perfect counterpoint to Bernini's lavish four-pillared canopy above the altar.

Within three concentric rings of tinted glass, the window depicts a dove suspended between heaven and earth, holding an olive branch in its beak. It rises above an extravagant sculpture in bronze – an empty throne, around which mitred, caped figures recoil and dispute, and a flurry of cupids and angels gather around pillars of smoke (or clouds of incense?) pierced by innumerable streaks of unearthly radiance, stabbing against a marbled backdrop.

With a very Italian talent for vivid imagery, the photograph managed to suggest that the Pope's soul, too, had fluttered free of its decomposing prison. The biological truth, that sweltering summer, was less lofty. Several of the young Swiss Guards posted by the catafalque succumbed to nausea. Large fans were then discreetly installed to circulate the air without a constant reminder of mortality.

There was a certain irony in the ceremonial exit of Paul VI. The functions of the Church performed in St Peter's perpetuate an atmosphere of worship which he did very much to consign to history. They tend to remind one of the unkind comparison made by a British writer of the 1930s, an addict of Byzantium, who declared that, while Haghia Sophia represented man's homage to the immanence of God, St Peter's was designed only as a salon for His agents. Paul VI was very definitely one of His paramount agents.

As Giovanni Battista Montini, the Pope had passed his early years in the service of papal diplomacy, then, as Cardinal of Milan, he had occupied the See of Saint Ambrose, adopting the benevolent, but firm, paternalism recommended by Pope Pius XII to his prelates. All his life had been passed in positions where the Church exercised authority, mingling with temporal affairs but officially not partaking of them, meeting ordinary folk but rarely on any terms other than those of diplomatic intercourse or conventional respect. Many thought him a hidebound relic, imprisoned by protocol, blind to modern theology, a bureaucrat whose own private thoughts were probably communicated in formal Latin.

Paul was the last pope who passed most of his life within the walls of the Vatican and imbibed all its customs. He was a very modest man, but he could not shake off the majesty of his office, even when its authority no longer commanded awe.

Pope Paul VI was granted a funeral rite in the most impressive setting allowed to any mortal. The great façade of St Peter's was hung in black, thus Carlo Maderno's columns and balustrades became a monumental frieze of mourning. In the belfry far beyond, to the rear of the basilica's dome, the toll of hollow chimes announced the grief of the universal Church. And in the curved piazza extending before the basilica, ambassadors tugged at their starchy collars, their wives employed the order of service to fan life into the stagnant air, priests and prelates perspired under layers of vestments, and nuns, apparently impervious to sweat in black and white habits, recited their liturgy. Tourists gazed in wonder and some incomprehension. A very few Romans, chiefly the old, the mildly infirm and those indifferent enough to August to stay away from the beach, stood chattering to each other.

The Requiem Mass for Paul was said before a congregation that barely filled half of the greatest auditorium on earth. Without a human throng, St Peter's Square appeared all but empty. The Pope's small coffin reposed upon a bier set on the gently ascending steps to the portals of the basilica. Robbed by his own liturgical reforms of the splendour accorded to his predecessors, Paul VI went out in a chant of bare simplicity, unacknowledged by the Roman crowd, unlamented by modernists who thought him reactionary, and damned by the guardians of tradition who considered him weak.

The Pope would have been most upset to hear their verdict. He personally drew up the arrangements for his own funeral. It embodied the virtues of humility and abasement in the face of God, which, he considered, were best expressed in simple liturgy, plain words and a minimum of pomp. Alas, the splendid backdrop confounded him, and even if the square stood half empty, even if his prescription was followed to the last chant, the farewell to Paul VI was of a grandeur that he could not diminish.

It was not until the dead Pope was conveyed into the silent crypt under St Peter's and entombed beneath a slab, bare except for his name, that Paul VI finally attained the retirement he sought.

From the Counter-Reformation to the Second Vatican Council, the Roman Catholic Church scarcely permitted itself a moment of doubt. Thereafter it seldom seemed to find anything certain. The Church into which Pope Paul was baptised was dust and ashes when he died, as remote from its present form as Manchu China is from the People's Republic. Many applauded, some lamented, probably all still feel slightly lost.

There followed an episode in the history of the Church which still seems so bizarre that it is necessary to dig out the yellowing newspapers, review the video tapes and, indeed, descend to the crypt of St Peter's once more to assure oneself that it actually took place.

Here lies Pope John Paul I, within a surprisingly ornate sarcophagus, inlaid with streaked marble, surmounted by angels of mourning, for all the world like an extravagant nineteenth-century tomb in the Parisian cemetery of Père Lachaise. In keeping with the other tombs, it bears only his name and does not record the dates of his pontificate. Yet the span of his reign is perhaps its most significant historical element, for John Paul I only lived for thirty-three days after his election. He was chosen as Pope on 26 August 1978, and was found dead, sitting up in his bed, on the morning of 29 September. Not since 1605, when the Medici Pope Leo XI reigned for a mere seventeen days, had a pontificate been cut so short.

Like a dark story out of the medieval papacy, the Pope's demise brought conspiracy and rumour from every cobwebbed recess of the Vatican. Two authors were to do very well out of his sad end, one asserting that he was murdered, the other seeking to prove that he was abandoned to die of a curable circulatory ailment. Neither thesis, though energetically sustained and argued in each case with thorough intelligence, could be regarded as proven.

Albino Luciani was out of the mould of John XXIII in at least one respect. He, too, was a homespun Patriarch of Venice whose instinctive humanity had outshone the formality of his office. Like John after Pius, he seemed to promise light, freshness and air after the austerity of Paul VI.

There, however, the similarities evaporated. John XXIII had not served the Curia, but he had laboured in the diplomatic service and was familiar with its workload. Albino Luciani shared his pastoral concern; indeed, he infused it with a warmth that granted him instant popularity. But there was evidence that Luciani was naïve about the papacy's dealings with Italy, unable to cope with the sheer workload presented to him by his officials, and bereft of a first-rate personal secretary who might have proved an intermediary between the Pope and the enormity of his task.

He was also a man who would have felt uncomfortable with the enclosed and confidential method of government and external relations so typical of the Holy See. He publicly suggested that if St Paul had been alive in 1978 he would have pursued his ministry by becoming the head of Reuters. (Evidently, Luciani did not enjoy the acquaintance of the self-styled gourmet who headed that organisation at the time.) To Curial officials steeped in the dignity of Paul's pontificate and nostalgic for the lost majesty of Pius, these were banalities. Whispers began to surface in the Italian newspapers that the new Pope was not up to the job. In conventional terms, he was not. But Cardinal Basil Hume of Westminster, emerging from the conclave, had spoken of him as the candidate through whom the cardinals profoundly felt the influence of the Holy Spirit. It would be left to conjecture whether the Luciani papacy might have moved the Church into a new age.

It has been suggested that John Paul I was ready to consider a revision of the teaching on birth control. He sent a sympathetic message to the parents of Louise Brown, the world's first test-tube baby, declining thereby to endorse the Vatican's previous censure of the process. This prompted worry among traditional theologians and brought private expressions of concern that the Pope, in a fit of benevolent naïvety, might be altering doctrine without clear thought.

These might hardly seem motives for murder. There were, however, darker affairs afoot within the Vatican that would later come to light. Some thought that John Paul 1 might order the Vatican Bank to conduct its financial dealings with rather more rectitude than its record suggested was the case. It had become enmeshed with two notable frauds, Michele Sindona and Roberto Calvi, now both dead in mysterious circumstances. Others suggested that he intended to expose a network of Freemasons within the Vatican who conspired with right-wing extremists to perpetuate an unjust status quo. Therefore, runs the argument, powerful men with much to lose within the Vatican and the Italian establishment arranged his death. All these suggestions may well be true. Unfortunately, they rely on testimony that will, by its nature, never be publicly vouchsafed.

The conspiracy theory also incorporates a certain amount of wishful thinking and hindsight. John Paul 1 died in September 1978. At that time the Vatican Bank pursued its operations behind a cloak of apparently profitable discretion. It was not until 1982 that the collapse of the Banco Ambrosiano and the death of its chairman, Calvi, fully exposed a network of fraud involving the Church's financiers and brought the Vatican into disrepute. The Freemasonry issue, too, did not arise until 1981, when the discovery by the fiscal police of a secret list of lodge members provoked the fall of the Italian government then headed by Arnaldo Forlani. It seems a little much to credit that the former Patriarch of Venice found time in his thirty-three days to perceive the workings of two scandals of immense complexity which were only to be revealed over time in the years ahead.

The Vatican did little to contribute to public understanding of the Pope's death. It was put about, at first, that he had been found dead by his secretary, the Irish priest John Magee. Many years later, Fr Magee, by then safely dispatched to a bishopric in Ireland, admitted that he had only been the second person to see the dead Albino Luciani. He confirmed that the body had been discovered by a nun, Sister Vincenza, whose duty it was to bring the Pope his morning coffee.

At that time, the elderly Secretary of State, Cardinal Jean Villot, appears to have been in such a state of doddering incoherence that he could not face the announcement that a woman was customarily the first person to see the Roman pontiff each morning. Thus a lie was concocted, and a risible one at that.

Then there was the matter of what the Pope might have been reading when seized by whatever fatal malady carried him off. The official version first had it that he was studying *The Imitation of Christ*, an improving medieval text written by a mystic named Thomas à Kempis and dedicated to that pursuit. As this is reckoned by some to be the best-selling work in Christendom after the Bible itself, nothing could be more anodyne.

A second statement from the Vatican dispensed with *The Imitation of Christ*. It maintained, instead, that the late Pope had been found clutching sheets of paper containing personal writings. These, it cautiously specified, contained 'sermons, discourses, reflections and notes'.

This came as manna to the conspiracy theorists. If the Pope did not expire of apoplexy while reading the balance sheets of the Banco Ambrosiano, then he was surely drawing up lists of Freemasons to be dismissed from the Curia!

There was no autopsy. Cardinal Silvio Oddi declared that the college of cardinals accepted no interference and would not be disposed to discuss the subject. The Vatican rejected calls for an examination from outsiders and dismissed the concerns of several senior prelates. Cardinal Benelli of Florence, a distinguished curialist who came himself within a handful of votes of the papacy, went to his own grave some years later, convinced that something terribly wrong had occurred on the night of 29 September 1978. But Luciani's death and Benelli's defeat in the subsequent conclave had rendered the Cardinal a spent force, and Curial politicians are as prone as their secular counterparts to bitter reflection in exile.

The unsavoury fashion in which Albino Luciani was bundled to his grave suggests much more a hysterical rustling of cassocks than a cold and calculating plot. The quavering tones of Cardinal Villot, the remarks disdainfully delivered by Cardinal Oddi and the opaque pronouncements of Father Romeo Panciroli, the unfortunate Vatican press spokesman, all contributed to an impression of ill-deed.

The Vatican staged a lying-in-state and a pompous funeral for Albino Luciani, and then he was consigned to the crypt, one suspects with some relief. Cardinals descended upon Rome from the four corners of the air routes once again, and this time there was no romantic whimsy about their choice. Karol Wojtyla, the Cardinal Archbishop of Cracow in Poland, was elected after eight ballots over two days. Once again, the cardinals had sought a change in style to match the hour.

That they certainly received.

So, in the pontificate of John Paul II, some fifteen years later, what aspect did the Vatican present to the world? Its outward splendours seemed untouched. Imagine an early summer morning, walking across the bridge between baroque Rome and the Castel Sant'Angelo, the circular fortress-mausoleum where the Emperor Hadrian reposed in death and where Puccini's Tosca met her doom. To the west, a wide vista opens up down the Via della Conciliazione, a broad thoroughfare lined with fake obelisks. It conducts the eye straight down to the façade of St Peter's, the perspective compressed by distance so as to make it more squat and solid than it appears close-up. Dawn mists around the trees and hills to the rear of the Vatican are dissipating, the beginnings of a brilliant day emerge, with pale sunlight turning to a reflective glare off travertine and marble. The Lungotevere, the road bordering the river, is already alive with cars like a trout stream in the time of migration, so, fording the streams of Fiats, you jump on to the safety of the opposite pavement and begin to walk up towards the basilica.

The Via della Conciliazione was created to celebrate the concordat sealed between Mussolini and Pius XI on 11 February 1929. It ended the open hostility between the new Italian state and the papal government displaced from its realms by the conquest of Rome in 1870 and the unification of Italy. The treaty gave financial compensation to the Vatican for the loss of the Papal States and guaranteed its sovereignty over the patch of western Rome around St Peter's. It also elaborated the mutual rights and duties of the Roman Church and the Italian government. Thus it resolved the so-called 'Roman Question', a subject of heated animosity, with popes declaring themselves 'prisoners in the Vatican' and secular politicians abusing the papacy, when not shunning it. In the words of the Pope's own newspaper, the *Osservatore Romano*, Italy was given back to God, and God to Italy.

The concordat, however, drew many detractors. The future Paul VI recorded his own unhappiness and many reservations among the senior clergy. Others, more outspoken, deplored the fact that the Pope had concluded a pact with a Fascist regime whose excesses were steadily on the increase, and which, in fact, were greatly to be bolstered by this resolution of an embarrassing domestic dispute. The men who were later to found the Christian Democratic Party amid the rubble of Mussolini's corporate state unanimously decried the agreement. Publicly, however, the Church expressed unreserved acclaim for the diplomatic achievement of the pontiff.

The vast and destructive project with which Mussolini proceeded to construct the Via della Conciliazione attracted almost as much odium. In order to provide the space for this pompous thoroughfare, his architects required the destruction of whole streets in the ancient Borgo, the warren of dwelling-houses, workshops, brothels, restaurants, taverns and emporia of pious works that clustered around the skirts of St Peter's. The project was started in 1936 and did not reach its conclusion until the Holy Year of 1950. By then the ancient, the characteristic, the mildly scandalous and the wholly charming had all been swept away, and the great cobbled driveway thrusting to the heart of the Piazza San Pietro had been put in their place.

There are glimmerings of the old life in the few streets off to the north, through gates pierced in the fortified walkway – the so-called corridor of Alexander VI, running between Castel Sant'Angelo and the papal apartments. Here the small shops selling salami, cheese and wine survive cheek-by-clerical-jowl with homely trattorias and the plethora of outlets selling religious objects, many of them the same beaming portraits of the Polish Pope. One has the sense, however, that the old spirits have fled muttering to the shades, and even on the darkest winter's night the Borgo seems no more to summon up the air of malice and plot so characteristic of its long history.

Let us not be too hard on the Via della Conciliazione, though. Fine palaces and churches adorn its sweep. The Palazzo Torlonia, newly burnished to a dazzling gleam, resembles the great Cancelleria built across the Tiber by Bramante and Cardinal Riario to house the tribunals of the Church. The stinging air emitted by dozens of coaches – most, it is to be noted, from Poland, Czechoslovakia or Hungary – has yet to corrupt its freshness.

In the small church of Santa Maria Transpontina, the funeral of a simple nun is under way. Fewer than a dozen relatives and sisters, all of them old, gather in the front benches. The hired pallbearers are shuffling their feet at the back of the church. A sleek grey hearse is parked outside. Its window carries an advertisement and a telephone number for the undertaker's services. The priest, shuffling on to the altar, seems at something of a loss. Searching in his perfunctory sermon for words to eulogise this anonymous helper of Christ, he falls back on the general. Every person possesses his or her human dignity and identity in front of God. A true reward will be conferred upon the Just. The love of the Lord is always requited.

Across the road, at number 5, Via della Conciliazione, the less altruistic temper of humanity is on display. The local Italian government tax office is open for business as the first cappuccinos are frothing in the café next door, and by eight-thirty it is already a contentious babel of outrage, despair and loud self-justification. A shopkeeper emerges clutching the ubiquitous form 740, on which the self-employed are supposed to declare their income. Usually the form provides space for a work of fiction worthy of the Nobel prize. This morning, however, all does not seem to have gone well. 'Robbery! Shame! Thieves!' are the only three discernible words in a torrent of authentic Roman dialect directed at his waiting assistant. Another man stares at a sheaf of papers, shrugs and joins the throng pressing around the few counters open and manned. Some members of staff lounge scornfully behind the counter, just out of reach and, apparently, earshot of the crowd. One wonders if the Papal States were any more effective in the collection of their taxes.

The number of coaches is building up, for it is the day of a papal audience, one of those carefully programmed occasions in which John Paul II receives his devotees. The public meeting will not take place until eleven-thirty, but the devout are already flocking to St Peter's to prepare themselves in prayer for the encounter.

After a restoring coffee, consumed while standing at the bar in a café full of Vatican workers and clerics, it is time to confront the square and basilica. Some people affect to find St Peter's Square overwhelming – certainly George Eliot and Cardinal Wiseman must have done – but its original effect has been diminished.

Far away, in the deserts of Jordan, there is a horseback ride through a narrow defile and into a wadi that houses the lost city of Petra. The first impression is overwhelming. Around a bend in the track, through a sheer gap in the cavernous rock, the sunlight illuminates the façade of the ancient treasury carved out of the rock by the architects of the Nabataean kingdom. The pinkish stone glows against the blackness like a sudden pillar of fire. Riding out of the defile and surveying the noble treasury, one realises that it is a perfectly agreeable, if rather ornate building. Its power lies in that miraculous first sighting, and every other monument of Petra somehow pales into inconsequence after the initial rush of excitement.

In the days of the old Borgo, St Peter's Square enjoyed something of the same effect. Bernini built two long colonnades to embrace the circular piazza, adorning them with saints and angels. When, therefore, the traveller stepped out of the darkened warren of houses, alleys and shops, and into the light and spacious harmony of the piazza, it was like rounding that final bend into the city of Petra.

Nowadays, the original spell has been broken. The Via della Conciliazione allows us to see straight into the square from far-off. The false obelisks mounted at intervals along its length detract from the great obelisk of Caligula, set on a plinth at the centre of the piazza. The space just before the colonnades begin has been cleared completely in the interests of – what else? – traffic, and the hulking modern buildings around it, which house papal offices, are, to put it mildly, unfortunate. The two wings of office buildings create the impression that the piazza is a continuum of the Via della Conciliazione, rather than a glorious open-air arena at the heart of a venerable quarter. Bernini's original effect, which one imagines to have been awe-inspiring, has been rendered merely grandiose, a salute to authority instead of a rush of inspiration that bordered on the divine.

None of these considerations count for much with the thousands flocking to the audience with John Paul II. Indeed, so short is the public memory that some have doubtless forgotten that this was the scene of the first attempt in modern times to assassinate a Roman pontiff. Not even in the wars to liberate Italy and the various occupations of Rome by the forces of Napoleon had anything of its kind occurred. Nothing marks the spot in the square where the shots were fired. Only the presence of armed Italian policemen and security barriers at the entrance to St Peter's recall the fear and suspicions surrounding that day.

The shooting of the Pope was one of the critical events of the 1980s. It came at a moment when Communism, then in power throughout eastern Europe, was losing its grip on the populace but continuing to hold its own in the conflict against the western capitalist powers.

As Cardinal Karol Wojtyla of Cracow, the future John Paul II was schooled in a rigorous version of Catholicism that abhorred atheistic rule and devoted itself to the veneration of all that was traditional. As a young priest, he was taken up under the patronage – so important in the Church – of Archbishop Adam Sapieha, a cleric imbued with aristocratic charisma and fervent Polish nationalism.

The occupation and division of Poland were succeeded by full-scale war across its territories as the German armies fell back towards the Vistula in 1945. Upon 'liberation', the Polish Church soon found itself the symbol of national resistance to a Communist regime imposed by the Soviet Union. For another three decades Wojtyla ascended through the Polish hierarchy, conscious that the clergy commanded great loyalty for this national role, and equally aware that life under a hostile government on occasion required less heroism than flexibility. The unhappy fruits of this special relationship between hierarchy and people would become evident only after the fall of Communism. In 1978, when John Paul II was elected, his rise to the papacy delighted anti-Communists almost everywhere.

The new Pope instantly made it clear that a firm Polish style was to prevail. No further questioning of Rome was to be tolerated. The liberal theologian Hans Kung was banned. At the same time the pontiff exalted the sect of Opus Dei, with its traditional base in the ideology of Franco's Spain. The Pope censured the priests of Nicaragua who involved themselves in local politics. At the same time he was directing the negotiations of the Polish Church with the Communist authorities. Such was the consensus of the mass media in the first years of the 1980s, flush with emerging bull markets and under the influence of conservative governments in most of the western powers, that little notice was paid to this uneven application of the magisterium of Rome.

Adept at playing to the crowds, John Paul II substituted the spectacle of the papacy for the substance of reasoning and debate overseen by Paul VI. He travelled constantly. His message was one of tradition, timeless authority and obedience. It was shot through with all the tendencies in modern Catholicism that remained unembarrassed by relics, prophecies and miracles.

When it came to the critical struggle against Communism, the Pope was not content to await miraculous change. It is now known that he agreed in private with Ronald Reagan to conduct a clandestine campaign of financial and political support for the free trade union, Solidarity, in Poland, directed against the Communist government of General Wojciech Jaruzelski. Both the United States and the Holy See recognised the regime as the legitimate authority in Warsaw. This, however, was viewed as a technicality to be overcome in the interests of a global struggle against Communism to which both men were committed.

It is difficult to over-estimate the fear and passion with which events in the Communist world were followed in the offices of the Vatican. From the papacy of Benedict xv, elected in 1914, to the rule of the present incumbent, the Church made little secret of its preference for right-wing dictators over Communist politburos. The confrontation, in the eyes of the Curia, was apocalyptic in its implications.

Cardinal Agostino Casaroli, the architect of the Vatican's *Ostpolitik* under John, and Secretary of State under John Paul II, summed up the position. His vision embodied the Vatican propensity to think in millennia. Casaroli considered the fight against Communism to rank with the early persecutions, the contest between Popes and Holy Roman Emperors, the Reformation and the French Revolution. Upon consideration, he believed that the conflict with Communist ideology was the most profound the Church had ever faced, for here was a notion of existence and social organisation that denied any being higher than man himself.

So when Ronald Reagan sat down in the library of the papal palace with John Paul, the two men had much in common. Both had recovered from assassination attempts and both were prone to ascribe their good fortune to providence. Both were communicators whose public esteem depended more upon the warm embrace of their image than upon close scrutiny of exactly what it was they stood for. Neither was overly worried about legalistic procedures within their own governmental systems. Each man saw in the other an ally.

It was already the practice that the station chief of the CIA in Rome would brief the Vatican regularly on events in eastern Europe. Through the long autumn and winter of 1981, these discussions hinged mainly upon an analysis of whether or not Leonid Brezhnev and the Soviet Politburo would intervene with armed force to preserve the Communist state in Poland. The Pope let the Kremlin know that he was prepared, if necessary, to go in person to his homeland to assume his responsibilities in the face of an invasion.

One night, after dinner, and in the company of an engaging monsignor from the Vatican, I was walking across a darkened St Peter's Square. Martial law had been proclaimed in Poland just a few days before. The world's media was clamouring for a reaction from the Polish Pope, but thunderous denunciation came there none. The lights were aglow in the papal apartments, high above the shadowy colonnade.

'You would not believe, my friend, how closely the Holy Father is following events across the Polish border,' chuckled the monsignor. 'They say the telephones are cut off! Well, let them believe it. I know the Pope talked to three bishops this evening. There are already devout people ready to go in and out across the frontiers with money, messages, help of any kind that we can provide. You should see him! He keeps very calm in meetings, but I can tell that he is relishing this whole thing. It is the fight of his life.'

A decade later, much more came to light. Ronald Reagan had brought to the Vatican his Director of the CIA, a devout Catholic named William Casey. The director was a buccaneering old sort, who thought nothing of blowing up Muslim civilians with car bombs in Beirut or dropping mines in the harbours of Nicaragua, provided that it was all in a good cause. He fitted into an international Catholic fraternity, rich, a member of the Knights of Malta, well connected to the hierarchy in America. Director Casey and Cardinal Casaroli were to implement the vision of their masters. Money and propaganda flowed to Solidarity. All manner of covert actions lent assistance to the cause of the Church in Poland and undermined the Communist regime. Yet this was all conducted with subtlety and balance.

Both Casey and Casaroli were far too sophisticated a pair of operators to allow the Polish situation to degenerate to the point where a Soviet invasion might actually occur. Apart from the obvious, each had his reasons. The Reagan administration, for all its belligerent rhetoric, was actually extremely cautious about committing America to the use of force, not least because dead soldiers failed to contribute to the feel-good aura so essential to President Reagan's public ratings. America's ill-fated expedition to Beirut and its low-intensity war against Iran were to bear this out.

The Vatican saw no merit in unleashing a situation of complete disorder, where anarchy might prevail if Soviet tanks did not. Nor, in private, did the Polish hierarchy relish the prospect of Solidarity emerging to claim the unique mantle of resistance, at present the property of the Church.

So the effort ran at a carefully calibrated rate. Where did the funds come from? There were rich Americans aplenty who stood ready to underwrite adventures of this kind. But the sums involved were too great, and the need too immediate, for this to suffice. International banking analysts do not doubt that the Vatican's own bank, the Istituto per le Opere di Religione, or Institute for Religious Works, provided the conduit.

Thus, for all these reasons, it was easy enough to believe that the KGB had dispatched Mehmet Ali Agca to St Peter's armed with a pistol and a burning faith in Islam that directed him to view the Pope as a dangerous crusader. His bullets wounded the Pope, who was rushed to hospital, but later made a full recovery.

Agca was later to proclaim in court that he was, in fact, Jesus Christ. An American television reporter asked if he could repeat the assertion in English. Agca gaped insanely through the bars and gave every impression of a demented fanatic. Unfortunately for those who saw the trail leading to Moscow, he had a lengthy history of violence connected to the Grey Wolves, a band of Turkish terrorists of extreme right-wing persuasion.

This did not prevent the Italian authorities from putting on trial a Bulgarian airline official and others suspected of involvement in a KGB–Bulgarian plot employing Agca to assassinate the Roman pontiff. Years later, when the episode had been largely forgotten and its propaganda usefulness long redundant, the Bulgarians were let go for lack of proof. By then Agca had received John Paul II in his prison cell to make a private reconciliation. This intimate spiritual moment was made into a publicity stunt, with colour photographs released exclusively to *Time* magazine. It was all a long way from the rarefied private ceremonies of Pius XII.

It appeared by the early 1990s that the Wojtyla papacy had triumphed. Communism lay in ruins. Poland was liberated. Churches from the Baltic to the Danube were opened up, dusted down and filled with worshippers. The Vatican appointed bishops where commissars had ruled. Missals by the million were dispatched to the East while the works of dialectical materialism mouldered on library shelves in Vilnius and Bratislava.

Appearances, however, were quickly and heartlessly to deceive. To listen to the Pope proclaim his Easter message was to hear a cry from Lamentations, not a shout of exultation. He had much to mourn. Catholic Croats were slaughtering Bosnian Muslims, while both in turn engaged the Orthodox Serbs in a contest of tribal savagery not witnessed in Europe since the late 1940s. 'I say it to all, again and again: Do not kill! Do not kill! Shame upon those who break God's law and use violence ...'.

Deaf to repeated pleas and exhortations from the clergy of all sides, the fighting men made a mockery of the spiritual and nationalist values so confidently invoked by the Pope in the early 1980s as an alternative to the godless creed of Marx. Post-war Communism, many reflected, may have been drab, deadening and conformist, but it had certainly not engendered massacres, deportations and pillage.

In Poland, the Church had lost the lustre of opposition and now fought an unpleasant political fight to reassert its values against abortion and consumerism. Throughout the liberated lands, the peal of the church bell resounded against the clash of arms or the rumble of long-buried hatreds climbing out of the earth.

Bathed in the sunshine of an Easter Sunday on the Via della Conciliazione, immersed in adulation and deafened by the applause of his devoted crowds, the Pope may not have heard the shades of Pius XII and Paul VI rustle at his side. But for anyone possessed of an ear for the echo of history, for all those who believe that a harsh judgement is visited upon men's posthumous reputation, their presence could not be escaped.

CHAPTER 7

Four diversions

Santa Maria Sopra Minerva

No adornment to the baroque, no competition against the Pantheon, which stands nearby, no architectural jewel in its own right, the church of Santa Maria Sopra Minerva is given little notice in most guidebooks. Yet it seems to me a hidden treasure, one of those uncrowded corners of Rome to which one may retreat in the guarantee of mental refreshment and tranquillity.

The façade is Gothic, an austere flat-fronted construction, all angles and stark definition. A solitary window pierces the centre of the frontage. The church looks out of place. It was constructed between 1280 and 1290 on a site where pagan priests paid by the mighty Pompey once venerated the goddess Minerva. A temple of Isis is thought to have stood later on the spot. One is used to the Gothic of northern Italy, overwhelming with its thickets of pinnacles and its array of grinning basilisks. Santa Maria possesses none of that intimidating weight.

Instead, the church actually tends to lighten the surroundings by its difference, its severity of line and the fact that it presents a face of plain pinkish stone to the passer-by. With the bulk of the Pantheon looming at a few paces' distance – a building of ethereal lightness within, massive solemnity without – the church enjoys a comparative spirit of frivolity.

In part, this is due to the elephant. In 1667, or thereabouts, the reigning Pope discussed with Bernini a fabulous tale of the early Renaissance, in which various lovers progress through a garden filled with esoteric and allegorical symbols. It is rather hard to imagine the present pontiff, or any recent occupant of the Holy See, enjoying a familiarity with a work of this kind. But manners and morals were different then. The joint fascination of the Pope and Bernini with this tale is said to have led to the commissioning of the odd but cheerful statue derived from one such strange fancy. It stands before the Gothic realms of Santa Maria, as if it was a joke.

On a plinth there is a baby elephant, splendidly caparisoned, his head turned left over one shoulder in a quizzical pose, his trunk curling playfully. On the elephant's back, there is perched a small Egyptian obelisk, supposedly a representation of strength supporting knowledge. A Latin inscription records the sentiment that only a robust mind may bear the weight of solid wisdom. The obelisk resembles another one positioned atop the fountain directly in front of the Pantheon itself. The two are reckoned to have come to light in the Middle Ages, together with other Egyptian statuary that once decorated the Campus Martius, the low-lying flatlands that bordered the Tiber in classical times.

This amusing statue lends an air of whimsy to the square, which is just as well, since it prepares one for the inconsistent charms of the church. Augustus Hare, in censorious mood, did not much like Santa Maria Sopra Minerva. One suspects it was a little Catholic for his tastes – after all, one may always console a devoutly Protestant mind with the thought that baroque merely reinforces the Church in its effete indulgence, but this theory is not supported by the Gothic. His description of this inoffensive building is etched in acid. Behind the 'mean ugly front' there lurk 'tawdry imitation marbles, which have only a good effect when there is not sufficient light to see them'.

Oh dear. One has been warned. As if the strictures of a Victorian aesthete were not enough, here comes another recent authority. 'The interior ... most unfortunately restored in the last century,' it is noted, sniffily conceding: 'but it has a beauty of its own when flooded with the golden afternoon light from the rose windows'. Well, indeed. One might note that it is luminescent, calm and uplifting as well. Add the soft notes of a Bach fugue and the figure of a black-cowled monk caught in a beam of that very same light, and the interior of this derided place becomes wonderful.

Anyone who has ever taken the train to Florence and got off at the main station will recall the church across the piazza that gives the station its name, Santa Maria Novella. For many people, this is the first Florentine or Italian Renaissance church they ever see. Its architect was the same Dominican monk who designed Santa Maria Sopra Minerva and, not surprisingly, there are traces of his imagination in both buildings. But whereas the Florentine church is of bleak internal austerity, Santa Maria Sopra Minerva possesses an altogether richer heritage.

During the centuries in which the popes reigned over the states around Rome, the church was a centre of annual ceremonies at various points in the cycle of the liturgy. It was renowned for a procession on the feast of the Annunciation, when the Pope himself was wont to ride upon a white mule at the head of a troupe of cardinals, acolytes and sundry divines. The day was customarily reserved for an expression of loyalty to the temporal master of the Roman lands; thus the bemused albino mule and his burden would be greeted with flowers and shouts of acclamation, while the more comfortable classes looked on from balconies draped in purple velvet. The ceremonies were still of regal splendour when Boswell witnessed them many centuries later in the life of this church.

Lest any of the audience should forget the dread authority which underwrote this jovial scene, they needed to look no further than the tomb within Santa Maria which bears the name of Torquemada – in this case, a cardinal related to the maestro of the Inquisition.

Should any of them confuse the fairground jollity of the white mule with the revealed truth, they could also turn for chastisement to the sepulchre of St Catherine of Siena, for whom revelation was an almost daily phenomenon. What is one to make of this quintessentially medieval figure, whose remains were enclosed in 1461 within the marble sarcophagus beneath the high altar? Candles and lamps burn eternally there in her remembrance. Ecstatic, gifted with charisma, hysterical and visionary at once, she grew aware of her gifts at an early age, promptly became a vegetarian and scourged herself whenever she deemed it necessary. She began to experience visions as a child (this was the time of the plague mentioned by Boccaccio) and would gather her playmates around to hear her preach. Refusing to countenance her parents' desire for a suitable marriage, she insisted upon embracing a religious life,

bearing with fortitude the menial household tasks which were in consequence forced on her. Eventually, she persuaded her parents to allow
her to enter a convent at the age of thirteen, permission which by then
they may well have granted with a sigh of relief.

Catherine's powers rose in tandem with the terrors of the age. She
emerged from the cloister as a fearsome political figure, dispensing
advice to monarchs and exhorting the backsliding citizens of central
Italy to greater piety. She moved amid a landscape of burning cities and
the unpurified dead, becoming the inspiration of at least one pope and
the flail of republicans and dynasts. John Addington Symonds, who
rather relished this kind of thing, records that she expired at Rome on
29 April 1380 at the age of thirty-three, 'worn out by inward conflicts,
by the tension of a half-delirious ecstasy, by the want of food and sleep
and by the excitement of political life'.

She sleeps placidly enough today, under the altarpiece, with frescoed
saints and apostles all around. Her repose is seldom disturbed, for Santa
Maria Sopra Minerva does not figure in any list of 'top ten sights' for
tourists or pilgrims to complete in a week, or even a month, in Rome.

Yet its riches are fathomless, homelier than St Peter's, quirky, more
redolent of myth, readier to evoke the guts of life in the medieval city.
Clement VIII, the Aldobrandini Pope, ordered the second architect of St
Peter's, Giacomo della Porta, to design two pompous tombs in the
church for his father and mother. Cardinal Oliveriero Caraffa, a discerning
prelate from Naples, brought in Filippino Lippi to represent St Thomas
Aquinas in a cycle of frescos – 'ruined by a recent restoration' lamented
Augustus Hare, but perfectly agreeable to a less rigorous eye. Then there
is the unabashedly grim tomb of Pope Paul IV. A fearsome individual
he appears, holding the keys of St Peter with an expression on his stone
face of such utter lack of charity that not even the most zealous canoniser
might elevate him to sainthood. Paul IV, Pietro Caraffa, embodied the
aspects of the medieval papacy that have remained fixed in the minds
of the Orangemen of Ulster and the dissenters of central Europe. He
upheld the Jesuits, abhorred the Jews, applauded the Inquisition and
exalted his own authority. His Latin epitaph, however, recalls only his
eloquence, learning, innocence, liberality and greatness of soul.

Thank heavens that Cardinal Bembo, friend of Raphael and admirer
of beautiful women, rests in peace only a few paces away, his cheerfully
humanist funereal inscription eschewing the sombre monosyllables of
the conventional epitaph.

What treasures lie in this half-forgotten church! One can lose count of the defunct cardinals who lie here, a roll-call of distinguished Italian families: Tornabuoni, Tebaldi, Bonelli, Capranica. Next come the tombs of two members of the House of Medici who rose to the papal tiara. Giovanni de'Medici reigned as Pope Leo X for seven years, befriending Cardinal Bembo, patronising the arts and enjoying the papacy as God intended him to. He was the son of Lorenzo the Magnificent, and his neighbour in eternity, Pope Clement VII, was the son of Giulio de'Medici, who fell to the daggers of the Pazzi conspirators in Florence.

Clement VII presided through less carefree times. He was unfortunate enough to rule at the climax of a long-festering dispute between the papacy and the Holy Roman Emperors. Spanish and German soldiers fought their way down the peninsula to Rome, breached the city walls and ran amok. The city was sacked as if by the Huns or the Goths. Clement fled down the fortified passageway from the Vatican to Castel Sant'Angelo, where Benvenuto Cellini – at least by his own self-serving account – masterminded the defences. Cardinals were robbed, bullied and harried to death, women were raped, smoke billowed from ruined palaces and the gold reliquaries were smashed and the precious contents flung on marble flagstones. Rome lay in despair. Business had ceased, rubbish putrefied in the muddy streets and people streamed out for sanctuary in the countryside. Artists, scholars and poets, lured to Rome in the high days of the Medici papacies, starved, fled or fell to the sword. The Pope slunk away to Orvieto, dressed as a peasant.

He returned only when a surrender on terms of humiliation had been concluded. His remaining days in the Vatican were dragged out between fever and blindness; he was reviled by the populace and when he died they rejoiced. A relative intervened to save his corpse from desecration by the mob, and Sangallo built him an adequate if not sumptuous tomb. On a still summer afternoon, when hardly a soul is about, the profound silence in the church teases one to strain for an echo of these clashing events. But sound comes there none, and the saint, her popes and their acolytes slumber on.

As if by an afterthought, Michelangelo's statue of Christ bearing the Cross stands near the altar. A crucifix attributed to Giotto hangs almost unnoticed in a side chapel. The tombstone of Fra Angelico, nearby, is moving in its brevity and self-effacing tone. It asks only that his goodness to the poor be recalled by God, for his art was a work for earth, while his generosity was a labour on behalf of heaven. A *Madonna with the*

Child in a small side chapel is attributed to Fra Angelico.

It might be unorthodox to sing the praises of Santa Maria Sopra Minerva. It requires valuable time to visit it. One might even have to exclude better-known monuments, museums and sanctuaries from the itinerary. But few churches in Rome provide such tranquillity, such richness and such reflected glory.

Da Enzo

Very early one January morning in 1982, for reasons too complicated to go into, I found myself sitting on the steps of the church of Saint Vincenzo and Saint Anastasio under a sky as ashen as my own all-night pallor. None of the local cafés had yet opened. It was also too fearsome an hour to call upon any of my friends in the neighbourhood, a call, in any case, that would have required as many explanations on my part as kindnesses on theirs.

There was, however, a consoling view from the steps of the Fontana di Trevi, Nicola Salvi's insane masterpiece of aquatic statuary. It is perhaps the most extravagant of all Roman monuments in its challenge to the conventional imagination. The fountain occupies the entire wall of a *palazzo* and two-thirds of the piazza that stretches before it. At daybreak its gushing streams were muted. The vast basin glistened like a stagnant pond. Its stone divinities and galloping horses, so lively amid the spray and cascades, seemed marooned. Only a few trickles fell apologetically from the founts.

A couple of policemen loitered around the door of the maroon stucco apartment building on the right of the fountain, where President Sandro Pertini resided at that time.

Then, around the opposite side of the fountain there came an odd procession. It was led by a very fat man indeed. He was clutching several wooden boxes containing vegetables. Two stricken-looking women trailed behind him, weighed down by heavy bags. An old fellow with white hair and fine features brought up the rear.

With a certain amount of confusion, it bore in on me that this unlikely parade comprised virtually the entire staff of our local restaurant. When one is accustomed to seeing familiar faces only over a lunch or dinner table, it can be rather disjointing to encounter them before breakfast. The fat man was the cook. The two women flitted around the kitchen, and the sharp-featured, sharp-witted individual at the rear was Severio, the waiter. (There was another waiter, but if you had been served by Severio on your first visit to the restaurant, you would forever be ignored by his colleague.) As they walked past, they all gave a cheerful '*buon giorno*' as if it was the most natural thing in the world to meet one of your regular dinner customers on a January dawn, clad only in a T-shirt and torn jeans, huddled on the steps of the local church.

These people worked fantastically hard. They were all part of an extended family from the Abruzzi, and each day except Sunday they drove all the way into Rome as the stars were lightening in the eastern sky. They went every morning to the meat and vegetable markets for fresh stock. They would stay in the cramped and hot surroundings of their restaurant until the last inebriated diner had wandered out at around eleven o'clock in the evening. This they did six days a week for years and years.

The place was called the Trattoria Scavolino, though everybody called it Enzo's. Eventually a sign went up conceding that Da Enzo was, in fact, the *nom de guerre*. It was not the most elegant of establishments. Hidden down a narrow alley, the Vicolo Scavolino, it comprised two rooms and one small galley kitchen, from which there wafted a perpetual stream of profanity and – on good days – the alluring smell of homely Roman cooking. In fine weather a few tables were placed outside in the alley. Most clients, however, sat in the second, larger room. There were clean tablecloths and napkins for every diner. The dishes, cutlery and glasses were spotless.

Da Enzo had pretensions to being a centre of artists and a talking shop for intellectuals. As proof of the former, a selection of hideous paintings, all framed at some expense, hung on the walls of the dining room. A handwritten sign informed the customers that all were for sale. One was said to be the work of Renato Mussolini, jazz-playing son of the late tenant of the Palazzo Venezia. It depicted a lonely castle at the summit of a grassy hill. At the foot of the castle a solitary tree, starkly outlined like a gibbet, stood against a lowering sky. Another canvas purported to convey a savage analysis of American consumerism. It showed a gasoline pump in the style of the 1950s, behind which something violently erotic was in progress. There was a portrait of a man with a red nose. And so on. It was generally best to select a table from which one did not have to view these works head-on, particularly if confronted at the same time by a plate of Enzo's Roman tripe.

As for being a talking-shop for intellectuals, most of the weight fell upon Severio, whose views were available gratis and at length to those customers favoured with his attention. Energetic and interminable arguments went on in the smaller, intimate dining room. But to judge by its inhabitants, one was only shown to a table there after approximately forty years of continuous patronage. Most of the debate centred on Lazio football club, their rivals at Roma, the weather, women and betting of various kinds. Although we lived in the years of the Red Brigades with all their sensations – kidnapping, murder and the like – I do not recall hearing politics mentioned once.

A scene ensued one Thursday, however, when a diner ventured to take issue with the quality of the fat chef's gnocchi. This provoked ire, indignation, appeals for understanding and finally a morose silence. Did the person not understand how the kitchen slaved all day, using only the freshest ingredients, standing up for hours at a stretch, and all this for the honour of being accused of producing inferior gnocchi? What was life coming to? There were no true Romans left, oh no! Once upon a time a serious restaurant might count on persons of taste and distinction at its tables. Hah! That was hardly so nowadays ...

The chef retreated behind his hatch, amid steaming cauldrons and spitting pans. Nobody ventured a word. The diner shrugged and went on eating his gnocchi. One did not complain at Enzo's.

Partly this was due to the fact that there was precious little to complain about. The food was certainly not refined. But it was freshly cooked, simple, well flavoured and served with amusement. It was also very, very cheap.

Upon arrival, even after hundreds of meals at the place – and I ate there almost every day for at least two years – Severio would produce a menu typed upon an elderly machine in the kitchen. 'Consult the horoscope,' he would say. There would be a list of dishes that never vanished from the menu. Then there would appear the day's favourites. On Thursday there was the infamous gnocchi. On Friday there was fresh fish. Other specialities varied with the whim of the gross chef. But one had to be early, or lucky. The best dishes would be greedily consumed by the regulars, leaving only the perennial dishes that had long simmered on many a Roman stove.

The pasta, of course, was sturdy and filling. Naturally it was always *al dente*, tossed in a fresh tomato sauce or a meat ragout. When the chef was in the mood, and fresh clams were available, he could make *spaghetti alle vongole* with as much panache as the most expensive place in town. But mostly one ate a simple plate of fettucine or spaghetti, with a dusting of grated Parmesan. On days when the consequences of the previous night were still particularly fearsome, Severio would produce a bowl of *capellini in brodo*, delicate strands of pasta in a clear soup. Light food was frowned upon. Ladies, who were treated with extravagant courtesy, would be permitted to order a caprese salad of tomato and mozzarella, or to consume Parma ham and melon as a main course. Similar desires on the part of young men were thought to be unnatural, Enzo's artistic pretensions notwithstanding.

The main course ... ah well, the main course could provide either a path to delight or a pitfall for the unwise. In general, the freshly tossed salad was good, so a steak, a breaded veal escalope or a pork chop to accompany it always constituted a safe option. On Fridays, the chef turned his attention to grilled sole, with outstanding results: a crisp, golden skin, luscious white flesh, moist and firm, within.

Alas, from these dizzy heights the menu descended rapidly to the likes of tripe, indeterminate stews – always optimistically labelled '*alla Romana*' – *polpettine* (meatballs) and *Coda alla Vaccinara* (oxtail simmered with carrots and celery). This is a dish that can be sublime. Unfortunately, the chef at Enzo's never realised that it is best when served at slightly more than room temperature.

There were a few byways into which one might safely escape during the menu's headlong plunge. *Vitello Arrosto* usually yielded a few delicate slices of roast veal. A *Brasato di Manzo* provided a trusty piece of beef simmered in red wine. Since Enzo's was not the warmest of places in the Roman winter, such fortifying dishes were a wise choice. Few concessions were made to modern or complicated desserts. The ice cream was fine, and Enzo turned a humble *tartufo*, or chocolate-coated ice cream, into a tempting conclusion to the meal by the simple expedient of drenching it in Roman brandy – the only known use for that otherwise undrinkable product. The bill, when it eventually appeared, would be scrawled on a piece of paper. One had the feeling that it was unlikely to figure on a tax return.

Da Enzo, then, had its weaknesses. But they were more than adequately compensated by its abiding strengths. Sun or snow, the place never failed to open. On a cheerful weekday lunchtime, you could appear with a few friends, sit outside in a noisy group and drink litres of the fresh Frascati wine, which Enzo kept in stone tanks. It varied somewhat with age, but never gave you a headache. People brought visiting friends, lovers and relatives for a cheap dinner. The lovers, often of a rather transient nature, received a gracious if indifferent reception from Severio. Fathers and mothers, of course, were greeted with delight and amusement.

Then on a lonely December evening you could come down from the evening shift in the Reuters office, around the corner, and ensconce yourself with a book over a drawn-out dinner, thence to stagger back to the office to send a message to London announcing that the bureau was closed for the night. In the solemn, computerised new age of journalism this practice would no doubt be frowned upon. Da Enzo offered a lifeline, however, in the shape of an ancient Bakelite telephone which sat next to the cook's hatch. If any item of urgent news came over the teleprinters of the Italian news agency, a wireroom operator back in the office would telephone to alert the diner. One could then rush back to the office and deal with the matter, thus conveying an entirely false impression of bustling efficiency. Severio, on occasion, would send a plate of food back to the chef to be kept warm while such vital matters as the latest issue of government treasury certificates – a grand name for debt – could be announced to an eager world.

Even this leisurely arrangement smacked of untoward haste compared with an earlier generation of journalists in Rome. The gentlemen would adjourn after a prolonged lunch to the swimming pool at the Parco dei Principi hotel, returning late in the afternoon to compose a few words on any subject thought likely to interest London.

Now, of course, such an arrangement would be unthinkable. All the loyal wireroom operators were pensioned off years ago, their places taken by inanimate screens. The prospect, too, that one's masters in London might remain in ignorance of an event for a vital few minutes – let alone half an afternoon – is unthinkable in an era of satellite television.

All this progress has certainly contributed to the increased speed, and no doubt greater revenue, of Reuters, but one cannot escape the sensation that a degree of civilised enjoyment – vital to the understanding of Italian culture, if not to the market in treasury bonds – has been lost. People were on occasion dispatched to unpleasant, bakingly hot, unpredictable and violent places from Rome. It seemed only fair to provide a balance of pleasure in their professional existences.

In those more languid times, the balance of pleasure was nearly always in the professionals' favour. In the 1950s one bureau chief resided in ambassadorial style in a beautiful apartment atop the Torre del Grillo, a medieval tower commanding a view of the forum of Trajan and the Palatine hill. Another purchased a villa in Tuscany. Yet another frequented the night clubs of Rome with such consistent energy that his aquiline features attracted the attention of Fellini, who cast him in a cameo role in his film *Casanova*.

Few of the distant managers in London could have imagined the abandoned behaviour that seemed to overtake the most ordinary Anglo-Saxon souls when exposed to an atmosphere of extreme heat, scanty clothing and chilled white wine at a derisory price.

Persons who in London showed the disposition of a timid bank clerk would conduct wild affairs, swim naked in Lake Bracciano, drink themselves into a frenzy at lunchtime and dance until dawn in seedy clubs. Dutiful spouses were apt to throw themselves wholeheartedly into what they fondly imagined to be a typically Italian indulgence in pagan pleasures, while their respectable Italian friends looked on in consternation. Work, while carried off with flair, could hardly have been said to provide the dominant ethic. On one immortal occasion a senior individual, due within ten minutes to present himself for an important interview with the governor of the Bank of Italy, lurched into the office dishevelled, unshaven and sporting a black eye. The staff, aware of his occasional difficulties at home, affected, in very English fashion, to notice nothing. Eventually the man turned to a junior colleague. 'I believe we should go now,' he said airily. 'I suppose it might be better if you were to bring the notebook.' He carried off the interview with complete aplomb and retired to salve the wounds of the day, where else, but at Enzo's?

For a long, long time, Enzo's seemed like an institution that would never die. It was at the core of a perfect little Roman village, between the Via del Tritone and the Quirinal palace. The area possessed its own market, shops, dry cleaners, newsagents and cafés, huddling around the mighty bulwark of the Quirinal walls. Tourists streamed into the piazza around the Trevi fountain, but they soon filtered off again, back to the main streets and the next impressive sight. One's regular dining companions dispersed to Beirut, Moscow or Rio de Janeiro. Yet every time one came back over the years, there was the narrow alley, the same few tables, the inimitable typed menu, and a warm, if never fulsome welcome. Severio and his ilk had no need for the effusive waving of pepper-mills.

In any case, one had eaten there so often and in such familiarity that it was like dining at home.

And then one day I arrived in Rome and walked down the alley and came up short. A new, brash sign adorned the grimy wall. Inside, the two rooms shone, newly painted in pastel pinks and blues. Flowers were arranged on each table. Candles were set next to them, in elegant designer holders. Snooty waiters, evidently having dipped their heads in hair-gel, flicked tablecloths and bent solicitously over the few customers. A gold-rimmed menu announced portentous food – fettucine with caviare, and so on – at prices that read like the national debt.

The hilarious art collection had gone, the kitchen was jammed with gleaming new equipment, a computerised till produced the receipts and, as the final insult, a portable telephone had replaced the old Bakelite, down which so many dramas had been announced.

The old Abruzzi family, it transpired, had just had enough. Years of backbreaking work, starting each morning in the dying light of the stars, had worn them down. By the middle of the 1980s Italy had caught up with the boom throughout the capitalist world and hideous sums of money were pouring in to transform ancient areas like that around the Quirinal. Once, the centre of Rome was full of family trattorias like Enzo's. Now, they are like lights going out all over the city, one by one, extinguished by economic growth – one hesitates to call it progress.

Eventually, a company had offered Enzo's people so much for the site that they had sold out and, no doubt, gone to a well-earned retirement with not an ounce of sentimental recollection. Alas, that it were so for the bereaved customers. For better or worse, perhaps because of the time in my life, Enzo's was the best restaurant I have ever known or ever will. It has gone, leaving a gap and a flood of memories every time I stroll down that narrow crooked passage where so much laughter and wine was spilt.

Stendhal's birthday

On the morning of a man's fiftieth birthday he does well to feel contented and at east. A lover of all things Italian, Stendhal chose his perspective with care for this auspicious moment, which fell, for him, on 23 January 1833. He walked to the summit of the Janiculum hill to survey the city of Rome laid out before him. The dome of Saint Peter's rose behind a screen of trees to his left, the triple fountain of Sixtus v splashed and gurgled to his right. He reflected that life was sweet, a thought which anyone in his position might share.

Cultivated, a discreet sensualist, hailed as a master of French prose while happily resident in his adopted Italy, Stendhal enjoyed a perfect harmony between his work, his philosophy and his agreeable daily existence. In those days the Roman skies were undarkened by pollution. Only the clatter of hooves on cobblestones disturbed the siesta. In the evenings, a rumble of eternal disputation, boast and plea resounded from the taverns.

Trastevere, the district beneath Stendhal's gaze, still looks from a distance much as the author would have seen it. The botanical gardens climb in unruly profusion up the slope of the Janiculum. Red-tiled rooftops, cupolas and spires, square watchtowers and proud campanile straggle towards the curve of the Tiber. At about three o'clock on an autumn afternoon, when the gardeners burn off the dead leaves and a hint of woodsmoke curls into the nostrils, Trastevere seems like a sleepy medieval village. Palm trees shade its courtyards and trellised vines cling to every roof terrace. The three arches of the Farnese palace, now the French embassy, rise across the river behind a curtain of withering branches. In the distance, following the Tiber's course to the south-west, the monastic churches on top of the Aventine hill ride like ships above the gap-toothed city skyline. This, in turn, is surmounted by a delicate tracery of television aerials.

The reverie breaks with cruel speed. 'Aooo!' comes the cry of the souvenir seller on the Janiculum, touting his plastic madonnas. The first huge coaches disgorge Grand Tourists from Osaka and Frankfurt, summoned by megaphones to admire a view that is, in that odd Italian expression, *suggestivo*. Down in the narrow streets, the roar of St Fiat and all his archangels sounds as a tocsin of damnation. Paris has its Haussmann boulevards, Los Angeles its freeways. Trastevere possesses nothing in its concept or layout to cope with the deathly twentieth-century marriage between Roman and motor car. In this it is paying the price of commercial greed, civic indifference and political larceny. It is slowly suffocating.

Its criminal reputation, hitherto roguishly folkloric, is such that the visitors from Osaka now employ armed guards to make the trek from coach to 'typical' restaurant. This followed the fate of a young Japanese lady foolish enough to carry her handbag on an evening visit to

Trastevere in search of Roman music and laughter. Two men on a motorbike swished by. One grabbed her bag, the strap snarled around her arm, and she was dragged fifty feet before smashing her head open on a characteristic old cobblestone. Her body was returned to Japan by the consulate, and the Japanese travel agencies decided to open contracts with a private security firm.

The culprits, of course, merited no more than an indifferent shrug from the police. Theirs is the most common crime against the person in the modern city, an event so banal that it no longer excites comment. From my window in Trastevere I used to watch at least one couple a week go through the ritual as they exited from the restaurant beneath my balcony. First complacency, a pleasing arm-in-arm stroll after lunch. Then shock, she whirling round in a daze, he open-mouthed, the scooter already haring up the street with an annoying whine of exhaust, her bag dangling from the hands of the thief. A second later came fury, shouts, a useless run for a few steps after the robbers, and appealing looks for help in every direction. She, by now, was usually in tears. The populace would look on in utter indifference, except for those who might pass comment on the stupidity of anyone carrying a bag in these streets.

Rome, lament the Italian newspapers, is nearing a state of collapse. Its quality of life grows worse, while its prices surpassed those in Manhattan some time ago. And should you wish to experience the full sickness of Rome, live in Trastevere for a year or two. In a Catholic symbiosis of beauty and ugliness, goodness and filth, piety and licence, extravagance and parsimony, the district offers a social map of Roman splendours and miseries.

Say 'Trastevere' to most Romans of a certain class and they will shake their heads and mutter some worldly wise piece of nonsense about the place. 'Full of foreigners – no Italians there.' 'Nobody lives there any more.' 'It's not a real area.' And so on. Self-styled Roman intellectuals are fond of complaining about the clichés to which their country is sometimes subject. No group is more ready to pass facile and false judgements on their own city, a place of which they remain, very often, in cocooned innocence. Trastevere is a case in point.

In fact, there are very few foreigners left in Trastevere, a medieval district that extends along the west bank of the Tiber from the Regina Coeli prison to the flea market at Porta Portese. None of them can afford the fanciful rents demanded by landlords today. Thirty years ago, it is true, the place developed as a version of the Left Bank in Paris, rather Bohemian, full of authentic working-class characters to lend atmosphere, attractive to foreigners streaming to Italy in search of heady sensations in everyday life.

Nowadays a tidal wave of new money generated during the 1980s has swept away this transient populace of writers, would-be artists, divorcees on fixed incomes, unhappy students and posturing Americans. The old Trastevere is no more, but it is new Italians that have sealed its doom – bankers, wheeler-dealers, drug traffickers and property speculators, piling in to buy up and renovate old apartments, each bringing their two noisy cars with them to jam the narrow streets and make life impossible. Rents have doubled, quadrupled within ten years, despite a law that supposedly regulates the amount a landlord can charge. Naturally this piece of legislation is widely ignored and a 'contract' for rents of thousands of pounds, dollars or deutschmarks is likely to consist of a scrap of white paper, innocent of any legal stamps.

I once signed the lease of an apartment in the Piazza Santa Maria in Trastevere on gold-embossed notepaper from the Oriental Hotel in Hong Kong, from where the owner, a cultivated octogenarian count, had returned at the conclusion of a painting tour. He was a charming man and had once used these great whitewashed rooms as a studio after the Second World War. He sought only a reasonable sum from a tenant who would keep the place in good repair. With the fall of the dollar and the artificial strength of the lira during the late 1980s, such deals were rare. Now one is far more likely to find expatriates living in the drab streets around the railway station than in the charming alleys and vine-clad *vicoli* of Trastevere.

The best way to arrive is often the most inconvenient. How many travellers are granted the first vision of Istanbul or Venice from the sea? So it is with Trastevere. Abjuring the convenience of buses and taxis across the two downstream bridges that link the area to central Rome, one should proceed on foot to the area of the Campo dei Fiori and then wend through narrow streets lined with antique sellers and furniture makers down to the Tiber. At the junction of the Via Giulia and the gruesome cobbled highway known as the Lungotevere there stands the most perfect bridge in all of Rome, the Ponte Sisto.

The Ponte Sisto was built between 1473 and 1475 at the command of Sixtus IV, who was then busily adorning the quarters near the Vatican with works of taste and magnificence. The city of Rome has been restoring it to unfortunate effect for almost a decade, and it may still be shrouded in ugly scaffolding and netted wire. The bridge replaced the classical Pons Janiculensis, so named because it leads directly to the foot of the Janiculum hill.

The Emperor Caracalla is supposed to have ordered the Pons Janiculensis built to reach a set of gardens in Trastevere, perhaps on the very site of the leafy botanical gardens remaining there today. If one is to believe the Christian historian Eusebius (and it must be noted that many do not), the bridge became the site of frequent martyrdoms, with at least four dead saints being cast into the Tiber at this point by their executioners. The Prefect Symmachus, an upholder of the old pagan order, rebuilt the bridge in the twin reigns of Valentinian and Valens. The early Renaissance bridge erected by the architects of Sixtus has, however, endured more or less unaltered until the present day.

When Augustus Hare made his way down to the Tiber in the latter years of the nineteenth century, he already found the prospect ruined. 'The bridge has been completely modernised and spoilt to carry out a ludicrous scheme, which unfortunately originated with the patriot Garibaldi, since the change of government in 1870,' he complained.

He was also to wax indignant about the destruction of a fountain of Pope Paul v, 'wantonly destroyed by the Italian government'.

'The fountain may be rebuilt,' he fulminated, 'but can never have its original design or beauty.' It has been, and it does. The prospect from the middle of the Ponte Sisto, drinking in the very same fountain on the west bank and its three-arched sister, high up on the Janiculum, is of unique delight.

There have always been foreigners clustered in the district opposite the Tiber island, as far back as the first emperors. It was the place to which those from the far-flung possessions of the Empire tended to gravitate, people from North Africa, Greece, the Levant and the rich province of Egypt. Jews and Syrians lived there without apparent antagonism. After the sack of Jerusalem in AD 70, many Jews had made their way to Rome to scratch a living. Some, it appears from the poets, became fortune-tellers.

Trastevere seethed and surged with the detritus of Empire. Juvenal's vicious *Third Satire* evokes the Syrians, who swarmed throughout the upper reaches of society employing their talents as musicians and wizards. 'The sewerage of the Orontes has emptied itself into the Tiber,' he scoffed, with the peculiar venom of a down-at-heel satirist. Syrian girls were known in Rome as early as the second century before Christ, raven-haired beauties with deep-set, luscious eyes and a deportment that spoke volumes of pleasures to come. They were much in favour to play the harp and timbrel at banquets, and figured among the upper ranks of the prostitutes of Imperial Rome.

It was only natural that among all these exiles from the shores of Tyre and Sidon, among the luteplayers of Damascus and the uprooted soothsayers of Galilee, there should coalesce a dim and early grouping of Christians, to meet in fervent conclave in the warren of alleys that led off from the Tiber quays. The grain ships would sail in from Ostia and up the river, then unsilted and clear for navigation, to deposit their golden cargoes in the warehouses whose ruins may still be seen beyond the Porta Portese. The mariners and those who braved the long sea journey from the Levant debouched into the foreigners' ghetto, a world apart from the rarefied salons of the Palatine.

Juvenal has left a description of urban life that probably focused on the Suburra but might equally apply to Trastevere. The *Third Satire* was penned with all the fierce odium of a self-made man, the son of a Spanish freedman, who had raised himself in Roman society by dint of military prowess and accession to the traditional priesthood. He reserved his scorn for the inflow of immigrants, the corruption of public life, the depredations of tax farmers, smooth Greek corrupters of youth, speculators who specialised in fraud and bankruptcy; in short, all the corrosive effects of new riches upon the old values of Rome. It is a pity he was not alive and writing in the Rome of the 1980s.

The world of the *Third Satire*, with some allowances for modern progress and laws, would strike resonant chords with any regular reader of the *Cronaca di Roma*, the local news pages in the city newspapers. It is a nightmarish chaos fit for an ancient Fellini, full of gimcrack tenements, jammed by rapacious landlords with hundreds of poor families, propped up by wooden struts, prey to fire and prone to sudden collapse, infected by contagion and domestic filth. Repeated attempts to enforce the building legislation were ignored, presumably due to bribery and influence at court. Trajan tried to limit the height of apartment buildings to sixty feet and the authorities attempted to impose some order after the Great Fire under Nero in AD 64. The speculative building craze did not abate.

The noise was appalling. Horsedrawn traffic was banned by the Emperor Claudius from entering the city for ten hours after dawn. This meant that all night the cobbled streets rang to metalled cart-wheels and the din of horses' hooves, the raucous shouts of drivers and the crash of loads coming and going. Such was a perfect example of a whimsical Imperial edict. Claudius, of course, slept in profound ignorance up in his boudoir high on the Palatine, while the penurious bourgeoisie, like Juvenal himself, tossed and turned all night. Insomnia caused more deaths than any other ill, the poet complained. The lot of the modern pedestrian in Trastevere is not much better than that of his counterpart in the late Empire, what with waggons and horses ploughing through the crowds, and the entourages of the rich casting those in their path into the gutters.

Wrapping his toga about him to go off to dinner, Juvenal considered it wise to make a will – so many objects were hurled out of windows or fell off the roofs that an evening out could be a perilous occasion. Then came the journey home, lit by guttering torches, in fear of drunken bullies or bands of robbers, airily disregarded by the palanquined speculator whisked past, burping, by his platoon of bodyguards, no doubt in the company of a perfumed boy from the Aegean isles.

No doubt as another provincial jealous of his *arriviste* status, Juvenal reserved particular venom for the Greeks, insidiously working their way through the beds of the men and women of the aristocracy and thereby into positions of comfort and wealth. In they came, schoolmasters, rhetoricians, surveyors, artists, tightrope-walkers, magicians and quacks, ever ready to adapt their charms to the requirements of whatever patron might secure them advancement.

Around the Imperial court they clustered, freedmen, honours-brokers, the purveyors of state borrowings and the administrators of public works. The scandals of the modern Italian Republic, in the light of this poetry, seem nothing more than a banal recitation of long-held practice. Here, in the first century after Christ, are upright Italians complaining of bribes and favouritism, scathing in their contempt for the municipal engineer and the public architect. The big public contracts, for temples, draining swamps, building new harbours and dredging the rivers all fell into the hands of frauds, who took the Imperial coin and then declared themselves bankrupt, protected by their paid friends at court from the consequences of their crime. Thus, amid a ruling order consumed with greed, did the bitter poet take refuge in private verse, for no such scurrilous and truthful satires could enjoy a public reading.

Amid the humid ant-warren of the poorer city, people clung to their inheritance, those who drew their first breath on the Roman hills and were nourished upon Sabine olives. Juvenal leads us to believe that in the brash Imperial time they could afford only vinegary wine and beans, or a sheep's head and dish of leeks. They dreamed of rural Italy, where the oppressive pace of life in Rome was unknown, of villas in cool Praeneste or on the slopes of Tivoli, where Hadrian built his pleasure dome. Cuckolded by Greeks, their sons led into oriental depravities, their fixed incomes ravaged by inflation and their city ransacked by speculation and profit, the Romans of Juvenal's class had yet to endure another humiliation. They could not even afford the professional fees of a middle-market tart for an afternoon's diversion.

It was in the pagan city depicted in these despairing verses that the Christians of Trastevere joined those from the Levant who followed their own esoteric cults in seeking spiritual relief. The area was known to be a stronghold of the worship of Mithras, a rite popular among the army and among the lower classes from Asia Minor. Mystical religion was entrenched in the daily practice of life. Little wonder, then, that the pagan historian Dio Cassius records that, on a day supposed to be that of the birth of Christ in far-off Palestine, a fountain of oil gushed forth without warning from a spot now marked by the Piazza Santa Maria in Trastevere. A Christian sanctuary was thus established within a few yards of the square in ancient times, and into the late Roman era the place was known as Fons Olei. Christian apologists suggest that the Emperor Alexander Severus gave his permission for a commemorative shrine, so impressed was he with the legend and the phenomenon.

By the third century, this site in Trastevere had assumed such importance that Pope Calixtus I commissioned a proper church to stand on the spot, and work was accordingly begun in the year 224. Calixtus himself did not live to witness it rising on the foundations of the old Mithraic temple, for he suffered scourging and martyrdom by defenestration nearby, in a little piazza that today bears his name and is boundaried by a grand palace belonging to the Vatican. The football-mad youth of Trastevere gather of an evening in the Bar Callisto, but it is doubtful if any know the origins of its title.

The church was modified down the centuries. It acquired a classic early medieval belltower. Shimmering mosaics were ordered to bring light into the darkened hollow of the apse. They are strange and hieratic divine figures, worthy to be matched with the great Sicilian masterworks at Cefalu and Monreale. A blithe façade was added during the Renaissance, providing a frame for the fading frescos that extend across the front of the old building. In the early morning, the first rays of light strike the façade of the church as if it were a sundial, creeping across each dilapidated fresco as if unveiling a work for the first time. Santa Maria in Trastevere is one of those churches in Rome that summons up the cool breath of deep antiquity from the moment you enter its portals. Within Carlo Fontana's eighteenth-century portico stand old gravestones and Christian carvings from the early centuries, with the dove, the olive branch and flowing river of grace recurring time and again among the roughly carved Greek letters proclaiming the undiscovered truth.

Once inside – there is seldom anyone there, for the Trasteverini are not a people prone to excessive observance – one might as well have entered the silence of the tomb. Only rarely do the cries and shrieks of the neighbourhood outside penetrate the gloomy interior of the basilica. There is little natural light. The nave is separated from the two aisles by twenty-two columns of granite and marble. A closer inspection shows that they are almost all of differing heights and have only a vaguely common breadth. Here is the proof of triumphal Christian plunder once again. It is all too easy to envisage the mighty columns dragged by horses and men from the fallen temples of pagan Rome, to be conveyed in victorious procession to the rising sanctuaries of the new religion. Some of the columns still bear the sculpted representations of classical deities. The effect, whether one follows the Christian religion or not, is haunting.

On Christmas Eve and Easter Saturday the church is plunged into darkness. Then, to a slow chanting of liturgy, one candle is lit, then another and another, until the lights are brought up and the world of the twelfth-century mosaic artists flares into life.

Stepping outside once again, the ochre and orange palaces arranged across the far side of the square appear in perfect proportions. A Bernini fountain, set upon a high plinth, occupies centre stage in the piazza, a useful prop for local motorbikes and a summer rendezvous for lovers and travellers, congregating at dusk to watch the effect of the backlit spray of the fountain and the glowing mosaics on the ancient façade of the church.

So much for the sacred. The profane is to be found every day in the square, in the shape of a fat man in his thirties with a little goatee beard. When he is not stoned, the fat man holds court with his little circle of hangers-on and fellow criminals. Deals are struck in one of the two cafés just off the piazza. Nobody messes with the fat man. When he reels into the local grocery store, see-sawing between displays of salami and crates of wine and laughing like a great bear, the folk behind the counter laugh with him, but there is loathing in their eyes.

The fat man at least has the virtue of living in the area he is destroying. The same cannot be said of the night-time denizens of Trastevere. *Figli di macellaio*, the old upper classes call them – butcher's children. They are the bored twenty-one-year-olds who live out in the boring satellite suburbs and descend on the medieval village after dark behind the wheel of daddy's car. As principal male accessory, the car is paraded through the narrow streets, its meagre engine roaring, stereo pounding and tyres screeching, usually with three other young males aboard to accompany the driver. Then it is double or treble parked, preferably blocking somebody else's exit, while the boys go off to strut their stuff. The car stereo – the second most important accessory – is detached to deter the numerous thieves and placed conspicuously upon the table in whatever establishment the boys choose to patronise. The more chrome and knobs the better. Sometimes the boys drink more than one beer and get frisky, but not too often. It is still considered a *brutta figura*, a loss of face, to get drunk. If the boys are out with the girls, the girls will be stunningly made-up and dressed, or semi-dressed, to kill. Trastevere is not really a place for quiet and intimate dinners, so the fun is forever *in gruppo*.

When they were seventeen, these same characters hung around the fast-food bars on the Viale Trastevere, a roaring four-lane artery that pulsates with traffic until three in the morning. The cult of the hamburger and its attendant bread roll, the panino, gave rise to the cult of the paninari in the 1980s. A whole style, vocabulary and dress accompanied this teenage fad, which even extended to comic books and television programmes. It was immensely innocent and hideously gauche.

Now that times are better and the gang have a little more cash, they can head for Ivo's pizzeria, one of the world's noisiest restaurants, where the waiters rush around as if they have had cocaine instead of mozzarella on their pizzas, while the girls look moody and glam. Teenage conferences are in permanent session in the ladies' loo. The main rooms resound with screams and laughter.

For the butcher's children with money to match their tastes, there is La Parolaccia, a restaurant where the cuisine is so mediocre that the management long ago thought up the ultimate gimmick: if you are insulting the diners with your food, why not insult them face to face?

'What does that lanky faggot with you want, signora?'

'No sir, you can come in, but the ladies ... well, we don't want whores in here tonight, please!'

'Is that slag in your party?' ... and so on.

Away from the *nouveaux riches* and the tourist traps around Santa Maria in Trastevere, fine restaurants of deep pride and tradition lurk down sidestreets and off little piazzas, Roman, Tuscan or Umbrian.

It is said that there were never any prostitutes in Trastevere because the local matriarchy proved so strong in resisting their influx. Indeed, there still appear to be very few, but in every other way the area sells itself as a fun palace to the city. Bars, clubs, 'cultural circles' and over-expensive eating houses have sprung up all over. The newcomers often seem to have limitless funds to invest in apparently loss-making enterprises.

Apartments are emptied of their tenants, renovated and sold off to politicians, bankers and bureaucrats. The small artisans, shoemakers, furniture craftsmen, metal-workers, jewellers and shopkeepers are all under pressure. Around Trastevere's market on the Piazza San Cosimato, the old streets are permanently choked with delivery trucks and builders' lorries.

And the square of Santa Maria with its haunting church is supposed to be free of the motor car, yet the local police invariably fail to prevent it becoming a squalid parking lot. The restaurant owners in the piazza complain that their well-heeled clients could not possibly walk to the front door. Remember that poor Japanese woman and those thieves!

Everyone has his or her own reason for being the exception to the rules that might preserve Trastevere from becoming a slum. Of course, nobody at City Hall is responsible for anything.

Should Stendhal ever return, in one of those dark Syrian cults of rebirth, I should advise him to be born a Finn and enter that country's diplomatic service. Thus he might be appointed ambassador to the Holy See by his fiftieth birthday and move into the official residence that goes with the job. It is a pink colonnaded villa on the brow of the Janiculum hill, from which he might permanently enjoy the same perspective of Trastevere as he did on that day in 1833, for only distance now lends enchantment to the view.

Contessa Donatella Pecci Blunt

The Contessa Donatella Pecci Blunt does not possess the oldest title in Rome, or the most austere *palazzo*, or a lineage traced back to *condottieri* of the Renaissance. She was, however, the pre-eminent Roman hostess during most of the decadent period of the late 1980s which preceded the collapse of the First Italian Republic. Therefore, as a reflection of its splendours and miseries, she is a personality without parallel.

Let us start with the *palazzo* itself. Modest enough on the exterior, a little inconvenienced by its next-door neighbour, the Syrian embassy, it none the less has the three principal merits required by estate agents in Rome as elsewhere on earth: location, location and location.

It stands at the foot of the Capitol in the Piazza Aracoeli. The *cordonata* of Michelangelo, a broad ascending avenue of steps, thrusts virtually from its doorstep to the Piazza Campidoglio, in which the bronze equestrian statue of Marcus Aurelius stood for centuries until modern pollution forced its removal. The Rome City Council, that model of civic virtue, meets in the *palazzo* nearby, when its proceedings do not descend into fisticuffs and interventions by the uniformed ushers.

The Palazzo Pecci Blunt is a short distance from parliament and from the headquarters of all the main political parties. It is a little further from the Vatican, but that did not deter clerical visitors, since Count Ferdinand (Dino) Pecci Blunt owed his very title to a family connection with Pope Leo XIII. His wife, the Contessa Donatella, is a lady of overflowing blonde charm and multilingual volubility. In the tradition of Italian aristocrats (recent or otherwise) she adopts political theories that sound, to blue-blooded northern Europeans, a trifle unconventional.

'Look, the French had a revolution,' she explains. 'Other countries had their revolutions. In Italy we never had a revolution until today. But now we have one. One led by the magistrates. And this is a revolution. It is, believe me. And I personally am for this revolution.'

It was a heady time, of party grandees toppling like so many pagan idols from their pedestals, of mass arrests, of tearful confessions and sudden recantations of lifetime behaviour. Most of those who provided the veneer of Italian business, government and society suddenly trembled. At a certain point the public understood that this was no mere settling of accounts within the establishment, for those under suspicion began killing themselves. Gabriele Cagliari, a man who headed the greatest chemical firm in the country, put a plastic bag over his own head, tied it tight and expired on the floor of the prison lavatory. Raul Gardini, a tycoon whose sharp practices caught up with him, read of his own impending arrest in the morning newspapers and retired back to his sumptuous bedchamber. There he placed a pistol to his temple and shot himself through the head, his servants rushing in to find a fountain of their master's blood drenching the linen sheets. Gardini was much mourned in his native Ravenna, but a crowd hurled insults at Cagliari's coffin while his widow stumbled from the funeral service.

At the offices of the Christian Democrats in Rome, the fax machine spat forth a simple message one morning in the week of these suicides. It read: 'Why don't you all kill yourselves?'

In the fascination of the purge, people awaited the next defenestration with sick interest, like a crowd in the Colosseum or the Roman mob surging up the Cordonata after poor, mad Cola Di Rienzo, whose statue remains in the garden nearby.

Such plebeian gestures did not appeal to the Contessa. She had, instead, adopted the most dramatic step that a woman in her station is capable of. The Pecci Blunt political salon, a place where, according to another contessa, 'all the Italian government could be found', is no more. The endless soirées at which ministers pontificated and prelates gossiped had come to an end. The Contessa still entertained, of course, but in these troubled times she preferred the company of artists and men of culture. 'I stopped giving parties for the politicians more than a year ago,' she said with a weary sigh. 'I had had enough, and the climate had changed.'

We were seated in a restful sitting room, furnished with the taste and objects, acquired over generations. French landscape paintings adorned the walls. A black and white photograph of the late President Kennedy and his wife, signed with warm best wishes from them both, reposed among silver-framed family groups and pictures of distinguished gentlemen in full evening dress, wearing their decorations. Coffee was served by a linen-jacketed servant. In the cool high-ceilinged chambers of the *palazzo*, the clamour of the Roman traffic receded to a distant murmur.

Men of every political persuasion, of devout religious faith and of none, all swanned through the Contessa's marbled ballrooms, took cocktails under the curving, frescoed ceiling of her loggia and dined in regal style, looking out, during hot summer evenings, upon fountains and a Renaissance garden set within a quiet courtyard.

'Sometimes we held parties for two hundred people', the Contessa recalled with wistful pride. 'We usually had a selection of people from every party in the house, Communists, Christian Democrats, almost all the others ...'.

She arose and swept through a panelled hallway. We passed through one gilded salon after another. Richly hung with tapestries, old Dutch masters and heavy drapes, they were furnished in a style that would not have looked out of place two hundred years ago. She entered the ballroom and turned with a flourish. In the mind's eye one could envisage it swirling, full of black-tied princes and glamorous consorts. Another room was set for what looked like some fairly serious card playing. Classical room succeeded luxurious chamber. Across one golden ceiling, the artist had cunningly painted a tangle of vine leaves running from beam to wooden beam, as if nature had intruded into the *palazzo* itself. 'Ah,' sighed the Contessa as I appreciated the touch, 'you could never get work like that nowadays.'

There was a splendid dining room fit for Metternich and Cavour, then a smaller, intimate salon. 'Hundreds of people are all very well but sometimes it's more interesting just to have eight for dinner, don't you think?' enquired the Contessa. It depended who they were, I replied. The Contessa threw back her blonde tresses and smiled indulgently. We proceeded to an alarmingly baroque private chapel. No confessional, I noticed, was provided.

That was a shame, for many of those who figured on the fabled guest lists were in disgrace. A collective act of self-abasement was in progress among the survivors. Some were fighting indictments for corruption. Others, already under formal investigation, had withdrawn from society as a wave of bourgeois revulsion, amply reflected in more select households such as this one, arose to consume the political class that had governed Italy since the Second World War. Only a few souls had thus far preserved their reputations and they were adopting a low profile. The ruling élite in southern Europe has always possessed a sixth sense informing it of when the time has come to disappear from view, check on its foreign bank deposits, and open up its property in Geneva or Chelsea.

But in the latest Italian revolution, events had moved without respite from the enlightenment almost to the terror. Suicides mounted by the week. The gaols were filling up with prosperous inmates. Other suspects disappeared to Latin America or the Caribbean. The former Socialist Prime Minister, Bettino Craxi, had even withdrawn to France with a much diminished retinue. He said that Italy was unsafe, a view enhanced by the mob who besieged his vine-clad Roman residence, the Hotel Raphael, to shout 'shame!' and 'thief!'.

'I did not like Craxi,' observed the Contessa, 'and he did not much like me. He did not come into this house.' It was murmured in society that the Contessa did not much like Mr Craxi's domestic arrangements when he was in Rome. He was not often seen in the company of his wife while staying in the capital. She, perhaps wisely, remained in their native Milan to preen herself at La Scala and to receive the acclaim of the Craxi acolytes.

Mr Craxi had served as Prime Minister for several years, a period marked by bombast and lavish claims on behalf of a mythical 'New Italy' overseen by himself. To some foreigners, especially to people unfamiliar with Italy, Mr Craxi presented a pleasing similarity to a Social Democrat from northern Europe. The effect was created by cunning on his part and gullibility on theirs. He professed to admire Garibaldi. But little of that hero's reputation for frugality or rectitude clung to his personage. He announced reforms and governed in a style he christened *decisionismo*. But this method consisted of little more than bullying, and when Mr Craxi parted company with government, the public finances remained in a disastrous state.

Eventually, pursued by a posse of magistrates investigating allegations of bribery and corruption, Mr Craxi also stepped down from the Socialist leadership, muttering about plots and a threat to the fine tradition of Italian democracy. He denounced all the charges as malicious lies, but his party evaporated as quickly as his reputation. And he was not invited to the Palazzo Pecci Blunt.

The Contessa had her political sympathies of course. She favoured the Republican Party. This body never captured more than a small percentage of the vote, but the system then pertaining guaranteed it a minor if prestigious role. It was Centrist, pro-business and pro-American. Members of the Agnelli dynasty lent it their support. Republicans liked to see themselves as the 'intelligent' party. They talked endless sense about reforming the state, putting right the public finances and banishing inefficiency, safe in the knowledge that the party's tiny influence meant that it would never, thankfully, be called upon to do so. It was the perfect party for rich intellectuals. Alas, however, even the simon-pure Republicans proved susceptible to scandal, and their future, too, fell into doubt. No wonder that the Contessa sighed repeatedly.

For many a long season, the paparazzi laid siege to the Palazzo Pecci Blunt, while government succeeded government and crisis followed crisis without noticeable effect. Roman political life was stuck in a fur-lined rut, while the national debt piled up and the standards of public services declined.

Although she existed within a cocoon of comfort and attention, the Contessa was a sharp observer of her guests. She gave the lie to that old canard about the aristocracy being out of touch. Much of what she said could have come from the lips of any middle-class Roman, fed up with fighting the traffic, the filth, the chaos and the arrogant bureaucratic servants of what everyone called 'the regime'.

'People had become tired of it all,' said the Contessa. 'Nothing ever changed. So much talk, then nothing. People were bored, bored, bored!'

The Contessa affected not to miss her old life amid the hurly-burly of cabinet ministers and their hangers-on. Frankly, she explained, she preferred Monte Carlo to Rome these days. The shopping was better in Milan and the service was nicer in New York. The boutiques that cluster invitingly around the skirts of the Piazza di Spagna had become common, the assistants were indifferent and the customers ... well, what could one expect? One came back to Rome only because one enjoyed location, location and location. Or because as one in love with Rome itself, she could neither leave it for good nor abandon hope of its improvement.

The Contessa went to a window that gave out upon pine trees and the ugly white block of the Victor Emmanuel monument. Outside the afternoon traffic began to seethe and bubble across the Piazza Venezia and beneath the famous balcony from which the Duce proclaimed his fantasies of empire.

'For twenty years the Italian people were asleep, just like they were asleep for twenty years when Mussolini was in power from 1922,' declared Contessa Pecci Blunt. 'Now they are awake.'

CHAPTER 8

Moro, the Red Brigades and the sack of Rome

Set into the stone wall at the south-east extremity of the Ponte Garibaldi there is a small commemorative tablet. It looks like one of the innumerable mementoes of those deceased in the service of the state to be found all over Italian cities. This one, however, is inscribed with simple ferocity.

It is dedicated to Giorgiana Masi, who was nineteen when she died. 'Killed by the violence of the regime, 12th May 1977,' it says. A poem written by a comrade provides an elegy for her lost friend: If all the tears in the world were flowers, a carpet of blossom could be laid for her to paradise.

The Ponte Garibaldi is one of Rome's busiest bridges, groaning each day under the weight of thousands of bustling Fiats and lurid orange buses. It spans the Tiber from the Via Arenula, the boundary of the Jewish quarter, to the fringes of Trastevere. Today few passers-by even cast an eye towards the epitaph. Commuters speed by in a rush of high-octane temper. The Sengalese and Poles who contend for the privilege of washing windscreens at the traffic lights lounge against the bridge wall.

Once, a few years ago, a friend, or a lover, or an old comrade had placed a spray of flowers, twisted about with kitchen foil, below the plaque, but they withered and browned in the fumes of a myriad exhaust pipes and then they were gone. Such is the ease with which great causes and small tragedies dissipate in Rome.

On that day in 1977 the bridge was the scene of a theatrical, violent contest between student revolutionaries, riot squads and the mysterious plainclothes figures who popped up at such moments wielding automatic pistols. The Ponte Garibaldi became the front line between the protesters and the forces of order guarding the approaches to the Ministry of Justice and the offices of the main political parties. A pitched street battle ensued.

A famous photograph exists from that time, showing masked men in jeans and casual shirts, in that semi-crouching position adopted by professionals about to open fire. It became an icon of left-wing protest, reprinted months and years later in an effort to prove that the disaster of the Left in Italy resulted from conspiracy and political sabotage. It was a question of little relevance to Giorgiana Masi, who fell that day, fatally wounded by gunfire at the edge of the bridge.

Was her death the work of the police, state *provocateurs* or urban guerrillas? It was a decade of plots and paranoia. Throughout the early 1970s, the Left grew in impatience and energy while the comfortable patrons of the political establishment sought in vain to preserve their own agreeable authority.

The political class had grown fat in the easy years of the late 1960s, when Italy underwent a second industrial 'miracle' to match the extraordinary growth it had witnessed between 1958 and 1963. There was money for everybody. A new wave of migration brought more people off the land and into the factories, and thence into the suburbs. In 1964 and 1965 the economy faltered, but it picked up again in 1966. An array of hitherto scarce products flowed from factories to the consumers. In 1965 fewer than half the families in Italy owned a television, about half possessed a fridge and only one family in five had a washing machine. Ten years later these appliances were to be found in almost every household.

Small and medium-sized companies flourished, providing the spine of Italy's manufacturing industries: textiles, electronics, leather, ceramics, and engineering parts. At the apex of the economy, a few mighty cartels, a tiny élite of businessmen and bankers reinforced their grip over trade. The political class, well funded, indulged its traditional predilection for patronage, inertia and the fluent, if futile, debate of arcane draft legislation.

The boom years generated sad consequences for the city of Rome. For those old enough just to remember the gentle stillness of the old papal city – almost unchanged since Shelley's time – the post-war construction mania sealed the capital's fate. Even in Mussolini's Rome, when grandiose buildings and thoroughfares were the order of the day, the place was still, by modern standards, a languid city. But in the 1950s a great rush of money and building transformed the periphery of the old papal domain into a hideous unregulated suburban sprawl. Gimcrack apartments sprouted up with neither shops nor services to support their inhabitants. Naturally, no serious plan for public transport was ever forthcoming. So the population acquired cars by the million and had no choice but to use their vehicles to descend upon the ancient city centre. That spelt the end for ever of the vestiges of old Rome that had survived since the Renaissance.

Amidst the rush to economic advancement, discontent and rage grew, often spurred by the dismal conditions of the suburbs. Italian students and trade unions caught on late to the great events of 1968. They made up for it with a 'hot autumn' of strikes and agitation one year later. By the early 1970s, the university of Rome, a great sprawling complex of undistinguished buildings, was brimming with bright-eyed admirers of the Chinese cultural revolution, orthodox Leninists, and the charming, irreverent adherents of 'Lotta Continua', a group whose title proposed 'Continuous Struggle'. These factions made up the largest New Left in western Europe. At the same time, young factory workers grew restive. Traditional trade union bosses found their authority challenged. To the dismay of the United States, the Communist Party advanced in every electoral contest. The head of Confindustria, the employers' federation, accused the unions of 'subverting the country's democratic institutions'. Giovanni Agnelli, the boss of Fiat, was moved to compare his declining profits to a cancer that might become fatal.

None of this prepared the Italian system for the shocks to come. In February 1973, the government decided to allow the lira to float, a hapless response to the flight of investment capital abroad. Not surprisingly, it plummeted. While the currency depreciated, the price of imported raw materials – of which Italy was naturally all but bereft – increased. Then, in October 1973, Egypt and Syria attacked Israel. The United States and the Soviet Union intervened to support their respective clients. King

Faisal of Saudi Arabia took the lead in imposing an oil embargo on the western powers. The Organisation of Petroleum Exporting Countries, known throughout the world thereafter merely as OPEC, proceeded to raise the price of crude oil at first by 70 per cent and then by whatever increments it thought the reeling markets might bear. It was the end of a golden age for Italy. In the 1960s, the supply of contentment had readily been purchased with little pain to the worker and almost no inconvenience to the ruling class. It was a miracle that would not be repeated.

Italy sucked in oil imports with the appetite of ancient Rome for African grain. Her biggest supplier was Libya, where the government had recently been abolished under the utopian rule of a young army colonel, Muammar Gaddafi. In vain did the Italians dispatch supplicatory missions to their former colonial domain. Colonel Gaddafi dreamed of the minarets in Jerusalem by day and practised his rhetorical imitations of the late Gamal Abdel Nasser at dusk before compulsory rallies held in the Italianate piazzas of Tripoli. No deals could be struck with such a figure, as impervious to diplomacy as he was proof against individual corruption.

From the reforms of Augustus to the inflation unleashed by Diocletian and the public works of Mussolini, Rome had echoed very quickly the effects of great change in the fortunes of the world. In 1974 the largest private bank in Germany, the Herstatt, collapsed. It is generally agreed that this marked the point at which the recession generated by high oil prices turned into a slump. In Rome, the government remained chronically weak, inflation proceeded to devalue the savings of the middle class, and investors chose to transfer their money into the currencies of Switzerland or Japan. Labour unrest increased once again.

The Communists, led by a Sardinian aristocrat, lingered upon the precipice of government, alternately lured by the prize and repelled by its responsibility. To young revolutionaries, the paralysis of the regime symbolised its decay. The vacillation of the Communist Party showed that it, too, was bankrupt. A small core turned to violence, shooting policemen, magistrates and 'slaves of the multinationals'. The Red Brigades and their splinter groups were born, and upon their ascendancy came the greatest plot to occupy Italian table-talk in modern times.

Through all this there moved like a spider the figure of Aldo Moro. The Italian newspapers called him '*il grande tessitore*'. It meant that he was the great weaver, the most dextrous spinner of strands into fabric. A man who had made his way to Rome from Puglia, the ancient Magna Graecia, Moro inhabited the rarefied world of the senior Italian politician, a place so remote from everyday reality that it might easily be confused with the inner courts of late Byzantium. He spoke in oblique, circumlocutory Italian. His philosophy – a profound, if superstitious, Catholicism aside – consisted of a devotion to compromise and a severe aversion to extremes. His speeches were of an intricate boredom such as to test the most patient observer of Italian parliamentary debate.

Moro approached politics with the relish reserved by a chess grandmaster for a particularly obscure manoeuvre. He once compared the stewardship of democracy to the skill of a cook preparing a slowly simmered dish of the thick white beans relished down in Puglia. On another occasion he described the respective policies of the Christian Democrats and the Communists as 'converging parallels'. This nonsense went unchallenged by his interviewer and passed into the Italian political lexicon, where it was marvelled at as an expression of infinite subtlety.

He brought to Roman politics the instincts of a shrewd provincial lawyer. Born in 1916, Moro grew up in the era of Catholic Action, when the Vatican turned from its ingrained reserve to the encouragement of popular political involvement by the devout. It believed that Catholic laymen, well organised, might guard against the Church's enemies: Communism, atheism and Freemasonry.

Moro fitted the description well. He presided over the Federation of Catholic Students at the university in Bari and smoothly entered the ranks of Christian Democracy after the collapse of Fascism. He ascended to the rank of Justice Minister in 1955, occupied the all-important post of Party Secretary in 1959 and became Prime Minister for the first time in 1963.

Yet in 1978 there was every reason to suppose that this paragon of post-war virtues, now president of his party, no longer suited the designs of those who made strategy in Washington or wielded the secret levers of power in Italy.

His hair was a statesman's silver. His eyes expressed wisdom and cynical humour. His cheeks were chubby, high-boned, running to jowls – those, in fact, of a well-fed bourgeois who consumed his pasta twice daily. His personal life appears to have been irreproachable to the point of satire; indeed, it was frequently laughed at. His piety was such that it attracted the admiration of Pope Paul VI. By contrast, in political matters he was corrupt and mediocre in equal measure. He preferred financial inducement to persuasion, and for many years he opted for stagnation whenever change offered itself. He could imagine no object higher than the continuity of himself and his friends in office.

None of this was exceptional; rather, it was the norm expected of Italian ministers. But Moro's desire to preserve the system he knew led him to an exceptional conclusion.

By the spring of 1978 Moro had served – if that is the word – as Prime Minister five times. There was no intricacy of parliamentary or cabinet procedure which escaped him. Although, like most Italian politicians, he remained parochial in outlook, he was also capable of realising when the times were out of joint. In short, he had decided that, for the first time since May 1947, the Communists had to be brought into the government. The moment had come for a 'historic compromise'.

The formula was not Moro's. It was first elaborated in a renowned collection of articles written by the Communist leader, Enrico Berlinguer, published by the party's theoretical journal, *Rinascita*, in October 1973. Across the Latin cultures, from Spain to South America, authority was clashing with reform. Berlinguer, like many thoughtful Italian leftists, was frightened by the military coup against the Socialist government in Chile. He was also aware that the attitude of the United States precluded a democratic Communist takeover in Italy. Where Communist enthusiasts saw power, their leader imagined tanks around the Piazza Venezia and glum files of activists lined up under guard in the football stadium. These were the ebbing years of America's losing fight in Vietnam. The values of the cold war, despite a period of *détente*, informed every aspect of international affairs. Berlinguer told the party faithful that a national alliance offered the only prospect of reform in Italy.

He sought a partnership between the Communists, the Christian Democrats and the Socialists. He had grander visions, too. He wanted Catholic and Communist virtues to coincide – Moro's 'converging parallels' – so that Italy might be governed on a moral and ethical basis that suited the traditional religion of its people and met the social needs of a growing industrial class. The world of Don Camillo, where village priest and Communist agitator existed as foes, would give way to a civilised, very Italian, understanding.

Moro and Berlinguer, both somewhat ascetic, both family men, both astute manipulators of their own parties, frequently discussed the project. They understood each other's heritage and mentality. It took five years, the slump and the growth of leftist terrorism, but the Christian Democrat eventually arrived at his conclusion.

On the morning of 16 March 1978, Moro kissed his wife Eleonora goodbye, descended to the front door of his apartment building and got into his chauffeured car. Five bodyguards awaited him. As the satirists noted with glee, Moro lived in a modern suburban development, devoid of architectural originality. Few people knew their neighbours. It was quite unlike the alleys and piazzas of the *centro storico*. Strangers came and went. Odd faces were not remarked upon.

In the chamber of parliament at Montecitorio, the deputies were congregating in a buzz of expectation. Giulio Andreotti, the new Christian Democrat Prime Minister, was due to present his government for a vote of confidence. For the first time, it would have the support of the Communists, who would enter a carefully crafted scenario. They were to lend external assistance to the coalition. Then they would begin to share power. Eventually, Communist ministers were to sit in the cabinet. Moro, the great weaver of this fabric, would contemplate his handiwork from outside the government, reflecting the Italian tradition that the president of the Christian Democrats is often a more powerful figure than the individual who sits in the office of the Premier.

The president's dark sedan car made it as far as the crossroads just down the street from his apartment where Via Mario Fani meets Via Stresa. Suddenly a small white Fiat reversed around the corner into its path. Moro's driver stamped on the brake pedal. A second car, containing three of his bodyguards, could not stop and smashed into the back of the vehicle.

Stunned, the bodyguards did not react in time to save their master. Four men dressed as Alitalia pilots, hanging around as if waiting for a crew pick-up bus, dropped their bags, pulled out guns and began shooting. Two other men leapt out of the Fiat. They began shooting too. A witness was later to describe how the principal gunman, who used a sub-machine gun, directed his fire with cool, professional precision.

When people are killed by gunfire in cars, the results are grotesque. Moro's men jerked and convulsed in awful pain. Their legs flew up and shattered the windscreens. Their arms twisted around their heads, as a child protects itself. The seats and carpets became soaked a hectic red. One man crawled from the second car and managed to fire two shots at the attackers. A spray of bullets threw him over on his back and he died in an attitude of crucifixion. When the noise of shots, car engines and squealing tyres gave way to a hush, the fearful inhabitants of Via Fani peered over the boxes of flowers on their balconies at a scene of desolation. Moro, brilliantly left untouched amid the rapid fire of his assailants, was gone.

For fifty-five days, Italians followed the agonies of his kidnapping with the awe of an audience at a tragic opera. There were photographs, communiqués, statements telephone messages, fruitless police searches and conspiracy theories. All the usual suspects were rounded up. The Red Brigades announced his trial before 'a people's court'. Then, in their sixth communiqué, they decreed a sentence of death.

Throughout the melodrama, there ran unmistakable elements of sinister farce. The Christian Democrats turned to the Sicilian Mafia and the Roman underworld for help. None was forthcoming. A series of false clues led the police to a frozen lake. The ice was solemnly broken and the lake was dredged, without result. Moro's family and friends even managed to make indirect contact with the kidnappers. Negotiations, of a kind, ensued. The Socialists, too, found a way to communicate with the Red Brigades, but it was to no avail. No fewer than five government security services were involved in the hunt, all at war with one another, each answering to a different power centre in the Italian labyrinth, none powerful enough to take the overall charge necessary for such a task. The chaos was such that many years later Moro's friends were to look back and wonder if it had not all been deliberate.

Moro was permitted to write to his family and political colleagues. He did so eloquently and, as one might expect, at length. As the moment of his own extinction neared, he grew bitter and gave vent to recriminations against his own party.

The Red Brigades demanded an exchange of prisoners by which Moro would be set free at the sake time as thirteen leftists held in prison. The Communists and the hardline Christian Democrats found themselves unexpectedly united in rejecting the notion. The Communists feared any sign that they might be suspect in their stand against terrorism. Cynics supposed that Moro's rivals in the Christian Democrat Party simply did not want to see him come back. Moro's allies and the Socialist Party argued in vain for a compromise, assuring all-comers that an exchange would be proof of the state's humanity, not confirmation of its weakness. Moro's letters – twenty or more were released by the kidnappers – grew persuasive, cajoling and impatient by turn. He also submitted to prolonged questioning by the captors and wrote a lengthy account of his political activity.

On 9 May the most prominent Christian Democrat in the Italian Senate, a dwarf-like rogue named Amintore Fanfani, intended to raise the possibility of a one-sided act of goodwill at a formal meeting of the party leadership. This formula, of which the president might have been proud, would have allowed the government to release some of the prisoners while proclaiming that it had not given in but merely exercised clemency. In the Vatican, Pope Paul was on his knees night and day, imploring divine intercession to save his friend.

It was all too late. Some time in the early hours of 9 May, an executioner proficient in the use of a pistol came to Moro in his darkened cell and extinguished all the genius, the scheming and the secret memory in that fertile brain. The captors stuffed his wounds with paper handkerchiefs to staunch the blood, wrapped his corpse in a blanket and placed it in the boot of a Renault 4. As a conclusive demonstration of the state's impotence, a final act of political theatre, the car was boldly driven right into the centre of Rome and parked in the Via Caetani, a street roughly equidistant from the headquarters of the Christian Democrats and the Communists.

The forensic experts found eleven bullet holes in the body, but thought that nine of them might have been inflicted after death. Just in case the public might remain in any doubt, somebody passed the black and white photographs of the post mortem to a weekly magazine, and there, for the whole nation to see, was this most fastidious of politicians sprawled naked on the slab, displaying his stigmata, front and back.

Eleanora Moro took her husband home and gave him a quiet family burial, rebuffing every effort by the party and the state to intrude with ceremonial upon her grief. As her years of widowhood slipped by, Mrs Moro would sometimes venture out of seclusion to defend her husband's memory and to attack in her lonely bitterness all those who had, in her view, contributed to her bereavement.

Who killed Moro? Arrests, investigations and trials produced an official verdict. A group of ten Red Brigades activists were convicted of the attack in Via Mario Fani. It was said that one Prospero Gallinari had actually executed Moro, although he was never charged with that crime. Gallinari was caught in 1979 and wounded in the head during his arrest. He now receives guests in prison and chats away about the ideological errors of the past. But he has never spoken of Moro's end, whether to confirm or deny his part in it.

There are, however, a few indisputable facts to be obtained by applying the antique judicial quest: *cui bono?*

The Italian Communists were the largest party of their kind in the western world in the 1970s, and had they entered office, even in coalition, the effects might have reinforced the Left in Europe and lent psychological strength to what was then the Soviet bloc. Yet Berlinguer was no authoritarian, nor did his party stand for conventional Communist forms of government. Berlinguer insisted that Italy would remain in NATO. The great social battles over divorce and abortion had already been decided by the people in a referendum. Consumer economics and institutionalised corruption – under the Christian Democrats – completed the decline of traditional Italian values, which successive popes had wrongly attributed to the works of Marx.

The Historic Compromise could have been a brave experiment in managing a western society. Detached from its international repercussions, the Italian model offered a path to growth far removed from the nostrums that were to emerge victorious in the decade after Moro's death. Those simple solutions, which brooked no alternative, would have co-existed most uneasily with a successful example of government by social compromise in a major western nation. Indeed, the cold war might have ended through evolution rather than the collapse of the Communist states into chaos, war and penury.

A gradual convergence of East and West would have suited the Italian conception of affairs. Moro himself might have helped to engineer it. But such thoughts were not permissible at the time.

Henry Kissinger, Richard Nixon's Secretary of State, came to the 'Italian problem' fresh from Cambodia and Chile. He was but the most vocal among a chorus of American voices warning Moro and the establishment against any accommodation with the Communists. The Kissinger philosophy on Italy persisted in Washington even after the Democratic victory that ushered in the presidency of Jimmy Carter. Italian leftists suspect that intervention in their country's affairs by the CIA and its paid associates inside the Italian establishment ensured Moro's doom and the failure of the Historic Compromise.

The dream of a national alliance died the day of Moro's kidnapping. Giulio Andreotti governed alone at the head of a Christian Democrat minority cabinet which was sustained for a while by Communist support but eventually gave way to the tired formula of Centre–Right coalitions employing the same venerable faces. Enrico Berlinguer saw his chance to occupy a critical place in Italian history recede, until, by the time of his own death, he realised that the great plans of the 1970s, the silken web spun by the great weaver, amounted to no more than a footnote. Berlinguer lived to witness the rise of Solidarity in Poland, the surge of the capitalist Right in the West and the decline of Soviet power. Giovanni Agnelli, who had complained of cancerous effects on his profits, defeated a major strike at Fiat in 1980. The Italian economy boomed once more, stoked by spendthrift deficit spending and riding on the back of market forces unleashed in London, Washington, Bonn and Tokyo.

One day in 1984, Berlinguer was felled by a huge cerebral haemorrhage. He died without recovering consciousness. Perhaps because he was only in middle age, he had prepared no testament. More than a million people crowded the streets and piazzas of Rome for his funeral. A forest of red banners saluted his passing, tears were shed in abundance and, from the microphones, the Central Committee declaimed their old slogans by way of eulogy. It was a requiem for Italian Communism, not mere salutation of a lost leader. The party never revived. When the Soviet Union collapsed, it finally changed its name and adopted a pink flower to replace the hammer-and-sickle, but its fortunes did not improve and its votes ebbed away. Eventually it underwent an inevitable schism, dividing into a moderate Social Democratic faction and a group of diehards. The moderates became the dominant party in central Italy but theirs was no longer a national movement, for northerners preferred antonomy and southerners stuck to the old order. Thus did the party of Gramsci and Togliatti peacefully expire.

Such are the arguments rehearsed late into many a Roman evening when the flasks of Frascati are drained and old leftists talk of how they were robbed. As in all the best conspiracy theories, there exists no proof. Few Romans credit the authorised version of the Moro affair. It is still as remote as the conspiracy of Catiline, as indifferent to historical truth as any Renaissance tale of Borgia depravity. It provides a staple of Roman conversation at the tables of the high and the low, and that, perhaps, is its only enduring tribute.

CHAPTER 9

Don Giulio, The Noblest Roman

In the quiet hour after dawn, when the centre of old Rome still slumbers in a halo of baroque peace, a hunched figure could be seen ascending the steps of the Gesù, the mightiest Jesuit church in the city, therein to kneel at Mass beneath the fresco by Gaulli that depicts the *Triumph of the Name of Christ*.

The honourable Giulio Andreotti, seven times Prime Minister of the Republic of Italy, for a third of this century the high priest of Mediterranean Christian Democracy, the confidant of popes, presidents and Arab dictators, was making his peace with God.

It was more than suitable that Mr Andreotti should have chosen the mother church of the most instinctive and subtle order in Christendom for his daily devotions. The Gesù, like the Society of Jesus, combines unrestrained glory with infinite varieties of light and shade.

On the one hand, it celebrates the sublime. Gaulli covered the entire ceiling of the nave with a vast, whirling cavalcade of princes, saints, angels, apostles, nymphs, the elect and those who appear to be damned; all cowering and in recoil at the resplendent glowing centrepiece of the Holy Name, from which there emanate rays of piercing brilliance. The pilgrim's eye is led from dark to light, through clustered groups of figures and tempestuous cloud, to contemplate irresistibly the depths of the sky and the Name itself. The effect employs fresco, painted stucco and the superimposition of painted parts on the architecture of the vaulting of the roof itself, so that the work appears to burst the bounds of ordinary confinement and to illuminate the whole church.

On the other hand, the Gesù exalts the dignity of the church. The altar and tomb of Saint Ignatius himself express the confidence of Catholicism restored, uniting sensuous, opulent colour with the finest marble. The tomb is inset with lapis lazuli and crowned by a globe of that exquisite material.

It is the very epitome of Jesuit triumphalism, a monument to the luxurious and worldly period through which the order passed in the seventeenth century. It invites the worshipper to look on and adore, but also to enjoy.

All the more reason, then, that an Italian Christian Democrat might feel at home in this environment, which so amply provides temporal glory and spiritual refreshment. Catholicism preached the merits of confession and redemption. The Jesuits, at least according to their critic Pascal, refined the doctrine that the end may, on occasion, justify the means. Devout servants of Christian Democracy, like Mr Andreotti, learned to confess in private and to stay in office.

The Gesù, its façade by Giocomo Della Porta newly restored and gleaming, was also most convenient. If Mr Andreotti's devotions ran true to the rest of his daily routine, then everything between himself and the Almighty was open to negotiation. And across the triangular piazza stands the headquarters of the Christian Democrats, an edifice wherein pacts with the Devil were concluded on an almost daily basis.

In Mr Andreotti's long life, the odour of incense has always been permeated by the whiff of brimstone. Born in Rome, he found shelter in a protected clerical job within the Vatican during the Second World War. Shuffling, black-suited, amid fusty library shelves and incense-scented chapels, he made acquaintances that were to last a lifetime.

One Alcide De Gaspari, had also passed years labouring in the Vatican. He came from the Trento, a province of the far north which began the century as part of Austria-Hungary. He had served as a Catholic deputy in the forgotten parliament of the Habsburg Empire. He had suffered at the hands of the Fascists, once kidnapped and once imprisoned for sixteen months. In the 1930s, the Vatican gave him a safe job in its libraries and he assumed the role of Catholic politician in exile, occasionally asserting his independence of thought. He took issue with the concordat between Pius XI and Mussolini. The Vatican required some years and underwent great soul-searching before it put its weight behind the Christian Democrats, possibly because Pius XII did not relish the second word in the party's title. Eventually, the quiet confidence won by De Gaspari among the monsignori and cardinals allowed the Christian Democratic politicians to inherit the ruins of Fascism, armed with a mandate from the papacy to resist the Communists.

Thus not long after De Gaspari and Andreotti emerged in 1943, Italy had found its principal new political force and the younger man had found a mentor. Andreotti took his first Italian government post under De Gaspari in 1947, while one Margaret Hilda Thatcher was an undergraduate in the chemistry laboratories at Oxford.

In one incarnation or another, Andreotti was in almost every Italian government for the next forty-five years: Under-Secretary, Foreign Minister, Minister of Defence, Minister of Finance and Prime Minister, effortlessly weaving the skein of alliances and appointments that under-writes every Italian coalition. Through the decades of office, attempts to lift his parliamentary immunity, allegations of corruption and criticism of his intimate links with political friends of the 'Honoured Society' – the Mafia – in Sicily, all left him untouched.

'Power,' he once observed, 'exhausts only he who does not possess it.'

By his seventies, he was rendering daily thanks to the Deity for granting him victory over all his foes, for preserving him from death or disgrace, and for conferring on him a measure of influence over his brilliant, contentious nation without rival in the history of Italian democracy. He epitomised his country in the second half of our century as no other European politician. His genius makes Machiavelli extinct. He may not have become President of the Republic, but his role as a lifetime member of the Senate ensured him a permanent forum for intrigue.

If any ghosts rustled in the sombre aisles of the Gesù, then they were probably old friends, for the old fox, as his fellow Romans call him, had outlived them all. One recalls the sibylline, silky-voiced, corrupt Aldo Moro, executed by the Red Brigades while his relieved colleagues piously invoked principles of state in exculpation of his abandonment. One should not forget the ascetic, tormented Pope Paul VI, dead on the rack of illness, with his heart broken at the close of that convulsive decade in Italian history, the 1970s. Then there was the crooked Sicilian financier, Michele Sindona, hailed by Mr Andreotti as 'the saviour of the lira', who choked to death through poison placed, some claim by his own hand, in the morning coffee served to him inside a maximum security prison. And Roberto Calvi, the fraudulent head of the 'priests' bank', the Banco Ambrosiano, found hanging one grey dawn beneath the arches of Blackfriars Bridge in London. Asked later about these two epic swindlers, Mr Andreotti assumed a pained look, then his face crinkled in the usual half-smile. 'I must say,' he observed, 'that I met Mother Teresa much more often than I met Sindona or Calvi.'

Witticisms – the celebrated *battute* or asides – of Mr Andreotti hang heavily in the air of the Gesù. The shades of dead legions flicker as motes of dust in the shafts of morning sunlight – policemen, magistrates and outspoken politicians who have fallen to the scythe of the gangster or the terrorist. It is curious how much of Mr Andreotti's career can be written through other people's obituaries.

As a prolific writer, Mr Andreotti has ensured that his own silky version of events is available to historians, although it may be doubted whether his observations will illuminate their task. Here he is on the strange death of Mr Calvi and its accompanying scandal of the Vatican Bank. 'Evidently one does not wish to prolong a dispute in which too many people have already tried to stoke the fire,' he wrote. 'The legal case is still open and, who knows, one day we may learn exactly what happened in those overheated times.' Who knows, indeed?

It takes even a connoisseur of the arcane world of Italian party politics an awfully long time to wend his way through Mr Andreotti's memoirs. So many crises, frivolous at the time, transient in their effect: resignations reshuffles, changes of party secretary, summits of the coalition, audiences with the President, interventions by the head of the Senate, emergency sessions to approve the budget, meetings with foreign dignitaries, prayerful sessions with the reigning pontiff . . . all of it so much insubstantial activity, played out against a backdrop of historic events for Italy and the world.

This is Mr Andreotti on the assassination of the government's top anti-Mafia officer, General Carlo Alberto dalla Chiesa, and his young wife in Sicily. The killings set off a storm over links between a faction of the Christian Democrats (the one, curiously enough, allied to Mr Andreotti) and the Mafia. 'The general had been pushed into an administrative role in which he could do very little. Unfortunately a perfidious example of political manipulation ensued, exploiting the memory of these two poor victims for its own ends.'

His only significant observation on Licio Gelli, head of the illegal P2 Masonic lodge, the existence of which was revealed in 1981 and brought down the government of Arnaldo Forlani: 'I always felt that it was a great exaggeration to attribute so much power to this person.'

The scandal over corrupt payments allegedly made by the state petrochemical concern ENI to intermediaries in Saudi Arabia: 'unfortunately this disturbing affair remains a mystery'. The reader might have expected a little more light shed on the mystery, given that Mr Andreotti was the Prime Minister who gave official approval to the contract ...

And thus it goes on.

His commerce with heaven complete, Mr Andreotti was wont to progress to the Piazza Montecitorio, a few minutes' walk from the Gesù. This was his routine through long years as a member of the lower house, faithfully elected year after year by his Roman constituents. The Chamber of Deputies opens the doors of its great, bow-fronted palace early, even as the guards on overnight duty at the Prime Minister's office, next door, still loll bleary-eyed at their posts. The first milky coffee of the morning may profitably be taken in its café, where political clients flock and cluster around the Minister. The Christian Democratic grandee in Rome, like the Liberal Democratic potentate in Tokyo, had to cultivate a permanent circle of those to whom obligation was satisfied and on whom favour was bestowed. Truly, it was the life of a modern prince.

The event that spelt the end of guaranteed innocence took place far away from Rome, in the avenues of lemon groves and villas that make up the seaside suburb of Mondello on the fringes of Palermo. On the morning of 12 March 1992, a distinguished gentleman with a mane of silvery hair and the hooded eyes of a *Capofamiglia* stepped out of his home and into a chauffeured car. Salvatore 'Salvo' Lima, the pre-eminent leader of Christian Democracy in Sicily, was one of the few dignitaries on the island who did not feel the need for a bullet-proofed and armour-plated vehicle to guard against the Mafia.

Mr Lima believed he had protection enough, which in a sense he had, because in a sense he *was* the Mafia. Throughout western Sicily, the Mafia families helped to deliver votes to his candidates. In return they gained preference in bidding for state contracts, were able to influence verdicts and sentences in court, and could win jobs for life in the bloated and bankrupt local administration for their cousins and in-laws.

Mr Lima, in turn, delivered his political support to Mr Andreotti. The votes from Sicily provided Mr Andreotti with the backbone of his *corrente* or group inside the party, without which his power to command cabinet office would be as nought. Thus while Mr Andreotti was sitting in the highest councils on earth as Foreign Minister or taking tea with popes, the quiet, steady machine of Mafia-dominated votes in Sicily was helping to ensure that he stayed there. Of course, the Mafia required favours in return. When Mr Lima could not meet their requests in person, he boarded the Alitalia flight to Rome and there he sought influence from on high.

By the morning of 12 March, however, Mr Lima's smooth career had reached a turning point. The political climate had changed. It was no longer possible to 'adjust' convictions through compliant judges. Hundreds of mafiosi, convicted in spectacular mass trials, faced the dismaying possibility of actually having to serve their sentences. This was all but unheard of. After years of mutual understandings, Mr Lima had failed to deliver.

As he got into the car, a pair of gunmen approached. They started shooting. Mr Lima, wounded, leapt from the car and tried to run down the street to escape. It was of no avail. The men chased him and fired again. The elder statesman of Sicily, the most powerful figure in its political firmament, choked out his last few minutes in a pool of blood – like so many innocent victims of the Honoured Society he had done so much to promote.

One wonders if, in his dying moments, Mr Lima recalled the face of Giulio Andreotti and his rousing speech to the seaside conference of Christian Democracy: 'Pay no heed to those who preach to you of false morality ... do not let the good name of Sicily be smeared ...'.

That is when it all began to unravel. 'I must say this, that in all the years I knew Salvo Lima in the party from 1968 onwards, in all those years up until his death, I never had any firm reason to believe, never had even a single idea that Salvo Lima led a double life or that he served the interests of the Mafia,' complained Mr Andreotti. 'Quite the contrary.'

In this he was speaking an absolute version of the truth. Of course the late and scarce-lamented Mr Lima did not serve the interests of the Mafia. He served the interests of the political class in its dealings with the Mafia, for power in southern Italy alternates between the civil and the underground authorities. To the Andreottis and Limas, therefore, it was a question not of bowing down to the Mafia, but rather of regulating economic and political affairs in tandem with it. Rather like forming an Italian coalition, in fact, but with perhaps more dramatic consequences for misunderstandings.

A year later the trail had led from Mr Lima's coffin, via the magistrates of Palermo and into the seventeenth-century courtyard of S. Ivo alla Sapienza, next door to the Senate in Rome. Within its precincts a committee of the Italian Senate was due to meet Mr Andreotti, now a Senator for life. The unthinkable had occurred. Mr Andreotti was to face the judgement of his peers, who were asked to remove his parliamentary immunity. The magistrates had sent a document of fifty-eight pages full of dreadful accusations and Mr Andreotti had been summoned to defend himself.

At seventy-four, Mr Andreotti looked as sharp as ever, with his hair brushed neatly back, his bright eyes shining behind thick glasses and his thin mouth, whose corners twitch upwards in a half-smile of perpetual irony. But in these stressful weeks he had acquired a patina of tiredness, as if he could not believe that after decades of immunity his good fortune had come to an end.

One watched his hunched figure step out of the armour-plated car with the habitual dignity of the statesman. Clad, as ever, in a well-cut charcoal suit from Angelo Litrici, his Roman tailor, Mr Andreotti was ushered through a baying pack of paparazzi to sit at the bar of the accused. His protestations were as nought. The Senators voted to strip him of the protection which every member of parliament enjoyed. It was, said many a newspaper reaching for historical analogy, like the meeting of the Fascist Grand Council which withdrew its support from Mussolini on 25 July 1943. The Duce lingered on, but that date fixed the end of his regime.

Mr Andreotti was famously imperturbable. But in the dark days after that decision his household was, one heard, a place of torment and recrimination. His wife, Livia, was said to be distraught. It was as if these people, omnipotent for so long, could see awaiting them the fate dealt out to many foes and to many great men who topple from their pinnacles.

One might easily imagine, up on the darkened Palatine hill, the unquiet spirits of the classical Livia and her husband Augustus, sighing in sympathy as they hurried through the roofless corridors of their old domain ...

There were grim and damning things said about the elder statesman. All of them were denied. He was said to have performed the function of the Mafia's political protector at the highest levels of the Italian state. He was alleged to have profited from the votes assiduously provided by the Mafia to Salvo Lima. There were tales – vigorously contested, of course – of secret encounters with the bosses of the Palermo underworld. One informer claimed to have seen the old fox turn up for a meeting with the fugitive head of the entire Sicilian Mafia, a nasty fellow named 'Toto' Riina. At the end of this encounter, it was claimed, Mr Andreotti had exchanged the traditional kiss upon both cheeks with this gentleman.

On the night that this revelation became public property and filled the airwaves, cafés and restaurants with excitable chatter, Mr Andreotti appeared in the marbled corridor of his *palazzo*. A blonde and comely television reporter thrust a microphone towards him. What did he have to say about the famous kiss?

The brow furrowed, the eyes hardened. A television light glared in his face, picking out the ridges and creases in his frown. For the first time in more than a decade of observing the man, I could see 'Don Giulio' – as, by then, we all knew him – lose his patience. 'Not only am I stupefied by the calumny of these lies,' snapped the statesman, 'but I'm stupefied by their very stupidity.'

Then there was The Plot. No Italian scandal could be complete without the added flavour of conspiracy. The fashionable version of The Plot ran approximately as follows. The cold war had drawn to a close. The United States – bulwark of Christendom and paymaster for Don Giulio's party – no longer required Italy as a strategic ally against Moscow. The Kremlin was no longer deemed to pose much of a threat and the Italian Communists had dissolved. A red takeover could no longer be summoned up to justify the most insalubrious manoeuvres of politics and finance; nor could the murky figures who operated, in effect, as Italy's death squads be called upon to blow up a train here or a bank there in a bid to blacken the Left.

Washington, in other words, had no further need to tolerate Don Giulio's Italian system, just as it had earlier discovered no pressing requirement to sustain Ferdinand Marcos in the Philippines.

Indeed, ran the theory, the American government and the powerful firms of Wall Street had determined that a united Europe posed a threat

to their economic predominance and had set out to undermine it –
starting, naturally, with the weakest link.

The proof? Why, on the very day that Don Giulio was called before
the Senate, the Director of the CIA, James Woolsey, had landed in
Rome to meet his Italian colleagues. In the overheated atmosphere of
the Italian capital, his appearance – on a long-planned visit, the American
embassy insisted – set off a delicious wave of speculation.

Woolsey's distant predecessor William Colby was left to deflate the
Italian press by telling them that 'Clinton's problems are Yeltsin and the
Federal deficit – no offense but he's dedicating no energy to Italy.'

No such reasoning could stifle the deep-seated Roman instinct to
search the heavens for an augury of evil. For Mr Andreotti there existed
nothing less than 'a skilful campaign of denigration, especially in America'.
His acolyte, Claudio Vitalone, radiated menace. There was, said Mr
Vitalone between clenched teeth, 'a destabilising conspiracy hatched in
foreign circles'.

There were reservoirs of support, of course, even in the weeks when
a generation of influence was visibly ebbing away from Don Giulio.
'Among people in the Vatican I've had no impression that they are
trying to distance themselves,' he observed. 'Indeed everybody in the
Church who granted me their esteem in the past has reconfirmed it.' He
showed signs of emotion when he attended a special Mass in a district
of Rome at which almost the entire Curial hierarchy was present. The
cardinal delivering the sermon spoke of the Vatican's thanks to him and
its appreciation of his advice. The Church particularly recalled his wise
counsel during the crisis of the Banco Ambrosiano (an affair for which
it ended up paying out $250 million). The deity for once forgotten, the
entire congregation of cardinals, bishops, priests and faithful broke into
applause. Don Giulio, moist-eyed, sat in his pew like a sculptured saint.

Away from such lachrymose ceremonies his sang-froid remained
intact. 'This is all really rather boring,' he said one morning at the
Foreign Press Club. 'You know, I'm having to take time off to deal with
all these legal matters. It is interfering with my reading, my writing, and,
of course, my work to encourage a dialogue between the religions.'

These holy pursuits aside, Don Giulio devoted laborious and subterranean efforts to his defence. There was, for example, the famous
correspondence of the pseudo-Cicero. Don Giulio assumed the role of
the Roman orator to pen a letter to an errant son. At turns paternal,
chiding, ominous and wistful, it invited the imaginary recipient to cease

his treacherous, unfilial criticisms. People rushed to identify the target as one or other of Don Giulio's erstwhile supporters. The letter of the pseudo-Cicero was in truth an epistle to all those who had supped at the fountain of Andreotti patronage. It sounded injured but still full of menace.

Then Don Giulio turned to his favourite use of witticism and irony to deprecate the motives of those who accused him. 'A little chorus of informers,' he mused, 'not even singing in tune.'

He conceded that there may have been a 'quietus vivere', a live and let live approach to the Mafia. Naturally, it was not his fault. Indeed, his governments, more than any others, had acted against the Honoured Society. 'I may have been inattentive in the past,' Don Giulio said piously, 'but in this I am more than an angel.'

To hear the authorised version, one could close one's eyes and imagine fleets of warships and squadrons of helicopters descending at Don Giulio's command upon Sicily. At the stern command of the Prime Minister (himself), a myriad incorruptible policemen invade the slums of Palermo to root out the criminals. Austere magistrates, under the benevolent gaze of the Premier, pursue malfeasance in the highest reaches of Sicilian society, while from the island's pulpits an upright clergy, wisely prompted by Don Giulio, anathematises the mafiosi. Proud Italian lawgivers commune with their American friends in the implacable pursuit of ill-gotten gains ... and so on.

It was, no doubt, unfortunate that few shared Don Giulio's particular impression of recent Sicilian history. It was even more unhappy for him that so many seemed to take issue with his own conduct of affairs. Indeed, the overwhelming impression in his hour of trial was one of an elderly individual who, like Pius xii, had removed himself to a higher plane of contemplation from whose perspective all contours were erased and the rough edges of history had been smoothed out into a slick and burnished veneer.

In Umberto Eco's novel, *Foucault's Pendulum*, the characters are Milanese intellectuals, serious to a man and long diverted from their days of idealism, who find excitement in the realms of magic, indulge in hidden ancient rites and pursue the lost secret of the Latin Kingdom of Jerusalem. Their brilliant emptiness epitomises the fate of Mr Eco's generation in Italy – the class of 1968 that never grew into power because the generation of Mr Andreotti stood Colosseum-like in its way. They stare into malt whisky in smoke-filled bars along the old canals of

Milan, once the scenes of heroic causes, now the haunt of bored people on the cusp of middle age, in search of a spark of imagination that religion, politics and prosperity cannot deliver.

The characters seek the occult secret of eternal power, only to fail, Mr Eco suggests, because while everybody cherishes the illusion of power, none but a handful understand its true substance.

To which the honourable Giulio Andreotti, genuflecting before the fresco in the Gesù that depicts the damned falling from the very rim of heaven, would surely murmur 'Amen'.

CHAPTER 10

Endpiece

One February in the late 1980s, the Pope, who took a close interest in his diocese beyond the Vatican walls, pronounced an anathema against the ills of Rome, its noise, dirt, chaos and overcrowding. The ruling Council did little or nothing to alleviate matters, concentrating instead upon polemic and self-enrichment. Parts of the city, said the Pope, 'were like the Third World'.

The next month, magistrates conducting one of nine separate inquiries into City Hall corruption warned the Christian Democratic Mayor, Pietro Giubilo, that he could face charges of abuse of office. These allegations arose out of contracts for the provision of lunchtime meals to thousands of Roman schoolchildren. Most, it seemed, had been allocated to firms controlled by a militant Catholic movement (much approved of by the pontiff) which rejoiced in the name of Communion and Liberation.

At the end of March, Mr Giubilo tendered his resignation but did not leave the Campidoglio. The four Centre–Right parties in the Council deserted their Christian Democrat allies in disgust. The Communists and their radical friends began a great hue and cry to expel the Mayor.

Mr Giubilo, however, was not alone. His patron in Roman politics was a cigar-chomping ex-Fascist, Vittorio Sbardella, known to all and sundry as 'the Shark'. And Mr Sbardella's patron, in turn, was the noblest

Roman of them all, our old acquaintance 'Don Giulio' Andreotti.

Abortive and theatrical sessions of the Council ensued, continuing into the steaming Roman summer. At times the invective from the Campidoglio became so heated that it is a wonder the shutters of the Palazzo Pecci Blunt, down the *cordonata*, were not blistered. At the end of May, when barometric pressure and thunder-filled skies combine to make most Romans murderous, forty-six out of eighty councillors resigned to try to bring about elections.

It is not known how the Pope felt personally about all this, for he is rarely given to vouchsafe his opinions on political personalities, unless they should happen to be wayward Jesuit priests. However, on 5 July that year his newspaper, the *Osservatore Romano*, accused the Mayor and his followers of 'keeping their hands on public affairs' (the Italian-language version implied 'the public purse') and 'aiming only to control votes and contracts'.

The clerics who edit the *Osservatore* had, quite clearly, endured enough of the city's government. They had already let fly against the Council's failure to enforce a ban on traffic over the Christmas and New Year holidays, 'plans which never became reality, with the holiday climate providing an alibi for improvisation and inefficiency'. The public should 'raise its voice ... because the quality of life in this city can no longer be contracted out to anybody' It was clear whose side the priestly journalists were on.

The Catholic world, though, is nothing if not a broad church, and the Mayor's faction soon found its voice. It transpired that Communion and Liberation (they of the school meals) controlled a weekly religious magazine entitled *Il Sabato*, and that 'the Shark', together with Mr Andreotti, were its political patrons. *Il Sabato* duly unleashed a volley of abuse against the reformist group within Christian Democracy and accused the *Osservatore* of 'defending Communist interests'.

The Mayor professed to be pained by the Vatican's outspoken opinions. 'Why,' he said plaintively, 'I've given the go-ahead to build six churches ... we've even named a street after Pope Paul the Sixth.' 'The Shark', not a gentleman to mince his words, detected 'the hoofprint of Opus Dei' behind it all, complaining of the influence enjoyed by that eccentric organisation under the pontificate of John Paul ii. He publicly reminded Cardinal Ugo Poletti, the Papal Vicar of Rome, of 'the few economic interest groups' he was organising to help diocesan funds.

Unabashed, Mayor Giubilo invoked a special law on 12 July and sat for seven hours in the City Hall with only eight other councillors. All of them were loyal Christian Democrats. This was one of the most remarkable municipal sessions in Rome since the days of the Gracchi. The nine men approved 1,200 long-delayed city decrees for contracts amounting to some £700 million. Most of these urban projects were related to the 1990 World Cup soccer finals in the capital.

Those of a critical and suspicious bent immediately recalled the *Osservatore Romano*'s immortal line about 'keeping their hands on public affairs'. It became quite clear what the papal journalists had meant. Unabashed, Mayor Giubilo and his friends even took out advertisements in the newspapers to boast of their efficiency. Cutting through all that red tape in one night! Why, surely this was what reform was all about!

Sadly and inevitably, the magistracy disagreed. Long after Mayor Giubilo had fallen from office and when the festivities of the World Cup remained but a distant hangover, the implacable machinery of justice was still investigating the deeds of that hot night on the Campidoglio. Lawyers and judges would be kept busy for many a month.

By then, of course, the caravan of municipal affairs had moved on, via special commissioners, new elections, juntas made or broken, mayors raised then expelled, all the while the city itself subsiding into murk, pollution, cacophonous traffic and services on the brink of collapse.

'It is quite horrible,' lamented Sandra Carraro, wife of yet another deposed Mayor of Rome. Signora Carraro was sipping espresso in one of the expensive, quiet trattorias hidden away in the pine groves of the northern suburbs. She was just back from the tennis court. 'There is a terrible nervousness in the air. Everybody is uncertain. Nobody knows what will happen next. And the way people are turning on other people is just awful.'

In the locust years, the Carraro *salotto* was another place of influence in the capital, perhaps less exalted than the Palazzo Pecci Blunt, but none the less a corner of society where the powerbrokers met to hammer out their deals. Franco Carraro, the Mayor, was a Socialist, but he was on good terms with the eternal, Don Giulio, and Sandra Carraro spoke to Mr Andreotti's wife Livia every evening on the telephone. The Mayor drew both Mr Andreotti and the Socialist leader Bettino Craxi into a tight circle that met over drinks and cards. It permitted the two apparent enemies to socialise far from the curious eyes of parliamentary deputies and Italy's uncontrollable newspapermen.

The subtle Roman, Andreotti, and the blustering Milanese, Craxi, found the *salotto* a comfortable hideaway to discuss their mutual needs. In any case, the Palazzo Pecci Blunt was off limits, because the Contessa would not have Bettino Craxi in the house. 'I did not like Craxi and he knew I did not like him,' she recalled. 'But my goodness, how some of these other women threw themselves at his feet!'

Don Giulio and the lumpen Bettino were the two most powerful men in Rome. Both having served as Prime Minister, both influential in business and politics alike, they were the political architects of the loudly proclaimed Italian economic Renaissance. In the mouth-watering Italian phrase, they 'carved up the tart', allocating ministries and contracts, deciding which company might be enriched overnight or which pliant functionary might be appointed ambassador to Washington.

Franco Carraro was made Mayor by their consent in December 1989, but his administration collapsed in 1993 amid a welter of recrimination and scandal, much of it dating back to the days of 'the Shark' and the Giubilo regime. At least eight of the councillors were hauled off to the Queen of Heaven prison downriver from the Vatican, and the police seized bundles of documents relating to the World Cup and other Pharaonic building projects. Not the least of these was a multi-billion lire railway terminal for the train link to Fiumicino airport, constructed in a location of no possible use to the passengers, but guaranteed not to interfere with the lucrative taxi drivers' racket, and of immense profit to the builders involved. Like a marooned white elephant, it stands echoing and deserted in a vast car park near the Pyramid of Cestius.

'Everybody knows that Franco stole nothing,' said Sandra Carraro plaintively. 'He just got caught in the middle'

Roman wisdom, Roman guile and Roman government performed their interlinked miracles for decades after Mussolini's abrupt departure.

Through the lifetime work of Mr Andreotti and his ilk, Italy prospered materially while retaining its unique national identity, complete with a creaking bureaucracy, a bankrupt public sector, absurd shopping hours and strictly regulated standards for the manufacture of spaghetti. It is, perhaps, the country in western Europe which has most carefully preserved its own language, music, philosophy and literature against the onslaught of transatlantic culture. It uncannily resembles another nation that is an enigma to outsiders, Japan.

Like the Japanese, the Roman ruling club contrived for years to oversee an economy in continuous expansion, without apparent hindrance from strong interest rates and an expensive currency. Only with the effects of the stock market crash of 1987, the end of Communism and the world recession that signalled the hangover after a long expansive party in the 1980s did either clique face the consequences of its stewardship.

In each country, one political group had maintained a stranglehold on parliamentary power and cabinet government since the armies of occupation marched out of their barracks forty years ago. The similarities pursue each other with eerie regularity. Subterranean power groups, esoteric societies or Masonic lodges, retain a subtle grip on the levers of influence. A well-developed underworld regulates criminal activity in close tandem with the political class and, increasingly, within the legitimate economy. Much of the business world is rigged by cartels, ringed by invisible Chinese walls against serious outside competition, and dominated by a few over-mighty players who answer to nobody, least of all the ordinary consumer or shareholder. For four decades, until the rival ideology collapsed, the entire enterprise was underwritten by a grateful superpower eager for stable premises on the underbelly of a threatening beast.

It was all outstandingly successful for the Roman governing élite and a total and unmitigated defeat for the forces in Italian society which since the Risorgimento had argued and fought for reform.

Ah, says the Anglo-Saxon outsider, but is Italy not inefficient, unstable and corrupt? The trains, it is true, frequently do not run on time. The telephones would exasperate the inhabitants of Lagos. The public hospitals could present scenes out of bedlam. The legal system owes more to Kafka than to Justinian. Companies present accounts according to whim alone, and on the Milan stock exchange, insider trading was no offence. As for the thousand banks, most owned by the state, or the post offices, or government departments, anyone obliged to conduct business with them is best advised to go equipped with an absorbing novel and boundless faith in the Madonna.

None of this is proof that the Italian system is inefficient. Quite the contrary. It demonstrates that the system works to perfect efficiency in the interests of those who share in it. The observer from Protestant northern Europe, alas, too frequently imports a concept of the rights and duties of rulers which fails to coincide with the evidence of Italian history.

Between the collapse of Fascism in 1943 and the revolutionary upheaval fifty years later, power in Rome was shared out through a multi-party democracy which dispensed the largess of the state via the patronage available to each political faction. Until the 1960s, the Christian Democrats had most of the cake. Then, bit by bit, the 'lay' parties, those not connected to the Vatican, the Socialists, Social Democrats, Liberals and Republicans, were brought into the network. Ministerial posts, lifetime appointments in the public service, grace-and-favour apartments in the centre of Rome, the esteem of one's supplicatory clients and the opportunity for personal enrichment: such were the spoils of power.

Refined to perfection by Mr Andreotti, the arrangement proved resilient enough to see off the challenge from the Communist Party in the 1970s, the onslaught of terrorism and the economic shocks dealt out by OPEC and the global recession.

Its success depended upon the mechanism elaborated by Cicero and savaged by Juvenal: that is, the relationship between patron and client, the reciprocal use of favour, the courteous mutual understanding that oils every transaction. If an ageing relative needs hospital treatment, then an arrangement can be made to provide the best. A telephone is required within less than six months? An acquaintance in the state monopoly company can probably be found – if you have the right connections.

Any Italian bank would laugh at an unknown entrepreneur who wanted venture capital to start a risky business like the Body Shop. In the early 1990s, many, no doubt, were splitting their sides. But with an introduction from, say, the Socialist politician whose party controls the chairmanship of the institution, the wildest schemes of dubious pro-fitability become possible. Foreigners imagine that Italian banks are inefficient because it can take a whole hour to cash a cheque. They simply fail to comprehend that the banks do not exist to redistribute funds or to provide financial services to retail customers. They exist to contain the flow of capital firmly within the *nomenklatura* and, *inter alia*, to maintain an army of underworked clerical employees with jobs for life in leisurely style. Clients who trusted in the advent of European competition at the end of 1992 soon found that they were prone to excessive optimism.

If services were freely and equally available to all on the basis of suffrage, taxation or market forces, where would lie the opportunity for the dispensation of favour and the glorious sensation of acquiring respect that marks an ancient civilisation? Without patronage, the Italian official or politician would be as Shelley's chameleon that feeds on light and air.

The second misconception, that the old Italy was unstable, arose from the fact that the revolving door to the office of the Prime Minister turned some fifty times since the foundation of the modern republic, and that the government perpetually appeared on the brink of another crisis.

Yet Italy was the only major European nation – East or West – that did not witness a democratic handover from government to opposition for more than forty-five years after the Second World War. Disputes were normally resolved between the secretaries of the five coalition parties: when they could not be settled in that way, the government 'fell' and was re-formed to take account of the shifting patterns of influence within the governing class. Foreign embassies then wasted a good deal of time and paper trying to analyse these events. There even existed a civil service directory of influence, the *Manuale Cencelli*, to be consulted as to precisely the amount of power accumulated in any one position and to determine its award accordingly. It was perhaps no strange thing that in its reverence for hierarchy, the *Manuale Cencelli* bore a striking similarity to the Vatican's dictionary of its own bureaucracy, the *Annuario Pontefice*.

It is true that the Roman establishment shuddered under terrorism. It had always made a virtue of avoiding conflict. Yet the state displayed a shrewd understanding of the Catholic psychology behind the Red Brigades. 'Repentant' informers were forgiven with mild penance in the manner of the confessional, the Red Brigades were infiltrated and the secret services sowed confusion and provocation in their ranks. In hindsight, there is little doubt that the kidnapping in 1982 of an American General, James Lee Dozier, was a 'sting' from start to finish. It flushed out the urban guerrilla cells and permitted the authorities to round up most of the dangerous activists. Disinformation, deals with the Mafia, a shoot-to-kill policy: the Italian system deployed every weapon to preserve itself against 'leftist' terror, and it won.

There was a heaven-sent bonus, too, for the ancient holders of power. The excesses of terrorism criminalised the Left in the eyes of the people and made any vigorous dissent subversive. Many of those who were active on campuses and factory floors in the 1970s are convinced that, while the initial violence of the Red Brigades was a spontaneous response to repression, its subsequent campaign of terror was manipulated by the state.

That may just be one of the conspiracy theories which proliferate in

Italy like olives on gnarled trees. The fact remains that in the 1980s the Communist Party never recovered its impetus, Italy accepted Cruise missiles with no significant protest, the radical student movement collapsed, big companies like Fiat 'restructured' with massive state-subsidised layoffs, and the ruling coalitions embarked on a deficit-driven boom that took years to come home to roost.

Through all this the key component in keeping Christian Democracy in power was the Socialist Party of Bettino Craxi. Theoretically committed to reform and opposed to Christian Democrat influence, the Socialists fought their way to an ever increasing share of the spoils through the 1970s, and Mr Craxi became Prime Minister for four years in the middle of the 1980s. British socialists viewed this process with satisfaction. But a corrective dose of northern European rationalism would have been in order. The labels of 'Left' and 'Right' mean very little in modern Italian history. The 'conservative' Christian Democrats maintained a vast and parasitical public sector in the interests of patronage, while the 'leftist' local council of Bologna was among the first to privatise services in the interests of efficiency.

Mr Craxi's version of socialism turned out to mean little more than equality of plunder inside the apparatus of government. Like every potential adversary of the Andreotti web, he and his party were inexorably drawn into its celebration of public office, like the Renaissance Pope Leo x, who remarked that, since God had granted him the papacy, it was now time to enjoy it.

So, to take the last Anglo-Saxon prejudice, was the Roman order of things corrupt? Of course it was. The architect Bruno De Mico, protagonist in a notorious bribery trial, declared that 'you cannot do business in Italy without paying people off'. The entire board of the state railways was forced to resign after a scandal involving, of all things, the contract for bed linen in sleeping cars. The chairman of the board was later murdered by hitmen. Even by local standards, the affair of the state railways was colourful. The reality of day-to-day malfeasance was more humdrum.

Everybody was 'just caught in the middle' under the Roman system. If the routine exchange of money for influence constitutes corruption, then political corruption was a way of life. The great majority of hardworking Italians run businesses or go about their salaried jobs without ever coming across such things in their lifetimes.

But how many times does the supplicant in the queue at the post office ask the sullen functionary behind the counter for '*una cortesia*' – a kindness – in fulfilling the task they are paid for? An enthusiastic Under-Secretary, Raffaele Costa, made headlines when he disclosed that most of the work that went on in the Ministry of Public Works involved shopping in illicit shops set up in the Ministry basement, the consumption of coffee and Camparis in the well-appointed Ministry bars, and the busy to-ing and fro-ing of unsackable civil servants maintaining their second jobs outside the building. Little wonder that public examinations for the most junior bureaucratic jobs are oversubscribed by the thousand.

Corruption deserves not forensic analysis, but cultural enquiry. Leoluca Orlando, a brave and honest man who became Mayor of Palermo on an anti-Mafia ticket, once sat in the Bourbon splendour of his office and explained that the problem in Italy was one of the old *cultura dell'appartenenza* – roughly speaking, the mentality that sought security in groups against a hostile outside world and an indifferent state. 'Then you naturally graduate to the *cultura della raccomandazione* where nothing can be achieved without a "recommendation", and here in Sicily the final form of that is the Mafia,' he said.

His point was that this ancient mentality lingers on, far from the somnolent villages of Sicily ... even unto the café at the Chamber of Deputies. Driving in from Palermo airport to the scene of a singularly bloody assassination, a group of foreign journalists once asked their taxi driver about the Mafia. 'Mafia?' snorted the man. 'You lot tell me – you come from Rome, don't you?'

So while the rest of Europe from Spain to the Baltic surveyed with amazement a decade of change and the substitution of old authority by fresh young blood, the 1990s began with Italy firmly in the hands of the *ancien régime*.

But while the earth moved around Italy, some of the rules under which its system enjoyed this prolonged renaissance had changed. Some economic analysts thought that the slow convergence towards a single European currency might finally force the government to face the consequences of a public sector debt equivalent to 100 per cent of GNP, hitherto financed by treasury bonds issued to a captive Italian market. But as delay succeeded crisis and each step towards union became more faltering, this happy prospect, too, began to recede.

One British ambassador, weary of trying to explain the vagaries of the Andreotti system to his bemused Thatcherite masters in London, observed that he could imagine 'no foreseeable way in which any Italian government wishing to remain in office can make significant reductions in the public sector deficit'.

On paper, there should come a reckoning. But it would be entirely consistent with past form for international commitments entered into on paper to fail to make their way into the light of reality. At the end of the century, moving capital in and out of Italy may be as tedious as ever, without a single official restriction remaining in force, and the government may still be up to its eyes in debt.

It was a similar tale with the prospects for 1992, a subject upon which Italian diplomacy rose to rhetorical flights of idealism consistent with the finest standards of *bella figura*. Not even the *ancien régime* was completely able to stave off the intrusion of mighty foreign banks, but any other international businesses seeking to inject competition or, heaven forbid, to provide lower prices for the Italian consumer, faced a myriad hidden obstacles. The Roman reality was that, while Italy has one of the best records of public commitment to implementing the European single market legislation, the gap between intention and fulfilment is enormous.

The ruined economies of eastern Europe lay gasping for investment, and the prospects for Italian industry and businesses in the north and centre of the peninsula became extraordinary. At the same time, economists could foresee the underdeveloped south slipping further away, undermined by waste, corruption, overmanning and the culture of 'recommendations', suffering from the expansion of the European market to the north-east, as it did when the unification of Italy drove the economic fulcrum of the nation to Piedmont and Lombardy.

Already one could sense the keen excitement in the north Italian air. The Northern League, a party dedicated to autonomy, if not outright secession, emerged as the most dynamic force in politics throughout the prosperous swathe of territory between the Alps, the Adriatic and the Ligurian riviera. Exhaustion with the mystic arts of bribery and corruption, impatience at the torpid pace of government, resentment at the taxes paid by northerners to subsidise a style of governance and life that seemed languid when it was not outright fraudulent – all combined to generate forces of a strength and unity of purpose not witnessed since the Risorgimento.

Milan, one sensed, strained towards the New World in the grandeur of its financial aspirations, and was linked more efficiently to Zürich, Geneva and southern Germany than it was to the nation's capital. Turin progressed each year towards the style and confidence of a great French city such as Lyon. Florence or Bologna echoed the civic spirit of Avignon or Salzburg, while Venice and Trieste awaited in wistful hope the regeneration of their old Habsburg hinterlands away towards Vienna and the plains of Hungary. A new Italy was indeed coming forth, but one in which Rome played a diminished part.

It is in the south that one senses both the dignity and the sadness of the old Italy, a world left behind in the rush to prosperity nurtured by tycoons like Gianni Agnelli of Fiat. The two worlds collide in Rome and in the antique persona of Don Giulio, their interests mediated by a priesthood of political hierarchs, but their confusions unresolved. The country underwent a revolution with the flight from the land to the cities after 1945. Then, in the last twenty years of the century, it experienced another in the explosive growth of the *terziario*, the service sector. There will be yet more Fiats, more Ermenegildo Zegna suits, more computers and more holidays in the Maldives for the lucky.

Yet something sweet and intangible was lost in Italy during the 1980s. In the wise words of the late Peter Nichols, 'they took away the old peasant values and substituted them with nothing more than the empty drive for acquisition'. While the time-worn structures of power remained in place, the rueful humour and the gentle, almost oriental courtesies that once regulated people's relations with one another have all but evaporated in the jostle of success. There is already a vogue for books and films recording the hardships of wartime and evoking nostalgia for the innocent days of the first great boom of the 1950s.

And the capital? A byword for inertia or greed, polluted beyond decent tolerance, abandoned to the overmighty motor car and awash in new money – much of it, alas, raised by government debt, private corruption or criminal enterprise – the city lay passive beneath this latest of her tribulations. If the jewels in the old crown of Italy, the prosperous city-states of the north and centre, were tugged ever closer to their European roots, never was it more pertinent that Rome lies closer to Tripoli than to Paris.

Yet the city itself, resilient down the centuries in defeat, grand in its moments of triumph, faced a new and inevitable transformation as the end of the millennium drew near. The truth was that in its heart it did not belong to a community composed chiefly of the states of northern Europe. Older, more powerful instincts tugged it towards the

Mediterranean basin, the Holy Land, the shores of Araby and the Levant. The new money ebbed away when the government's indebtedness reached its zenith. Then the collapse of the Republic disrupted the profitable flow of bribes and funds into manicured Roman hands. When the economic recession finally arrived, Rome was left with none of the residual assets of its dominance – no brilliant buildings, no gems of transportation, no public reminders of the regime's power as bequeathed to their capitals by rulers as diverse as Mussolini and Mitterrand.

Instead the city resumed its habitual torpor. It languorously edged forever southwards, towards its ancient familiarity with the Levantine entrepôts of Beirut and Tyre. It came to feel closer to Istanbul in its daily life than to any city of central Europe, except that civic affairs on the shores of the Bosporus were settled with greater charm than those on the poisoned banks of the Tiber. Business was once again conducted at an Alexandrian rhythm, and the life of a middle-class resident became more and more adapted to standards of services and traffic that were frankly Cairene. On a working day, one might sit profitlessly in a car for an hour or more in an attempt to reach a destination that Shelley might have reached on foot in twenty minutes, and on the frequent public holidays, a great stinking crocodile of motionless, honking vehicles extended down the old legionary roads to the coast, their presence marked by a humid fog of heat and noxious dust.

Yet at the centre of the metropolis, hemmed in by an ever-expanding ring of gruesome suburban estates, the dream of a grand and tranquil civilisation could still become fleeting reality.

Take the view from the Ponte Sisto, a slender footbridge I would cross every day returning to Trastevere from the Campo De'Fiori. The bridge was built by Sixtus IV and tinkered with by every Roman regime from Garibaldi to the present day. In fact, at the time of writing it is still garbed in scaffolding so venerable that it has become streaked with rust.

I would always pause, half-way across its span. At the western end there is a small piazza, where a single marble fountain plays, matched by its sister, the great triple fountain of the Acqua Paola, far up amid the greenery on the Janiculum hill. The red-tiled roofs of Trastevere straggle from riverbank to hillside, the dome of Saint Peter's rises through a curtain of trees on the right and the Tiber island resembles a great ship's prow downstream to the left, crowned, on a clear day, by the distant peaks of the Alban hills. In the mid-afternoon lull, when the roar of Mr Agnelli's Fiats has fallen to an adagio, you can – just – imagine the peace of the old papal city, hear the echo of carriage wheels on cobblestones and perhaps even hear the poets' footfalls, lightly, just behind you.

There are capitals more efficient, more cosmopolitan than Rome; there are cities with brighter nightlife, better bookstores, superior theatre, more efficient telephones, more industrious bank clerks, less traffic and fewer thieves of all kinds. None, however, will ever grant the subtle, infusing pleasure of an afternoon view such as this to the human heart.

Acknowledgements

The late Peter Nichols, for thirty years a great Rome correspondent of *The Times*, showed kind generosity to younger journalists taking their first halting steps along that road. In that sense, he may be said to have inspired this book.

Annette von Broecker at Reuters and Stephen Glover, then foreign editor of *The Independent*, were in their different ways perhaps the best employers one could have wished for as a correspondent in Italy.

I am indebted to Eugenio Scalfari at *La Repubblica*, who extended help and a warm welcome, and to Carlo Caracciolo, whose interest and hospitality have been unfailing.

Among the many people who contributed over the years to my own slow comprehension of the place are Pino Arlacchi, Wolf Achtner, Lucia Annunziata, Guido Barendson, William Barnes, Klaus Bender, Marco Borsa, Francesca Bossi, Marella Caracciolo, Deirdre Campbell, Brian Childs, Marina Cicogna, Paolo Filo Della Torre, Robert Fox, Paolo Garimberti, Francesca Gee, Tim Jepson, Monsignor Carlo Kasteel, Roger Lewis, Nicola Marinaro, Fr Peter Newby, Martine Newby, Leoluca Orlando, Don Pierfranco Pastore, Carlo Rossella, Victor Simpson, Bill Scott, Uli Schmetzer, the late Giorgio Signorini, Sir Derek Thomas, Gabrio Tosti di Valminuta, David Willey and Sir Terence Wood.

In researching the Ciano period I benefited from the guidance of Nicola Caracciolo in Rome. Norman Stone first provoked my interest in the mechanics of history during long autumn evenings in Cambridge. I must also register my thanks to the staff of the Public Records Office at Kew.

I owe a double debt to Richard Holmes, first, for writing a biography of Shelley which transformed my teenage years and, much later, for agreeing to spend valuable Roman hours discussing his subject. In the same breath I should thank the curator of the Keats–Shelley Memorial House, Baathsheba Abse, and her staff for allowing me to work among its books, papers and memorabilia. Dennis Redmont kindly gave permission for me to consult the files of the Associated Press in Rome.

Natasha Fairweather encouraged me at a critical moment to develop the original idea, while Anne McDermid at Curtis Brown and Ion Trewin at Weidenfeld & Nicolson made the book possible.

Most of all I have to thank my wife, Sophy Fisher, who lived with Rome, and me, and it, with patience and love.

Bibliography

Telegrams and letters of Sir Percy Loraine and dispatches from His Majesty's Legation to the Holy See are in the Public Record Office, Kew, mainly under FO 371.

The text used for the Ciano diaries was that in *Galeazzo Ciano, Diario 1937–1943*, ed. Renzo De Felice, Rizzoli Libri Spa, Milan, 1980.

The 1839 edition of poems by Percy Bysshe Shelley with introduction by Mrs Shelley is reproduced in *Shelley, Poetical Works*, Oxford, 1919, and this has been used for most quotations.

Other works and papers in the library of the Keats–Shelley Memorial House include:
The Journals of Mary Shelley ed. Feldman and Scott-Kilvert, Oxford, 1987.
Letters of Mary Shelley ed. F.L. Jones, University of Oklahoma Press, 1944.
Unpublished letters of Mary Shelley 1817–1820
Percy Bysshe Shelley: Letters from Abroad, Letters to Leigh Hunt, Letters to T.J. Hogg.
Notes on sculptures in Rome and Florence.
Unpublished letters from Italy, 1818–22.

A selection of other books consulted

Andreotti, Giulio, *Governare Con La Crisi*, Milan, 1991

Bagnard, Gilbert, *The Roman Campagna and its Treasures*, London, 1929

Barzini, Luigi, *The Italians*, London, 1964

Bowersock, G.M., *Julian the Apostate*, London, 1978

Caracciolo, Nicola, *Tutti Gli Uomini Del Duce*, Milan, 1982

Chadwick, Owen, *Britain & the Vatican during the Second World War*, Cambridge, 1986

Chastel, André, *Italian Art*, London, 1963

Ciano, Edda, *La Mia Testimonianza*, Milan, 1975

Cornwell, Rupert, *God's Banker*, London, 1983

François-Poncet, André, *Au Palais Farnèse Souvenirs d'une Ambassade à Rome*, Paris, 1961

Gibbon, Edward, *Memoirs of My Life*, ed. Betty Radice, London 1984

Gibbon, Edward, *The Decline & Fall of the Roman Empire*, abr D.M. Low, London, 1966

Ginsborg, Paul, *A History of Contemporary Italy*, London, 1990

Guerri, Giordano, *Galeazzo Ciano, Una Vita 1903–1944*, Milan, 1979

Hare, Augustus, *Walks in Rome*, London, 1893

Hebblethwaite, Peter, *John XXIII*, London, 1984

Hibbert, Christopher, *Rome: The Biography of a City*, London, 1985

Holmes, Richard, *Shelley: The Pursuit*, London, 1974

Innocenti, Marco, *I Gerarchi del Fascismo*, Milan, 1992

Juvenal, *The Sixteen Satires*, tr Peter Green, London, 1967

Leigh Hunt, *Selected Writings*, Manchester, 1990

Macchiavelli, Niccolo, *Il Principe*, ed. Luigi Firpo, Turin, 1961

Mack Smith, Denis, *Mussolini's Roman Empire*, London, 1976

Masson, Georgina, *A Companion Guide to Rome*, London, 1965

Nichols, Peter, *The Pope's Divisions*, London, 1980

Pansa, Giampaolo, *Lo Sfascio*, Milan, 1987

Spinosa, Antonio, *I Figli del Duce*, Milan, 1983

Tipographia del Senato della Repubblica, XI Legislatura, *Domanda di Autorizzazione a Procedere contro il Senatore Giulio Andreotti*, Rome, 1993

Waterfield, Gordon, *Professional Diplomat*, London, 1973

Willan, Philip, *Puppet Masters, The political use of terrorism in Italy*, London, 1991

Willey, David, *God's Politician*, London, 1992

Wittkower, Rudolf, *Art and Architecture in Italy 1600–1750*, London, 1958

Vene, Gian Franco, *Mille Lire al Mese*, Milan, 1988

Yallop, David, *In God's Name*, London, 1984

Index